To

Larry Niksch

This was beyond my ability
to do alone. You helped a
whole lot. Many Thanks.

John

AMERICA'S
S M A L L
WARS

Other Titles of Related Interest

Bacevich et al. AMERICAN MILITARY POLICY IN SMALL WARS:
THE CASE OF EL SALVADOR

Barnett OLD BATTLES AND NEW DEFENCES:
CAN WE LEARN FROM MILITARY HISTORY?

Collins GREEN BERETS, SEALS AND SPETSNAZ: U.S. & SOVIET
SPECIAL MILITARY OPERATIONS

Hilsman AMERICAN GUERRILLA: MY WAR BEHIND JAPANESE LINES

Mazarr LIGHT FORCES & THE FUTURE OF U.S. MILITARY STRATEGY

Paschall LIC 2010: SPECIAL OPERATIONS &
UNCONVENTIONAL WARFARE IN THE NEXT CENTURY

Vaux TAKE THAT HILL!: ROYAL MARINES IN THE FALKLANDS WAR

Related Journals*

Armed Forces Journal International

Defense Analysis

Survival

*Sample copies available upon request

An AUSA Book

AMERICA'S SMALL WARS:

LESSONS FOR THE FUTURE

John M. Collins

Frederick Hamerman
and
James P. Seevers,
Assistants

BRASSEY'S (US), Inc.

A Macmillan Publishing Company

Washington • New York • London • Oxford
Beijing • Frankfurt • São Paulo • Sydney • Tokyo • Toronto

U.S.A. (Editorial)	Brassey's (US), Inc. 8000 Westpark Drive, 1st Floor, McLean, Virginia 22102, U.S.A.
(Orders)	Attn: Brassey's Order Dept., Macmillan Publishing Co., Front & Brown Streets, Riverside, New Jersey 08075
U.K. (Editorial)	Brassey's (UK) Ltd. 50 Fetter Lane, London EC4A 1AA, England
(Orders)	Brassey's (UK) Ltd. Headington Hill Hall, Oxford OX3 OBW, England
PEOPLE'S REPUBLIC OF CHINA	Pergamon Press, Room 4037, Qianmen Hotel, Beijing, People's Republic of China
FEDERAL REPUBLIC OF GERMANY	Pergamon Press GmbH, Hammerweg 6, D-6242 Kronberg, Federal Republic of Germany
BRAZIL	Pergamon Editora Ltda, Rua Eça de Queiros, 346, CEP 04011, Paraiso, São Paulo, Brazil
AUSTRALIA	Brassey's Australia, P.O. Box 544, Potts Point, N.S.W. 2011, Australia
JAPAN	Pergamon Press, 5th Floor, Matsuoka Central Building, 1-7-1 Nishishinjuku, Shinjuku-ku, Tokyo 160, Japan
CANADA	Pergamon Press Canada, Suite No. 271, 253 College Street, Toronto, Ontario, Canada M5T 1R5

First edition 1991

Brassey's (US), Inc., books are available at special discounts for bulk
purchases for sales promotions, premiums, fund-raising, or educational use
through the Special Sales Director, Macmillan Publishing Company,
866 Third Avenue, New York, New York 10022.

Library of Congress Cataloging-in-Publication Data
Collins, John M., 1921–
    America's small wars : lessons for the future / John M. Collins,
Frederick Hamerman and James P. Seevers, assistants. — 1st ed.
        p.   cm.
    Includes index.
    ISBN 0-08-040583-5
    1. Low-intensity conflicts (Military science)—United States—
History—20th century.   2. United States—History, Military—20th
century.   I. Hamerman, Frederick.   II. Seevers, James P.
III. Title.
E745.C63   1991
355′.033573—dc20   90–24477
                                                            CIP

British Library Cataloguing in Publication Data
Collins, John M.
    America's small wars : lessons for the future.
    1. Small scale military operations by American military
    forces, history
    I. Title   II. Hamerman, Frederick   III. Seevers, James P.
    355.40973

    ISBN 0-08-040583-5

Published in the United States of America

To:
CONGRESSMAN DAN DANIEL (*D-VA*)

A "true believer," who fought for better U.S. low-
intensity conflict capabilities until his final day.
He is fondly remembered.

PUBLISHER'S NOTE

The United States is at a major turning point in providing for its security in the next century. To inform the deliberations on that crucial subject, John Collins's *America's Small Wars: Lessons for the Future* was developed at the request of the U.S. Congress. Brassey's (US) has commercially published this important historical study in its original form to make it available to the general public.

TABLE OF CONTENTS

Maps:

FOREWORD

The Persian Gulf crisis that erupted in August 1990 was still a classic low-intensity conflict when this foreword was drafted five months later. Both sides employed shows of force and other threats in attempts to achieve their objectives without risking a major war after Iraq annexed Kuwait. Political, economic, and psychological warfare took precedence over armed combat. Saddam Hussein briefly detained foreign nationals for bargaining purposes on a grand scale.

This book, written in simple, straightforward terms, contains lessons that might have expanded U.S. options before a big war erupted in the Persian Gulf, January 16, 1991, and shows how past experience could help improve future U.S. performance elsewhere. The 60 cases selected clearly indicate that military power often is the least important "weapon" used in low-intensity conflicts, confirm that U.S. interservice and interdepartmental/interagency collaboration is imperative, and highlight needs for area-oriented low-intensity conflict specialists able to work well with key leaders in foreign countries of particular interest to the United States. Annex B, which summarizes key congressional actions, is unique. There is nothing else like it in print.

I participated actively in five of the cases covered herein and helped plan U.S. operations in several more since 1950. As Commander-in-Chief, first of the U.S. Rapid Deployment Joint Task Force, then of U.S. Central Command, I prepared for many contingencies in an area of responsibility that encompassed 19 countries from Africa's northeast horn to Afghanistan and Pakistan. This book nevertheless provided me with perspectives I never had before. Officials who presently exercise similar responsibilities will find it helps them see forests instead of trees. Other readers who simply want an introduction to the intricacies of low-intensity conflict couldn't find a better place to start. This treatise, in short, promises to be a valuable reference for anyone with an interest in the subject.

Robert C. Kingston
General, U.S. Army (Ret.)

ACKNOWLEDGMENTS

Congressman Earl Hutto (D-Fl), Chairman of the Readiness Subcommittee, House Armed Services Committee, requested this unclassified assessment of U.S. low-intensity conflict (LIC) experience in the Twentieth Century to help Congress evaluate present and future LIC plans, programs, operations, force requirements, and requests for funds. Fred Hamerman, following my guidance, produced a first draft that most reviewers agreed overemphasized military power. That false start took six months, but was very useful, because the scope thereafter expanded considerably and cases selected are much better balanced. Jim Seevers, a Presidential Management Intern on loan for six months, added key congressional actions, which previously were slighted.

Associates who furnished source materials and comments occupied two categories: low-intensity conflict experts, active and retired; regional and functional specialists in the Congressional Research Service (CRS). More than 100 organizations and individuals made valuable contributions. I salute them all, but those listed below were most prominent.

General Bob Kingston, who wrote the foreword, amended many drafts. Scot Crerar and Gene Russell of BETAC Corporation did likewise. Pete Bahnsen, their compatriot, was especially helpful with LIC logistics.

Pentagon spokesmen who responded to requests for information and co-ordinated critiques included Lynn Rylander, since deceased, and Bill Olsen (Office, Assistant Secretary of Defense for Special Operations and Low-intensity Conflict); Colonel Tom Wilkerson (JCS Chairman's Staff Group); Major Bill McCoy (Army); Lieutenant Colonel Russell Craft (USMC), and Lieutenant Tom Duffy (Navy); Major Barbara McColgan (Air Force); Lieutenant Colonels H.T. Hayden and J.R. Pruden (Marine Corps). Brigadier General Sidney Schachnow spoke for U.S. Special Operations Command at MacDill AFB, Fl. Major Bill Burgess was my basic contact with the John F. Kennedy Center for Special Warfare at Fort Bragg, NC. Colonel Tom Swain and Lieutenant Colonel Charles Ciccolella represented the Army-Air Force Center for Low Intensity Conflict at Langley AFB, Va.

The Foreign Affairs and National Defense Division of CRS, as usual, was a superlative sounding board and fount of information. Bert Cooper, in collaboration with Doris Condit, a former colleague, donated out-of-print works that this study cites in 17 of its 60 LIC cases. Substantive assistance came from Steve Bowman, Bob Goldich, Mark Lowenthal, Charlotte Preece, and Jim Wootten (overviews); Larry Niksch and Bob Sutter (Asia); Brenda Branaman and Ray Copson (Africa); Dianne Rennack, Nina Serafino, Larry Storrs—I spent more time in his office than in mine—Mark Sullivan, and Maureen Taft-Morales (Latin America); Ellen Laipson, Clyde Mark, and Al Prados (Middle East); Dick Grimmett and Larry Nowels (foreign aid); Ted Galdi and Bob Shuey (economic sanctions); Marjorie Browne (peacekeeping); Raphael Perl (narco conflict); and Ellen Collier (presidential war powers).

Joseph Olszar typed the text. Dianne Rennack, a computer whiz, handled the complex tables. Paul Graney computerized my cartography. All three patiently incorporated repeated revisions. Carolyn Hatcher provided peerless reference support. Jim Robinson, the chief CRS reviewer, approved the final draft for publication.

No acknowledgments would be complete without special mention of Swift, my uncomplaining partner, who knows at least as much as I do about low-intensity conflict, because she heard no other topic of conversation at home for many months, morning, noon, and night.

John M. Collins
Alexandria, Virginia

BACKGROUND, PURPOSE, AND SCOPE

The first, the grandest, the most decisive act of judgement
that statesmen and generals exercise is to understand the
war in which they engage.

Carl Von Clausewitz
On War

Multifarious low-intensity conflicts (LICs), which occupy the imprecise
space between normal peacetime competition and combat equivalent to that
in Korea and Vietnam, have threatened or supported important U.S. interests
throughout the Twentieth Century. Recurrence seems certain, perhaps at
increased rates, because successful LIC operations allow highly-developed
states to achieve selected objectives while reducing risks in a world where the
proliferation of mass destruction weapons, missile delivery systems, and other
sophisticated devices makes mid- and high-intensity warfare increasingly
unattractive to rational decisionmakers. LIC techniques that are cheap to
employ but costly to counter also may enable weak nations and subnational
groups (such as transnational terrorists, insurgents, and narcotic cartels) to
compete effectively with powerful opponents, much like Lilliputians tied
Gulliver.

Officials responsible for U.S. national security consequently need abilities
to deter and, if necessary, conduct LIC operations of all kinds whenever and
wherever situations require. Incompetence otherwise might result in
destabilized friendly governments, isolate them from the United States
politically and economically, reduce U.S. access to crucial resources and sea
lanes, deprive America of important privileges (particularly transit rights and
overseas facilities), and open opportunities for opponents to exploit resultant
U.S. weaknesses.

The threefold purpose of this report is to:

• Define and describe low-intensity conflict

• Capsulize U.S. performance since 1899;

• Relate findings to future U.S. requirements.

Appraisals of U.S. LIC experience open with the Philippine Insurrection and Moro uprisings of 1899-1913. Earlier examples, including roots that predate the American Revolution, may be equally relevant, but 60 Twentieth Century cases that comprise a cross-section amply illustrate key points. Annex A puts each case in context, with special attention to where, when, why, and how the United States was involved. Annex B summarizes congressional authorizations and legal limitations. Annex C defines LIC terms.

Coverage of lengthy LICs treats crucial stages as subsets of a continuum. The Azerbaijani altercation (1946), Berlin Blockade (1948), Berlin Wall (1961), and Cuban Missile Crisis (1962), for example, punctuate the so-called U.S.-Soviet Cold War that still persists to some degree after more than four decades. The 11-minute U.S. raid on Tripoli, Libya (1986) was just one episode of a low-intensity conflict with Libya, now in progress for nearly 20 years.

Some of this survey is subject to reasonable dispute, partly because low-intensity conflict is an exceedingly complex subject, much discussed but seldom studied. The transition from "peace" to "war" often is barely perceptible. Termination may be equally indistinct. Ambiguities and intangibles abound, especially in covert action cases. Cause/effect relationships rarely are clear. Several U.S. LICs, for example, culminate in failure according to majority opinion, although the United States accomplished all important objectives. Others ended well for reasons that had little to do with U.S. skill.

First efforts herein therefore emphasize facts that help readers evaluate various opinions and proposed improvements. Subjective interpretations need clarifications, confirmations, and refinements. The product will be most useful if it encourages further in-depth research.

LIC DEFINED AND DESCRIBED

French philosopher René Descartes was fond of the phrase, "if you would speak with me, define your terms." Well said. Senior U.S. decisonmakers and staff must define low-intensity conflicts realistically before they can draw clear lines of responsibility. Official attempts to delineate LIC unfortunately confuse more issues than they clarify.

DEFINITIONAL CONFUSION

The *National Security Strategy of the United States*, which places LIC "at the lower end of the conflict spectrum," asserts that "low-intensity conflict involves the struggle of competing principles and ideologies below the level of conventional war." Many other motives, such as economic aspiration and self-determination, nevertheless are evident, and small conventional wars are commonplace. U.S. National Security Strategy also emphasizes the utility of armed forces in LIC, although nonmilitary power consistently is important and often is central.[1]

JCS doctrine replaces the term "conflict spectrum" with an "operational continuum", which comprises "three political-military states of world affairs: war, conflict, and peacetime competition. A fourth state, shown outside of the military continuum, is . . . routine peaceful competition," identified as "a situation where the political, economic, and informational elements of national power operate without the need for [armed forces]." Those semantic distinctions seem excessively subtle and are partly incorrect, since bloodless combat can and does occur independently under conditions that scarcely qualify as "routine peaceful competition." [2]

LIC, according to JCS doctrine lies only within "the *military* operational continuum -- peacetime competition and conflict" (emphasis in original). "Conflict" is defined as "an armed struggle or clash between organized parties within a nation or between nations in order to achieve limited political or military objectives." LIC, however, habitually occupies nonmilitary parts of that continuum. Some distinction between U.S. goals and those of other belligerents is essential, because parties battling for survival or regional

---

[1] *National Security Strategy of the United States*, Washington, The White House, March 1990, p.28.

[2] *JCS Pub 3-0: Doctrine for Joint Operations*, Washington, Joint Chiefs of Staff, January 1990, Appendix D.

supremacy seldom have limited objectives.[3]　　Finally, JCS doctrine acknowledges "peacetime contingencies" as a distinctive category of low-intensity conflict,[4] albeit *all* LICs normally are contingencies and technically transpire in peacetime, because none have yet been declared wars.　Low-intensity "sideshows" during World War II are salient exceptions.

DEFINITIONAL CLARIFICATIONS

This survey locates LIC on the conflict spectrum between normal peacetime competition and any kind of armed combat that depletes U.S. forces slightly, if at all (Figures 1 and 2 graphically contrast LIC with mid- and high-intensity conflicts).　Limitations on violence, rather than force levels and arsenals, determine the indistinct upper boundary of LIC.　Large military formations conceivably could conduct low-intensity operations for limited objectives using the most lethal weapons (perhaps for signalling), provided few U.S. casualties and little U.S. damage ensued.　The lower boundary, where nonviolent LICs abut normal peacetime competition, is equally inexact. Political, economic, technological, and psychological warfare, waged for deterrent, offensive, or defensive purposes, occupy prominent places.　So do nonviolent military operations, typified by shows of force and peacekeeping.

Insurgencies, counterinsurgencies, coups d'etat, transnational terrorism, anti/counterterrorism, minor conventional wars, and narco conflict lie between those poles.　Variations within each category, overlaps, and interlocks are virtually endless.

Most LICs occur in or are connected with developing countries.　Many, however, have regional (even global) implications.　U.S. participation almost always requires interdepartmental/interagency coordination.　The National Security Council is best able to accomplish that task for top layers of the Federal Government.　Most low-intensity conflicts are politically sensitive. The Department of State therefore is best able to coordinate LIC policies, plans, programs, and operations overseas, through ambassadors and embassy staffs.　The Department of Defense is primarily responsible for all military matters.　The Director of Central Intelligence coordinates LIC endeavors of the U.S. intelligence community.　Opportunities for congressional influence are proportionately greater than during mid- and high-intensity conflicts, provided Congress receives sufficient information in time to act.

---

[3] LIC is a relative term.　Conflicts that are low-intensity from U.S. perspectives may be mid- or high-intensity to U.S. opponents and/or partners.

[4] *JCS Pub. 3-07: Doctrine for Joint Operations in Low-Intensity Conflict*, Final Draft, Washington, Joint Chiefs of Staff, January 1990, Chapter V, p. 1-18.

Figure 1

CONFLICT SPECTRUM
(U.S. Perspectives)

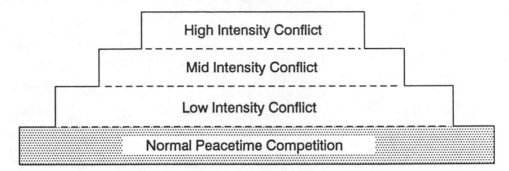

Typical Type Conflicts

Conflict Intensity [1]		
Low [2]	Mid [2]	High [2]

Violent Conflicts
   Insurgency (Phases I, II)
   Counterinsurgency
   Coups d'etat
   Transnational Terrorism
   Anti/Counterterrorism
   Narco Conflict
   Conventional War (Minor)
Nonviolent Conflicts
   Political Warfare
   Economic Warfare
   Technological Warfare
   Psychological Warfare
   Peacekeeping
	Limited Wars
	   Nuclear
	   Conventional
	
	Insurgency (Phase III)
		Nuclear Wars
		   Global
		   Regional
		Conventional War (Major)

[1] Chemical and biological warfare may augment nuclear and/or conventional capabilities at any conflict level, but do not constitute a separate type.

[2] Phase I and II insurgencies exclude employment of large paramilitary formations, which supplement undergrounds and guerrillas during Phase III.

Figure 2

LIC CHARACTERISTICS
Compared With Other Conflicts

	Conflict Intensity		
	Low	Mid	High
Types	Most		Fewest
Frequency	Greatest		Least
Duration	Most variable		Least variable
Violence	Variable	Inevitable	Inevitable
Threats to U.S.A.			
Direct	Abnormal	Abnormal	Normal
Ambiguous	Abnormal	Abnormal	Abnormal
Relative Complexity			
Causes	Greatest		Least
Deterrence	Greatest		Least
Relative Importance			
National Power			
Military	Least		Most
Paramilitary	Most		Least
Technological	Least		Most
Implements			
Diplomacy	Most		Least
Assistance	Most		Least
Reform	Most		Least
Sanctions	Most		Least
Force	Least		Most
Armed Forces			
Nuclear	Least		Most
Conventional	Least		Most
Special Operations	Most		Least
Special Capabilities			
Covert Actions	Most		Least
Area Orientation	Most		Least
Foreign Language	Most		Least
Public Approval	Most variable		Least variable
Budgetary Costs	Least		Greatest
U.S. Participation			
Predominant Roles	Indirect	Direct	Direct
Predominant Officials	NSC, State	DOD	DOD
Predominant Control	Variable	USA	USA

LIC ROLES AND MISSIONS

U.S. military roles and missions are defined in considerable detail for each type of LIC. Nonmilitary duties are less well developed or unaddressed. The following discussion and Figure 3 at the end of this section reflect those conditions.

INSURGENCIES/RESISTANCE

Insurgencies are protracted efforts by relatively large indigenous groups to overthrow governments or compel reforms, and sometimes to alter social systems (Viet Cong vs Republic of Vietnam, for example). Resistance movements employ similar forces and tactics to sap and, if possible, oust occupying powers (Afghan *Mujahiddin* vs USSR).

The principal U.S. role in insurgencies and resistance movements is commonly called unconventional warfare (UW). Main missions are to advise and assist local leaders who organize, equip, train, and employ undergrounds, guerrillas, and other paramilitary formations that specialize in clandestine infiltration/exfiltration, raids, ambushes, sabotage, subversion, psychological warfare, and other offensive operations. Political and economic programs always are important. Participation by U.S. combat forces depends on case-by-case decisions.[1]

COUPS D'ETAT

Popular participation characterizes resistance movements and insurgencies. A few conspirators, in contrast, normally plan and execute

---

[1] *JCS Pub 3-07: Doctrine for Joint Operations in Low-Intensity Conflict*, Final Draft, Washington, Joint Chiefs of Staff, January 1990, Chapter II, p. 2-7, 12-14, 17-18. For fundamentals of insurgency see, for example, Molnar, Andrew R., et al., *Underground in Insurgent, Revolutionary, and Resistance Warfare*, Washington, D.C., Special Operations Research Office, American University, November 1963, 358 p. and *Human Factors Considerations of Underground in Insurgencies*, Department of the Army Pamphlet No. 550-104, Washington, D.C., Headquarters U.S. Army, September 1966, 291 p.; *Selected Military Writings of Mao Tse-Tung*, 2d Ed., Peking, Foreign Langauages Press, 1966, 410 p.; Giap, Vo Nguyen, *People's War, People's Army*, N.Y., Praeger, 1962, 217 p.; ;Thompson, Robert, *Revolutionary War in World Strategy*, 1945-1969, N.Y., Taplinger Publishing Co., 1970, 171 p.; *Modern Revolutionary Warfare: An Analytical Overview*, Kensington, MD., American Institute for Research,May 1973, 126 p.

coups d'etat. Preparations may be prolonged, but implementation invariably is precipitate and the climax comes quickly.[2]

Ten of the 60 cases in this study were coups, but no doctrine as yet describes U.S. roles and missions for that type LIC.

COUNTERINSURGENCIES

Counterinsurgencies are internal defense (ID) programs that indigenous governments take to forestall or defeat insurgencies, whether they be anticolonial (FRELIMO in Mozambique), secessionist (Eritreans in Ethiopia), reformist (Sandinistas in Nicaragua), reactionary (Muslim fundamentalists), or revolutionary (Viet Cong). Occupying powers employ analogous techniques against resistance movements.

Foreign internal defense (FID) is the fundamental U.S. role in counterinsurgencies. Political, economic, military, legal and other advice/assistance are complementary. Associated skills bear little resemblance to those that promote UW. Civil affairs, civic action, countersubversion, public administration, and site security are representative activities. U.S. combat operations, when required, are strategically defensive and usually overt.[3]

COMBATTING TERRORISM

Terrorism, for purposes of this report, is public, repetitive violence or threats of violence intended to achieve sociopolitical objectives by intimidating innocent people and disrupting community routines so severely that afflicted parties eventually capitulate to avoid continued torment. Domestic terrorism, which originates within and is directed against one country, is a favorite tool

---

[2] For fundamentals see Luttwak, Edward, *Coup d'Etat*, NY, Alfred A. Knopf, 1969, 209 p.

[3] *JCS Pub 3-07: Doctrine for Joint Operations in Low-Intensity Conflict*, Chapter II, p.7-12, 14-16, 18-25. For fundamentals of counterinsurgency see, for example, Condit, D.M. et al, *A Counterinsurgency Bibliography*, Washington, D.C., Special Operations Research Office, American University, 1963, 269 p. ; Galula, David, *Counterinsurgency Warfare: Theory and Practice*, N.Y., Praeger, 1964, 143 p. ; McCuen, John J., *The Art of Counter Revolutionary War*, Harrisburg, PA., Stackpole, 1966, 349 p. ; Thompson, Robert, *Defeating Communist Insurgency*, London, Chatto & Windus, 1966, 171 p, ; Trinquier, Roger, *Modern Warfare: A French View of Counterinsurgency*, N.Y., Praeger, 1961, 115 p.

of some insurgents. Transnational terrorism, instigated by groups that renegade governments may sponsor and support, emanates from foreign bases.[4]

U.S. steps to combat terrorism subdivide into two basic roles.
Antiterrorism, the first line of deterrence and defense, emphasizes passive
protection for personnel and installations. Counterterrorism may attack
terrorists before they strike or be reactive. Timely, accurate intelligence
underpins all missions. Antiterrorists cannot accurately anticipate terrorist
incursions in its absence, counterterrorists can neither find terrorists nor
rescue hostages, and sensitive operations are apt to backfire with great
embarrassment to the sponsor.[5]

OTHER ARMED COMBAT

DOD roles and functions for low-intensity conventional combat, not
always clearly delineated, are scaled down and appropriately modified versions
of those that pertain during mid- and high-intensity conflicts. Title 10,
United States Code and Department of Defense Directive 5100.1 specify
primary and collateral functions for each service.[6]

NONCOMBAT OPERATIONS

Crisis management is the main U.S. military role in noncombat
operations. The mixed bag of contributory missions ranges from posturing

---

[4] *JCS Pub 3-07: Doctrine for Joint Operations in Low-Intensity Conflict*,
Chapter III. For fundamentals of terrorism see, for example, Watson, Francis
M, *Political Terrorism: The Threat and the Response*, N.Y., Robert B. Luce
Co., 1976, 248 p.; *The Terrorism Reader*, Ed. by Walter Laqueur, N.Y.,
Meridian Books, 1978, 285 p.; Kupperman, Robert and Darrell Trent,
Terrorism: Threat, Reality, Response, Stanford, CA., Hoover Institution Press,
1979, 450 p.; Moss, Robert, *Urban Guerillas*, London, Temple Smith, 1972, 288
p.; Marighella, Carlos, *Minimanual of the Urban Guerilla*, Vancouver, Canada,
Pulp Press, 1974, 38 p.; Jenkins, Brian M., *The Future Course of International
Terrorism*, Santa Monica, CA., RAND, September 1985, 13 p.

[5] A brief compilation of anti/counterterrorism issues and reference
materials is contained in U.S. Congress, House, Armed Services Committee
Print, *United States and Soviet Special Operations*, Washington, U.S. GPO,
April 28, 1987, p.56-63, 80-81, 86-67, 139-143, 150-151.

[6] *Title 10* specifies Army functions in Chapter 307, Section 3062; Navy
and Marine Corps functions in Chapter 503, Sections 5012 and 5013; Air
Force functions in Chapter 817, Section 8062. *DOD Directive 5100.1*,
"Functions of the Department of Defense and Its Major Components,"
elaborates.

and peacekeeping to noncombatant evacuation, other humanitarian acts, and assorted support (Figure 3). Most are self-explanatory.

Peacekeeping encompasses all efforts of any unilateral or multilateral force to maintain a truce and/or otherwise discourage hostilities, pending the restoration of true tranquility. Buffer operations, undertaken by mutual consent of all belligerents, conform to a mandate that often prescribes force size, composition, arms, dispositions, legal status, and other preconditions. Prowess at diplomacy, negotiations, mediation, and arbitration is imperative, because enforcement plays little or no part.[7] (Peace*keeping* becomes peace*making* when compulsion is employed).

Interposition between belligerents is the paramount U.S. peacekeeping role. The salient mission is to supervise one or more of the following: international territory (such as straits); cease-fires; withdrawals; disengagements; demilitarization; demobilization; prisoner of war exchanges; orderly transfer of power.[8] Logistic support, especially airlift, is the U.S. mission in some instances.

There are no officially defined U.S. roles and missions for political, economic, psychological, and technological operations that qualify as low-intensity conflicts or play prominent parts in any LIC. Assistance for friends and sanctions against foes are common methods. Psyop can be employed equally well, whether the purpose is deterrence, offense, or defense.

NARCO CONFLICT

Interdiction is the main U.S. role related to international narco conflict. The intent is to inhibit and, if possible, block all illicit drug traffic from foreign countries into the United States. Implementing missions, shared mulitnationally, seek to disrupt the production and distribution of illegal narcotics before shipments reach U.S. borders. Many U.S. organizations, including the military establishment, contribute to that process.[9]

---

[7] JCS Pub 3-07: *Doctrine for Joint Operations in Low-Intensity Conflict*, Chapter IV. *Peacekeepers's Handbook* (International Peace Academy), N.Y., Pergamon Press, 1984, P. 22; Rikhye, Indar Jit, "Peacekeeping and Peacemaking," in *Peacekeeping: Appraisals and Proposals*, Ed. by Henry Wiseman, N.Y., Pergamon Press, 1983, P. 6-7.

[8] JCS Pub 3-07: *Doctrine for Joint Operations in Low-Intensity Conflict*, P.IV-13 through IV-16; *Peacekeeper's Handbook* p. 21-41; Diehl, Paul F., "Peacekeeping Operations and the Quest for Peace," *Political Science Quarterly*, Fall 1988, p. 485-507.

[9] *National Drug Control Strategy*, Washington, The White House, January 1990, P. 49-72, 83-98, 111-112.

Figure 3

DOD LIC ROLES AND MISSIONS
Present Policies

	Insurgency, Resistance	Counter-Insurgency	Combatting Terrorism	Conventional Operations [1]	Noncombat Operations [2]
PRIMARY DOD ROLES					
Unconventional Warfare	X				
Foreign Internal Defense		X			
Anti/Counterterrorism		X	X		
Traditional Warfare				X	
Crisis Management	X	X	X	X	X
MAIN DOD MISSIONS					
General Purpose Forces					
Shows of Force					X
Offensive Combat				X	
Security Operations [3]		X	X	X	
Peacekeeping [4]					X
Special Operations Forces					
Direct Action [5]	X	X	X	X	
Hostage Rescue			X		
Psychological Operations	X	X	X	X	X
Evasion & Escape	X	X	X	X	
Support Forces					
Intelligence	X	X	X	X	X
Communications	X	X	X	X	X
Logistics [6]	X	X	X	X	X
Civil Affairs		X		X	X
Miscellaneous Forces [7]					
Law Enforcement [8]		X	X	X	
Drug Interdiction			X		
Advice [9]	X	X	X	X	X
Assistance [10]	X	X	X	X	X

[1] Conventional combat, peacemaking, and rescue operations not related to counterterrorism.

[2] Posturing, peacekeeping, sanctions, plus political and economic support. Peacemaking that confines armed combat to brief incidents.

[3] Sites, personnel (includes noncombatant evacuation), frontiers, lines of communication.

[4] Territories, ceasefires, demobiliations, demilitarization, disengagements, POW exchanges.

[5] Surgical antipersonnel actions, strikes, raids, ambushes, sabotage.

[6] Supply, maintenance, transportation, construction, medical evacuation, hospitalization, services.

[7] General purpose forces, special operations forces, and support forces as required.

[8] Includes crowd control and other military police missions.

[9] Politcal, economic, military, sociological, legal, technological.

[10] Funds, education, training, equipment, supplies, construction, services.

VARIOUS OVERVIEWS

Two world wars constitute the only U.S. high-intensity conflicts since 1899. Korea (1950-53) and Vietnam (1966-72) were mid-intensity in terms of American participation. Twentieth Century LICs, in stark contrast, outnumber all other hostilities in U.S. history and nearly blanket the globe (Figure 4 and Map 1).

The 60 cases picked for study purposes disregard borderline entries on several long lists[1] and span a broad spectrum from nonviolent conflicts to armed combat. Selections are exemplary, instead of exhaustive, to make the study manageable. Many more LICs might have been assessed, such as U.S. operations against the Soviet Union before World War II, Trieste in the late 1940s, Cambodia in the 1960s, and Vietnam after 1975, but their exclusion does not elementally alter study conclusions. Analyses disregard U.S. involvement in most "little wars" that overlaid and/or prolonged larger ones (Northern Russia and Far Eastern Siberia, 1918-1920 are illustrative.[2] So is the North Atlantic, 1940-41[3]). Resistance movements in the Philippines, Burma, and France during World War II are included, because they are the

---

[1] Blechman, Barry M. and Stephen S. Kaplan, *Force Without War: U.S. Armed Forces as a Political Instrument*, Washington, Brookings Institution, 1978, 584 p. (See especially lists on p. 547-556); *Armed Actions Taken By the United States Without a Declaration of War, 1789-1967*, Research Project No. 806A, Washington, Historical Studies Division, Dept. of State, August 1967 (never updated), 30 p.; Collier, Ellen, U.S. Congress, House *Background Information on the Use of U.S. Armed Forces in Foreign Countries*, 1975 Revision, 94th Congress, 1st Session, Washington, Subcommittee on International Security and Scientific Affairs of the Committee on International Relations, U.S. GPO, 1975, 84 p.; Kaye, G.D., D.A. Grant, and E.J. Edmond, *Major Armed Conflict: A Compendium of Interstate and Intrastate Conflict, 1720 to 1985*, ORAE Report No. R 95, Ottawa, Canada, Operational Research and Analysis Establishment, Dept. of National Defense, November 1985, paginated by section (see especially Annex C, p. 42-23)

[2] See, for example, Dupuy, R. Ernest and William H. Baumer, *The Little Wars of the United States*, NY, Hawthorne Books, 1968, p. 169-213, 217-218; Kennan, George F., *Russia and the West Under Lenin and Stalin*, Boston, Little, Brown and Co., 1961, p. 64-119.

[3] Morison, Samuel Eliot, *History of United States Naval Operations in World War II*, Vol. I, *The Battle of the Atlantic*, Boston, Little, Brown, and Co., 1954, 434 p.

Figure 4

SIXTY FOREMOST U.S. LICs
Since 1899

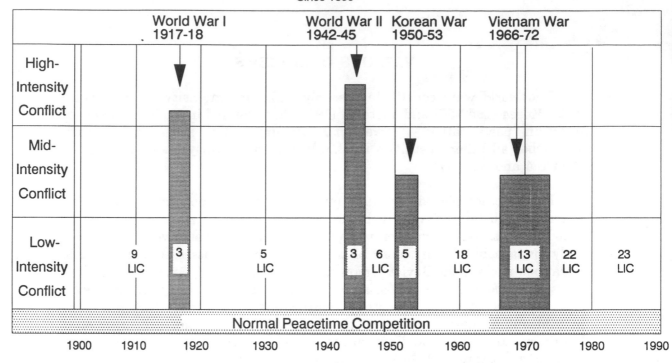

1. Philippines (1899-1913)
2. China (1900)
3. Colombia/Panama (1901-14)
4. Morocco (1904)
5. Cuba (1906-09)
6. China (1912-41)
7. Mexico (1914-17)
8. Haiti (1915-34)
9. Dominican Republic (1916-24)
10. Nicaragua (1926-33)
11. Philippines (1942-45)
12. Burma (1942-45)
13. France (1944)
14. China (1945-49)
15. Greece (1946-49)
16. Philippines (1946-55)
17. Indochina (1946-54)
18. U.S.S.R. (1946 -)
19. Israel vs. Arabs (1948 -)
20. Iran (1951-53)
21. China (1953-79)
22. North Korea (1953 -)
23. Guatemala (1953-54)
24. Vietnam (1955-65)
25. Laos (1955-65)
26. Lebanon (1958)
27. Cuba (1960 -)
28. South Africa (1960 -)
29. Dominican Republic (1960-62)
30. Zaire (1960-64)

31. Brazil (1961-64)
32. Vietnam (1963)
33. Dominican Republic (1965-66)
34. Guatemala (1965-74)
35. Thailand (1965-85)
36. Jordan (1970)
37. Libya (1970 -)
38. Chile (1970-73)
39. Iraq (1972-75)
40. OPEC (1974-75)
41. Cyprus (1974-78)
42. Mayaguez (1975)
43. Cambodia (1975 -)
44. Nicaragua (1978-79)
45. Iran (1979 -)
46. Syria (1979 -)
47. El Salvador (1979 -)
48. Bolivia (1980-86)
49. Afghanistan (1980 -)
50. Nicaragua (1981-90)
51. Falkland Islands (1982)
52. Lebanon (1982-84)
53. Grenada (1983)
54. Philippines (1984 -)
55. Philippines (1985-86)
56. Haiti (1985-86)
57. Angola (1986 -)
58. Narco Conflict (1986 -)
59. Persian Gulf (1987-88)
60. Panama (1987-90)

NOTE: LICs on the graph total 107, rather than 60, because many cases start in one time period and overlap one or more others. The U.S.S.R., for example, is part of every tally since 1946.

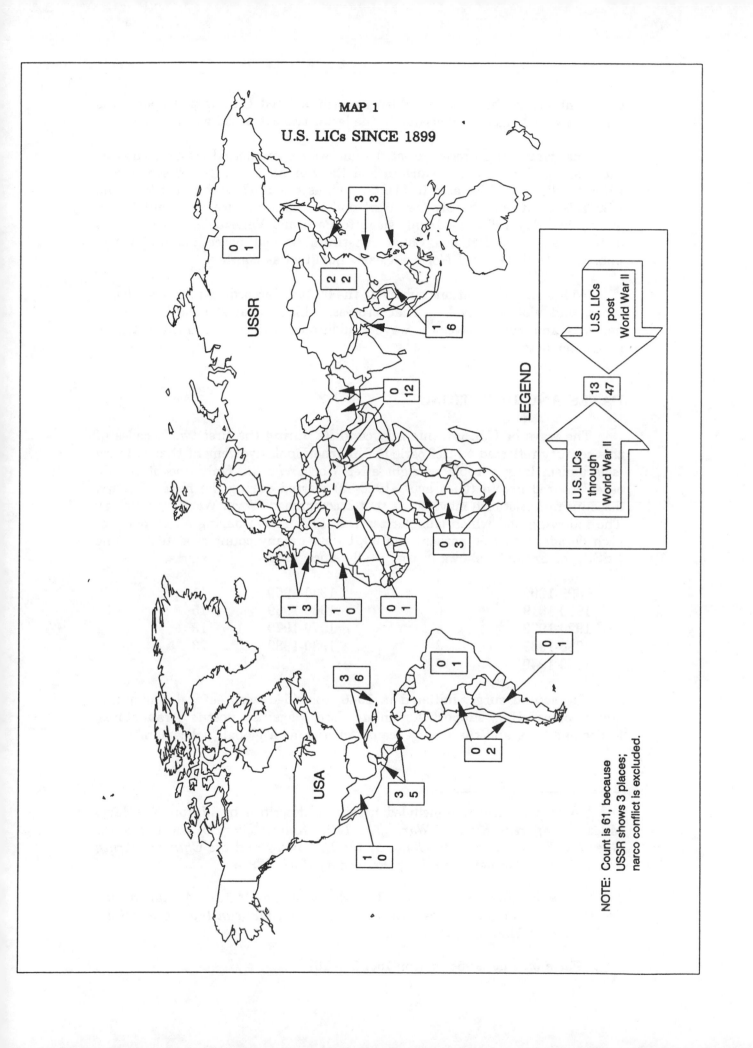

MAP 1

U.S. LICs SINCE 1899

LEGEND

U.S. LICs post World War II

U.S. LICs through World War II

13
47

NOTE: Count is 61, because
USSR shows 3 places;
narco conflict is excluded.

only conflicts in that category during which isolated U.S. special operations forces saw prolonged combat and, in the latter two cases, led guerrilla bands.[4]

The winnowing process treated some widely publicized clashes, such as those along Europe's Iron Curtain and the Korean DMZ, as parts of larger LICs. It disallowed isolated incidents, such as the 1967 Israeli attack on the USS *Liberty* during the Six Day War[5] and assaults on Vice President Nixon during his May 1958 "good will" visits to Peru and Venezuela.[6] Continuous disputes over the Panama Canal constitute normal peacetime diplomacy; imbroglios with General Noriega clearly qualified as conflict.

Preliminary evaluations subdivide the 60 cases according to times, places, types, and violence levels. That process, which isolates elemental cycles, patterns, and trends, paves the way for additional review of each LIC category in greater detail.

DATES AND DURATIONS

The wave of U.S. low-intensity conflicts during the first two decades of this century reflected a brief period of international involvement that military isolationism largely replaced right after World War I. Only one of the 60 cases covered herein (Nicaragua, 1926-33) started during the next 25 years, discounting resistance movements that accompanied World War II (Figure 4). The following list, which summarizes U.S. LICs active during all or parts of each decade, totals 96 rather than 60, because many count repeatedly. The USSR, for example, shows in every tally since 1946:

1899-1909	5	1950-1959	11
1910-1919	6	1960-1969	15
1920-1929	4	1970-1979	19
1930-1939	3	1980-1989	23
1940-1949	10		

The second surge, initiated in 1946, coincided with several communist power plays, U.S. support for infant Israel against hostile Arab states, anticolonialism, and the emergence of America as a global "policeman."

---

[4] A fourth case, not included herein, is described by Milton E. (Mary) Miles, *A Different Kind of War : The Little Known Story of the Combined Guerrilla Forces Created in China by the U.S. Navy and the Chinese During World War II*, Garden City, NY, Doubleday, 1967, 629 p.

[5] *Facts on File*, 1967, p. 203, 324; Ennes, James M., Jr., *Assault on the Liberty: The True Story of the Israeli Attack on an American Intelligence Ship*, N.Y., Random House, 1979, 299 p.

[6] *Facts on File*, 1958, p. 159-160, 166-167.

Further sharp increases in the 1960s and 1970s coincided with U.S.-supported coups, the onset of insurgencies that seemed to threaten U.S. interests at home and abroad, and governments that sponsored or sustained transnational terrorism. U.S. involvement in 14 of the 60 conflicts started during the 1980s, more than any other decade. Several responded or were related to the Reagan Doctrine, which still fosters modest economic and military assistance for anti-communist insurgencies and resistance movements.[7] Drug interdiction and miscellaneous entries made up the remainder. Fourteen cases remain active in 1990, compared with 11 in 1979, 8 in 1969, and 5 in 1959.

Thirty-four of the selected U.S. LICs (57%) lasted fewer than five years, but 20 (33%) exceeded ten years. Eleven of those continue:

40+	2	Soviet Union (1946-), Israel vs. Arabs (1948-),
30-39	3	North Korea (1953-), Cuba (1960-), South Africa (1960-),
20-29	4	Thailand (1965-85), China (1912-1941), China (1953-1979), Libya (1970-),
10-19	11	Philippines (1899-1913), Colombia/Panama (1901-14), Haiti (1915-34), Philippines (1946-55), Vietnam (1955-65), Laos (1955-65), Cambodia (1975-), Iran (1978-), Syria (1979-), El Salvador (1979-), Afghanistan (1980-),
5-9	10	
1-4	34	
	60	

Whether those trends will persist is problematic. Soviet preoccupation with problems at home, Qadhafi's quiescence, and less evangelism from post-Khomeini Iran, for example, could help prevent conflict proliferation or prompt

---

[7] Copson, Raymond W. and Richard P. Cronin, *"Reagan Doctrine": Assisting Anti-Marxist Guerrillas*, Issue Brief 86113, Washington, Congressional Research Service, May 1, 1987, 17 p.; Bode, William R., "The Reagan Doctrine," *Strategic Review*, Winter 1986, p. 21-29.

trends toward fewer U.S. LICs in the future. Long cases, however, likely will remain in style, because drug interdiction, resistance movements, counterinsurgencies, and anti/counterterrorism usually feature protracted operations.

GEOGRAPHIC LOCATIONS

Three-fourths of the selected U.S. LICs since 1899 took place in Latin America, the Orient, and Middle East (Figure 5). That distribution, however, is deceiving, because the half-way mark separates two distinctive trends. The total is 63 instead of 60, because the USSR counts globally and in three regions:

	Pre-World War II	World War II	Post-World War II
Global	0	0	2
North America	1	0	0
Latin America	4	0	17
East Asia	3	2	13
Middle East	0	0	12
Africa	1	0	4
Europe	0	1	3
	9	3	51

Two regions contained 7 of 9 U.S. LICs before World War II. Most Latin American cases entailed "Yanqui imperialist" protectorates in so-called "banana republics" (Colombia/Panama, Cuba, Dominican Republic, Haiti, and Nicaragua).[8] Expeditions against Pancho Villa in our own backyard comprised the sole exception. The Philippine Insurrection and Moro uprisings of 1899-1913, followed by the Boxer Rebellion and gunboat diplomacy in China, were East Asia's contributions. U.S. policies that long ago disappeared prompted all cited conflicts, the last of which ceased in 1934.

The proliferation of LICs after World War II indicated growing U.S. interests in every geographic region. Latin America and East Asia lead the list with 17 and 13 respectively. Middle East conflicts, which began in Iranian Azerbaijan (1946) put 12 on the scoreboard. Four in Africa are fewer than might be expected, given lively competition for strategically important positions and/or critical raw materials in countries that are politically, economically, and socially underdeveloped. The most persistent LIC in post-war Europe directly involved the Soviet Union, as might be expected. Several episodes elicited vigorous U.S. responses between 1946 and 1968.

---

[8] Lieuwen, Edwin, *U.S. Policy in Latin America: A Short History*, N.Y., *Praeger*, 1967, p. 29-60; Herring, Hubert, *A History of Latin America: From the Beginning to the Present*, 2d Ed., N.Y., Alfred A. Knopf, 1967, p. 407-411, 429-433, 440-441, 464-466, 473-480.

Figure 5

SIXTY FOREMOST U.S. LICs
By Region

	1899 - 1919	1920 - 1939	1940 - 1949	1950 - 1959	1960 - 1969	1970 - 1979	1980 - 1989	Total
Global			1	1	1	1	2	2
Western Hemisphere								
North America	1							1
Central America	1	1		1	1	3	3	8
South America					1	1	2	4
Caribbean	3	2			4	1	3	9
Total	5	3		1	6	5	8	22
Eastern Hemisphere								
Europe			3	1	2	1	0	4
Middle East			1	3	1	6	6	12
Africa	1				2	2	3	5
East Asia	3	1	6	6	6	5	5	18
Total	4	1	10	10	11	14	14	39
Grand Total	9	4	11	12	19	20	24	63

North America

1. Mexico (1914-17)

Central America

1. Colombia/Panama (1901-14)
2. Nicaragua (1926-33)
3. Guatemala (1953-54)
4. Guatemala (1965-74)
5. Nicaragua (1978-79)
6. El Salvador (1979 -)
7. Nicaragua (1981-90)
8. Panama (1987-9C)

South America

1. Brazil (1961-64)
2. Chile (1970-73)
3. Bolivia (1980-86)
4. Falkland Islands (1982)

Caribbean

1. Cuba (1906-09)
2. Haiti (1915-34)
3. Dominican Republic (1916-24)
4. Cuba (1960 -)
5. Dominican Republic (1960-62)
6. U.S.S.R. (1962)
7. Dominican Republic (1965-66)
8. Grenada (1983)
9. Haiti (1985-86)

Global

1. U.S.S.R. (1946 -)
2. Narco Conflict (1986 -)

Europe

1. France (1944)
2. Greece (1946-49)
3. U.S.S.R. (1948, 1956, 1961, 1968)
4. Cyprus (1974-78)

Africa

1. Morocco (1904)
2. South Africa (1960 -)
3. Zaire (1960-64)
4. Libya (1970 -)
5. Angola (1986 -)

Middle East

1. U.S.S.R. (1946)
2. Israel vs. Arabs (1948 -)
3. Iran (1951-53)
4. Lebanon (1958)
5. Jordan (1970)
6. Iraq (1972-75)
7. OPEC (1974-75)
8. Iran (1979 -)
9. Syria (1979 -)
10. Afghanistan (1980 -)
11. Lebanon (1982-84)
12. Persian Gulf (1987-88)

East Asia

1. Philippines (1899-1913)
2. China (1900)
3. China (1912-41)
4. Philippines (1942-45)
5. Burma (1942-45)
6. China (1945-49)
7. Philippines (1946-55)
8. Indochina (1946-54)
9. China (1953-79)
10. North Korea (1953 -)
11. Vietnam (1955-65)
12. Laos (1955-65)
13. Vietnam (1963)
14. Thailand (1965-85)
15. Mayaguez (1975)
16. Cambodia (1975 -)
17. Philippines (1984 -)
18. Philippines (1985-86)

NOTE: LICs total 63, rather than 60, because the U.S.S.R. is listed globally and in three regions.
Totals do not always add on the table, because many cases start in one time period and overlap one or more others.

Figure 6

SIXTY FOREMOST U.S. LICs
By Type

	Insurgency, Resistance	Coups d'Etat	Counter-Insurgency	Combatting Terrorism	Conventional Operations [1]	Noncombat Operations [2]
1. Philippines (1899-1913)			X			
2. China (1900)					X	
3. Colombia/Panama (1901-14)					X	
4. Morocco (1904)					X	
5. Cuba (1906-09)					X	
6. China (1912-41)					X	
7. Mexico (1914-17)					X	
8. Haiti (1915-34)					X	
9. Dominican Republic (1916-24)					X	
10. Nicaragua (1926-33)					X	
11. Philippines (1942-45)	X					
12. Burma (1942-45)	X					
13. France (1944)	X					
14. China (1945-49)						X
15. Greece (1946-49)			X			
16. Philippines (1946-55)			X			
17. Indochina (1946-54)			X			
18. U.S.S.R. (1946 -)						X
a. Azerbaijan (1946)						X
b. Berlin Blockade (1948)						X
c. Hungary (1956)						X
d. Berlin Wall (1961)						X [3]
e. Cuban Missile Crisis (1962)						X
f. Czechoslovakia (1968)						X
19. Israel vs. Arabs (1948 -)						X
a. War (1956)						X
b. War (1967)						X [3]
c. War (1973)						X
d. Sinai (1976 -)						X
20. Iran (1951-53)		X				
21. China (1953-79)					X	
22. North Korea (1953 -)					X	
Pueblo (1968)						X [3]
23. Guatemala (1953-54)		X				
24. Vietnam (1955-65)			X			
25. Laos (1955-65)			X			
26. Lebanon (1958)					X	
27. Cuba (1960 -)	X	X				X
a. Anti-Castro Acts (1960-65)		X [3]				
b. Bay of Pigs (1961)	X [3]					
28. South Africa (1960 -)						X
29. Dominican Republic (1960-62)		X				
30. Zaire (1960-64)			X		X	

Figure 6 (cont.)

SIXTY FOREMOST U.S. LICs
By Type

	Insurgency, Resistance	Coups d'Etat	Counter Insurgency	Combatting Terrorism	Conventional Operations [1]	Noncombat Operations [2]
31. Brazil (1961-64)		X				
32. Vietnam (1963)		X				
33. Dominican Republic (1965-66)					X	
34. Guatemala (1965-74)			X			
35. Thailand (1965-85)			X			
36. Jordan (1970)						X
37. Libya (1970 -)				X	X	X
a. Gulf of Sidra (1981, 86)					X [3]	
b. Tripoli Raid (1986)				X [3]		
38. Chile (1970-73)		X				
39. Iraq (1972-75)	X					
40. OPEC (1974-75)						X
41. Cyprus (1974-78)						X
42. Mayaguez (1975)					X	
43. Cambodia (1975 -)	X					X
44. Nicaragua (1978-79)	X					
45. Iran (1979 -)				X		
a. Desert One (1980)				X		
b. Lebanese Hostages (1984-)				X }[3]		
46. Syria (1979 -)				X		
47. El Salvador (1979 -)			X			
48. Bolivia (1980-86)						X
49. Afghanistan (1980 -)	X					
50. Nicaragua (1981-90)	X					
51. Falkland Islands (1982)						X
52. Lebanon (1982-84)					X	X
53. Grenada (1983)					X	
54. Philippines (1984 -)			X			
55. Philippines (1985-86)		X				
56. Haiti (1985-86)		X				
57. Angola (1986 -)	X					
58. Narco Conflict (1986 -) [4]				X		
59. Persian Gulf (1987-88)					X	
60. Panama (1987-90)		X			X	
Totals [5]	**10**	**10**	**11**	**4**	**20**	**13**

1. Conventional combat, peacemaking, and rescue operations not related to counterterrorism.
2. Posturing, peacekeeping, sanctions, political and economic assistance.
3. Episodes indicated do not count in totals.
4. Narco conflict is closely connected with transnational terrorism.
5. The grand total is 68, because cases 29, 43, 52, and 60 count in two categories; cases 26 and 37 count in three.

The Middle East and East Asia boast 6 of the 11 ongoing LICs that currently exceed 10 years. Only conflict with the USSR shows clear signs of abatement:

Global	1	USSR
Middle East	4	Israel, Iran, Syria, Afghanistan
East Asia	2	North Korea, Cambodia
Africa	2	South Africa, Libya
Latin America	2	Cuba, El Salvador

About one-third of the cases that involved U.S. armed forces occurred far inland. Actions in another third were on or fairly close to coasts.

TYPES BY TIME AND PLACE

Six LIC types compete for attention (Figure 6 lists related conflicts chronologically). Zaire, Cambodia, Lebanon (1982-84), and Panama fit in two categories apiece. Cuba and Libya count in three. Miscellaneous combat and noncombat operations account for half of the 60 conflicts addressed by this study. Insurgencies/resistance movements, coups, and counterinsurgencies equally share most of the remainder.

Distribution by decade depicts a different pattern, as the table below indicates:

	Insurgency Resistance	Coups d'Etat	Counter Insurgency	Combatting Terrorism	Other Combat	Noncombat Operations
1980-89	3	3	3	4	5	8
1970-79	3	1	2	3	3	7
1960-69	1	4	5	0	3	4
1950-59	0	2	4	0	3	2
1940-49	3	0	3	0	1	3
1930-39	0	0	0	0	3	0
1920-29	0	0	0	0	4	0
1910-19	0	0	1	0	5	0
1899-09	0	0	1	0	3	1

Variform combat by U.S. conventional forces predominated before World War II, when the United States backed the first of 10 insurgencies and resistance movements. The Bay of Pigs fiasco, which failed to dislodge Fidel Castro in 1961, discouraged further actions of that sort until the Reagan Doctrine revived resistance 20 years later. No coups d'etat appeared before 1953, when the CIA helped unseat Iran's Prime Minister Mussaddiq. The United States has instigated or encouraged several more since then, with peaks in the 1960s and 1980s. U.S. counterinsurgency experience, with one exception (Philippines, 1899-1913), opened with three lengthy conflicts immediately after World War II. Two, three, or four have been in progress simultaneously each ensuing year. U.S. noncombat LICs, the most prevalent type since their onset in 1945, include the five longest conflicts (over 30 years). Anti/counterterrorism, which emerged in 1970, remains the least common U.S. LIC form, even counting narco conflict, which is closely affiliated.

U.S. involvement in insurgencies, resistance movements, and noncombat LICs was evenly dispersed through several regions. Over half of all U.S.-supported counterinsurgencies since 1899 occurred in East Asia. Latin America accounted for most coups and peacemaking operations (the latter are listed under "other combat"). Narco conflict, a global LIC, also centers on that region. The Middle East and North Africa (Libya) are the locus of most U.S. conflicts classed as "combatting terrorism."

	Insurgency, Resistance	Coups	Counter Insurgency	Combatting Terrorism	Other Combat	Noncombat Operations
East Asia	3	2	7	0	4	3
Mid-East	2	1	0	2	2	5
Latin Am.	3	7	2	0	8	3
Europe	1	0	1	0	0	1
Africa	1	0	1	1	1	4
USA	0	0	0	0	0	0
Global	0	0	0	1	0	1

VIOLENCE LEVELS

Force or threats of force were conspicuous elements of U.S. LICs until after World War II, as Figure 7 shows. U.S. "saber rattling" and military combat during low-intensity conflicts actually increased after 1970, despite widespread belief that the so-called Vietnam Syndrome and the Nixon Doctrine dampened such proclivities. The table below omits U.S. armed combat in Guatemala (1965-74), because much of it occurred between the two periods portrayed:

	1945-1965	1970-1990
Threats of Force	Azerbaijan (1946) China (1950-65) North Korea (1953-) Lebanon (1958) Berlin Wall (1961) Cuban Missile Crisis (1962)	Jordan (1970) Syria (1979-) Libya (1981-) Nicaragua (1981-90) Narco Conflict (1987-) Panama (1989)
Armed Combat	Formosa (1950-56) Vietnam (1955-65) Bay of Pigs (1961) Dominican Republic (1965)	Mayaguez (1975) Iran (1980, 87-88) Libya (1981, 86, 89) Lebanon (1984) Grenada (1983) Persian Gulf (1987-88) Panama (1989-90)

Figure 7

SIXTY FOREMOST U.S. LICs
Emphasis on U.S. Armed Forces

	1899-1919	1920-1939	1940-1949	1950-1959	1960-1969	1970-1979	1980-1989	TOTAL
No U.S. Military Units								
Global			1	1	1	1	2	2
Latin America			0	1	3	2	4	8
Europe			1	0	1	1	0	2
Middle East			1	2	1	5	2	6
Africa			0	0	1	2	2	3
East Asia			3	2	3	2	3	8
Total			6	6	10	13	13	29
U.S. Military Units, but no Combat Units								
Latin America			0	0	0	1	1	1
Europe			1	1	0	0	0	1
Middle East			0	0	0	0	0	0
Africa			0	0	1	0	0	1
East Asia			0	1	2	1	0	2
Total			1	2	3	2	1	5
U.S. Combat Units, * but no U.S. Combat								
Latin America	2			0	1	0	2	7
Europe	0			0	1	0	0	1
Middle East	0			1	0	1	1	3
Africa	1			0	0	0	0	0
East Asia	0			1	1	1	1	1
Total	3			2	3	2	4	12
U.S. Military Combat								
Latin America	3	3	0	0	3	1	2	9
Europe	0	0	3	0	0	0	0	1
Middle East	0	0	0	0	0	0	3	3
Africa	0	0	0	0	0	1	1	1
East Asia	3	1	3	2	0	1	0	8
Total	6	4	6	2	3	3	6	22
Grand Total	9	4	13	12	19	20	24	68

* Except isolated incidents.

NOTE: Totals do not add on the table, because many LICs overlap time periods and five countries count in two or more categories (Cuba, Iran, Israel, Libya, U.S.S.R.).

Figure 7 (cont.)

SIXTY FOREMOST U.S. LICs
Emphasis on U.S. Armed Forces

No U.S. Military Units

1. China (1945-49)
2. U.S.S.R. (1946 -)
3. Greece (1946-49)
4. Philippines (1946-55)
5. Indochina (1946-54)
6. Israel vs. Araba (1948 -)
7. Iran (1951-53)
8. Guatemala (1953-54)
9. Cuba (1960 -)[1]
10. South Africa (1960 -)
11. China (1960-79)
12. Brazil (1961-64)[1]
13. Vietnam (1963)
14. Libya (1970 -)[1]
15. Chile (1970-73)
16. Iraq (1972-75)
17. OPEC (1974-75)
18. Cyprus (1974-78)
19. Cambodia (1975 -)
20. Nicaragua (1978-79)
21. Iran (1979 -)[1]
22. Syria (1979 -)
23. Bolivia (1980-86)
24. Afghanistan (1980 -)
25. Falkland Islands (1982)
26. Philippines (1984 -)
27. Haiti (1985-86)
28. Philippines (1985-86)
29. Angola (1986 -)

U.S. Military Units, but no Combat Units [2]

1. U.S.S.R. (Berlin Airlift, 1948)
2. Laos (1955-65)
3. Congo (1964)
4. Thailand (1965-85)
5. El Salvador (1979 -)

[1] See * for brief exceptions.

[2] Excludes combat units employed in advisory and training capacities.

U.S. Combat Units, but no U.S. Combat

1. Colombia/Panama (1901-14)
2. Morocco (1904)
3. Cuba (1906-09)
4. North Korea (1953 -)
5. Lebanon (1958)
6. Dominican Republic (1960-62)
7. U.S.S.R. *
   a. Berlin Wall (1961)
   b. Cuban Missile Crisis (1962)
8. Brazil (1964)
9. Jordan (1970)
10. Iran (1980)
11. Nicaragua (1981-90)
12. Israel (1982 -)
13. Narco Conflict (1986 -)
14. Panama (1987-89)[1]

U.S. Military Combat

1. Philippines (1899-1913)
2. China (1900)
3. China (1912-41)
4. Mexico (1914-17)
5. Haiti (1915-34)
6. Dominican Republic (1916-24)
7. Nicaragua (1926-33)
8. Philippines (1942-45)
9. Burma (1942-45)
10. France (1944)
11. China (1953-59)
12. Vietnam (1955-65)
13. Cuba (1961) *
14. Dominican Republic (1965-66)
15. Guatemala (1965-74)
16. Mayaguez (1975)
17. Iran (1980) *
18. Libya (1981, 1986, 1989) *
19. Lebanon (1982-84)
20. Grenada (1983)
21. Persian Gulf (1987-88)
22. Panama (1989-90) *

Six of the seven U.S. post-Vietnam combat cases occurred during the 1980s. Three in the Middle East marked a new era, because earlier employment of U.S. armed services in that region had been confined to shows of force.

Americans commonly applaud short, successful wars and disapprove those that are lengthy and inconclusive, but experience thus far neither proves nor disproves whether they will tolerate sustained low-intensity combat. Few shooting wars in this study exceeded two years. Most of them preceded World War II: Philippines, 1899-1913; China, 1912-41; Mexico, 1914-17; Haiti, 1915-34; Dominican Republic,1916-24; Nicaragua, 1926-33. All involved sporadic, small unit actions with short U.S. casualty lists. None caused a serious public outcry.

Sharp U.S. setbacks and unexpected reversals more often provoke adverse public response and drastic policy revisions. The Bay of Pigs (Cuba 1961), Desert One hostage rescue disaster in Iran (1980), and the sudden death of 241 American military personnel when terrorists destroyed a headquarters building in Beirut (1983) are three prominent examples.

The U.S. Army or Marine Corps contingents predominated in most cases that included U.S. combat, although naval or air power (often both) habitually played important supporting roles. Two LICs in China (gunboat diplomacy 1912-41 and the defense of Formosa), Dominican Republic (1962), Jordan, and Persian Gulf were primarily Navy shows. The Air Force took precedence during the Berlin airlift and LICs in Zaire, the Falkland Islands, and the Philippines (1989), none of which involved U.S. combat.

Joint operations that no single U.S. military service dominated nevertheless began with the Boxer Rebellion and have been the rule for the last 40-plus years, whether employed for armed combat or shows of force. All LICs that include relatively large deployments reside in that category: Vietnam, 1965; Dominican Republic (1965); Grenada (1983); Persian Gulf (1987-88); and Panama (1989-90).

Half of the conflicts in this study excluded American military forces entirely. Security assistance (broadly defined) has been the basic U.S. instrument 17 times since 1946, when the U.S. Government extended economic and military aid to Greece and Turkey in response to the Truman Doctrine.[9] Sanctions have been the predominant U.S. instrument even more often.

OVERARCHING OBSERVATIONS

Only three of the 20 longest conflicts (10-40 years) involved much military combat by any belligerent: Israel (1956, 1967, and 1973); Cuba

---

[9] *U.S. Security Assistance: The Political Process*, Ed. by Ernest Graves and Stephen A. Hildreth, Lexington, MA., D.C. Heath & Co., 1985, 194 p.

(1961); and Vietnam (1960-65). Cold war with the Soviet Union, the longest running, has not been very explosive since the 1960s. Four of the 13 other active LICs, however, have great potential for unexpected and steep escalation (Map 2):

HOT	WARM	COOL
Israel	Cambodia	Afghanistan
Narco conflict	El Salvador	Angola
North Korea	Iran	Cuba
Philippines	Libya	South Africa
	Syria	USSR

The diverse characteristics and geographic distribution of those critical conflicts indicates a need for specialized, area-oriented, interdepartmental/interagency U.S. assets, civilian as well as military, skilled at low-intensity conflict. Strong U.S. strategic airlift and sealift capabilities are also essential, because no region is reachable overland. Rapid response and staying power both are required.

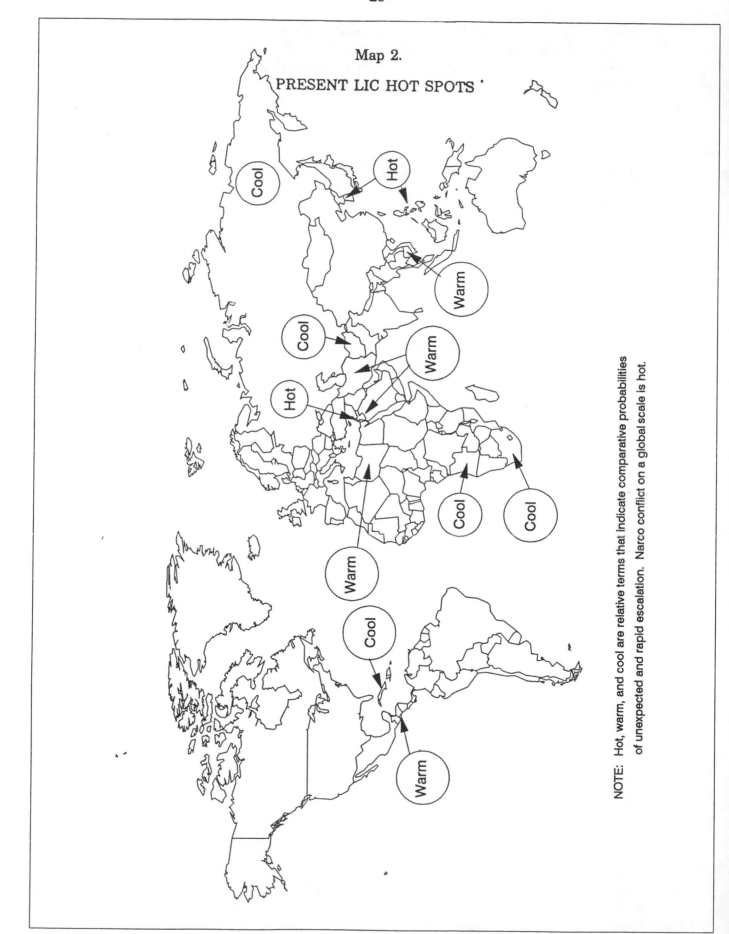

Map 2.

PRESENT LIC HOT SPOTS

NOTE: Hot, warm, and cool are relative terms that indicate comparative probabilities of unexpected and rapid escalation. Narco conflict on a global scale is hot.

U.S. LIC HIGHLIGHTS

Every low-intensity conflict has unique features. Strategic (as opposed to tactical) experience seldom can be transferred successfully from one time period to another without precise appreciation for changes that transpire in the interim. U.S. special operations forces and security assistance as we know them today, for example, did not exist before World War II. Lessons are equally tricky to transplant from place to place, unless the original region and new locale are analogous.

This section accordingly scrutinizes cases within each LIC category to isolate similarities and differences that constitute patterns and confirm or refute the presence of trends. Interests, objectives, policies, strategies, and instruments are typical topics for comparison. See Annex A for case summaries that include political-military contexts. Annex B summarizes congressional prescriptions.

INSURGENCIES/RESISTANCE

Support for insurgent and resistance groups constituted 10 of the 60 U.S. low-intensity conflicts selected for this study. Four continue:

		Annex A-B Case Numbers
1980s	Angola (1986-)	57
	Nicaragua (1981-90)	50
	Afghanistan (1986-)	49
1970s	Nicaragua (1978-79)	44
	Cambodia (1975-)	43
	Iraq (1972-75)	39
1960s	Cuba (1960-)	27
1950s		
1940s	France (1944)	13
	Burma (1942-45)	12
	Phillipines (1942-45)	11

The list above excludes resistance movements in East Germany (1953), Hungary (1956), and Czechoslovakia (1968), which comprised parts of the lengthy LIC called the Cold War. NATO policy in each instance was to contain communism, not roll it back, and the risk of war with the Soviet Union made direct intervention seem unattractive. U.S. support consequently was limited largely to public and private exhortations that encouraged uprisings we were poorly prepared and ill disposed to support.[1]

Common Characteristics

Resistance movements that opposed invaders or puppet governments in the Philippines, Burma, France, Afghanistan, and Cambodia constitute half of the cases in this category. The rest were some form of insurgency, including counterrevolutions in Cuba, Nicaragua, and Angola. The Soviet Union or its clients were U.S. rivals in five of seven cases since World War II.

All but two (Afghanistan, France) took place in jungles or swamps, where the climate is warm and wet (Map 3). France was the only arena with a highly developed infrastructure. Rudimentary road, rail, and communications nets otherwise were the rule. Large airfields were rare. Recipients of U.S. assistance almost invariably were located in remote and/or hostile territory inaccessible by sea.

All 10 LICs in this class featured armed conflict by the principal protagonists or their proxies. It was prolonged, except for operations in Cuba (1961). U.S. combat, mainly by Army and civilian special operations forces (SOF), was consistently small scale, usually *sub rosa*, and casualties were few, even during World War II, when they saw most action. Each U.S. unconventional warfare (UW) element comprised carefully selected, superlatively trained personnel who were organized and equipped to perform unorthodox tasks.

The main U.S. role switched from leadership to security assistance following the Bay of Pigs failure. The Nixon Doctrine (1969) institutionalized that trend. Afghan *Mujahiddin* and anti-Sandinista Contras received more than 90% of all aid to undergrounds and guerrillas. The former benefitted substantially from covert shipments, despite a flawed conduit. Overt assistance to the Contras was less successful, largely because Contra plans and U.S. programs were very loosely linked. A skeptical Congress, which questioned cost-effectiveness, allocated inconsistently and discontinued military aid after September 1987. Fewer funds ever reached Angolan and Cambodian

---

[1] U.S. Congress, House, *U.S. Relations With the Countries of Central and Eastern Europe*, report prepared by Francis T. Miko for the Subcommittee on Europe and the Middle East of the Committee on Foreign Affairs, 96th Congress, 1st Session, Washington, U.S. GPO, December 1979, p. 1-4.

Map 3

INSURGENCIES/RESISTANCE AND COUPS

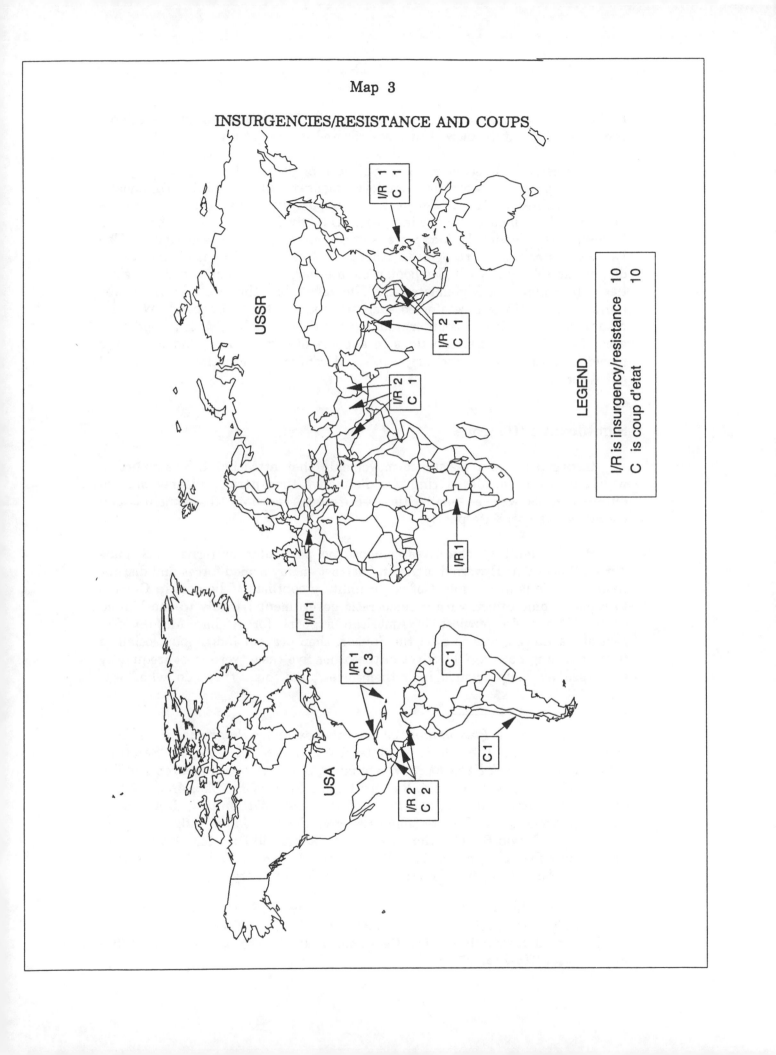

LEGEND

I/R is insurgency/resistance   10
C is coup d'etat   10

backwaters. In short, it seems safe to say that U.S. security assistance seldom promoted U.S. interests well in cases covered by this study.[2]

Stringent U.S. economic and political pressures designed to improve resistance prospects were first employed against Cuba in 1960. Diplomatic relations ceased in 1961. Severe export-import and other restrictions have been in effect since the following year. U.S. rivals in the four other cases, including the Soviet Union, were subsequent targets for sanctions. The United States never recognized Angola's Marxist government and broke diplomatic relations with Cambodian counterparts. We maintained marginal ties with regimes in Afghanistan and Nicaragua, but they were by no means normal. U.S. officials reinforced such strictures with embargoes.[3] Whether results were positive or counterproductive is debatable but, with the possible exception of Nicaragua, sanctions in support of insurgencies and resistance movements have not yet clearly expedited conflict termination on U.S. and allied terms.

Significant Differences

Insurgencies and resistance movements that attracted U.S. support in widely dispersed locales during two distinctive time periods display marked differences, as well as similarities. Purposes, concepts, instruments, and consequences correlate poorly.

Political-military objectives compose no particular pattern. U.S. aims during World War II were designed to distract enemy armed forces and disrupt their operations in the midst of major military conflicts. The goal in Cuba is to replace communism with a democratic government friendly to the United States. The main purpose of American support for Afghan *Mujahiddin*, partially achieved, was to evict the Soviets, then prevent indigenous socialists from retaining power. Objectives of the other five cases were most frequently expressed as "help friends help themselves," but help them do what was

---

[2] *Congressional Presentation for Security Assistance Programs, Fiscal Year 1990*, Washington, U.S. Dept. of State, 1989, p. 6-8, 74, 100-101; Serafino, Nina M., *Contra Aid, FY82-FY88*, Washington, Congressional Research Service, August 18, 1988, 14 p.; Cronin, Richard P., and Francis T. Miko, *Afghanistan: Status, U.S. Role, and Implications of a Soviet Withdrawal*, Issue Brief IB88049, Washington, Congressional Research Service, January 6, 1989, p. 9-10; Ottaway, David B., "CIA Removes Afghan Rebel Aid Director," *Washington Post*, September 2, 1989, p. 1; Collins, John M., *Green Berets, SEALs, and Spetsnaz*, N.Y., Pergamon-Brassey's, 1986, p. 50 and note 47, p. 135.

[3] Galdi, Theodor W., and Robert D. Shuey, *U.S. Economic Sanctions Imposed Against Specific Foreign Countries: 1979 to the Present*, Washington, Congressional Research Service, December 1, 1989, p. 5-8, 13-16, 37-42, 55-62, 141-148, 213-216.

unclear. Resultant ambiguities laid a wobbly foundation for plans, programs, and budgets.[4]

U.S. strategic and tactical UW doctrine was tailored in each case to suit special circumstances. Supreme Headquarters Allied Expeditionary Force (SHAEF), for example, centrally controlled U.S. SOF in France to ensure that their activities were coordinated closely with conventional military operations. General Eisenhower, in fact, called resistance forces the equivalent of 15 divisions.[5] OSS Detachment 101, which trained 10,000 Kachin tribesmen to conduct guerrilla warfare against the Japanese in Burma, was much more autonomous.[6] Resistance movements in Luzon and Mindanao, led by U.S. officers, remained isolated from each other and war efforts elsewhere; their endeavors never were as well integrated with grand schemes as analogous actions were in France.[7]

U.S. LICs in this category since World War II have been cast in much different molds. The Bay of Pigs (1961), a clumsy conventional invasion on Cuba's south shore, came to symbolize incompetence. Plans and implementation both were seriously flawed.[8] The Shah of Iran, at U.S. behest, helped Kurdish separatists bedevil pro-Soviet Iraq a decade later (1972-75), but chastened U.S. officials avoided direct support for insurgencies and resistance movements until the Reagan Doctrine blossomed 20 years after the Bay of Pigs.

U.S. strategies and tactics for the four active cases are distinct from each other and all six predecessors. The political and economic war of attrition against Castro's Cuba, basically above board, denies sustenance to an opponent. Aid to Cambodia through convoluted channels provides sustenance

---

[4] Collins, John M., *Green Berets, SEALs, and Spetsnaz*, p. 47-50, note 44 p. 134.

[5] Paddock, Alfred H., Jr., *U.S. Army Special Warfare: Its Origins*, Washington, National Defense University Press, 1982, p. 27-29; Miller, Russell, *The Resistance*, N.Y., Time-Life Books, 1979, p. 184-191.

[6] Peers, William R., and Dean Brelis, *Behind the Burma Road: The Story of America's Most Successful Guerrilla Forces*, Boston, Little, Brown, & Co., 1963, 246 p.

[7] Volkman, Russell W., *We Remained: Three Years Behind the Enemy Lines in the Philippines*, N.Y., W.W. Norton, 1954, 244 p.; Harkins, Philip, *Blackburn's Headhunters*, London, Cassell & Co., 1956, 326 p.; Asprey, Robert B., *War in the Shadows: The Guerrillas in History*, Vol. I, Garden City, N.Y., Doubleday, 1975, p. 562-578.

[8] Wyden, Peter, *Bay of Pigs: The Untold Story*, N.Y., Simon and Schuster, 1979, 352 p.; Kirkpatrick, Lyman B., Jr., "Paramilitary Case Study--The Bay of Pigs," *Naval War College Review*, November-December 1972, p. 32-42.

to potential friends. Behind-the-scenes support for resistance forces in Afghanistan and Angola emphasizes covert assistance. Nicaragua, the only U.S. LIC since 1961 that accentuated military strategies, tactics, and covert action, attracted even more criticism than the Bay of Pigs. The sale of arms to radical Iran and use of resultant revenues to fund the Contras created an international scandal[9]. Paramilitary Contras harassed the Sandinista Government and probably helped multiply its economic problems, but never developed a strong constituency inside Nicaragua. Sandinistas, who feared a U.S. invasion, built an Army that outnumbered counterparts in eight NATO nations: Belgium, Canada, Denmark, Iceland, Luxembourg, the Netherlands, Norway, and Portugal.[10]

Culminating Comments

U.S. support for insurgencies and resistance movements includes no unqualified success since World War II. The Bay of Pigs was an unqualified failure. None of the four active cases seems likely to escalate sharply, but neither do any seem near culmination. It is too early to tell if Afghanistan, the most promising, will combine tactical success with strategic failure, but the Brezhnev Doctrine, designed to prevent reversals of socialism, apparently still applies to that beleaguered country, despite the Soviet withdrawal.[11]

Experience from the 10 cited cases suggests that some essential skills which served well during World War II now need sharpening:

---

[9] U.S. Congress, Report of the Congressional Committees Investigating the *Iran-Contra Affair*, S. Rept. No. 100-216, H. Rept. No. 100-433, 100th Congress, 1st Session, Washington, U.S. GPO, November 1987, 690 p.; *Report of the President's Special Review Board*, Washington, U.S. GPO, February 26, 1987, 281 p.; U.S. Congress, Senate, *Preliminary Inquiry Into the Sale of Arms to Iran and Possible Diversion of Funds to the Nicaraguan Resistance*, Report of the Select Committee on Intelligence, 100th Congress, 1st Session, Washingotn, U.S. GPO, February 2, 1987, 57 p.

[10] *The Military Balance, 1988-89*, London, International Institute for Strategic Studies, 1988, p. 58-61, 72-76, 200-201; Lynch, David J., "Defector: Ortega OK'd Military Buildup," *Defense Week*, December 21, 1987, p. 10; Branigan, William, "Nicaragua Describes Major Arms Buildup," *Washington Post*, December 13, 1987, p.1.

[11] Ottaway, David B., "U.S. Misread Gorbachev, Official Says," *Washington Post*, September 10, 1989, p. 1; "Yuli Vorontsov: Afghanistan Will Hold Out," *News and Views from the USSR*, Washington, Soviet Embassy, March 20, 1989, 4 p.; Cronin, Richard P. *Afghanistan After the Soviet Withdrawal : Contenders for Power*, Washington, Congressional Research Service, March 2, 1989, 39 p.

- Unconventional warfare (UW) techniques.

- Paramilitary techniques.

- Proper employment of security assistance to insurgents and resistance forces.

- Proper employment of sanctions against their opponents.

COUPS D'ETAT

Ten coups d'etat that the United States helped plan and/or implement were selected for study. One (Cuba, 1960-65) is part of a much longer conflict that continues:

		Annex A-B Case Numbers
1980s	Panama (1989)	60
	Haiti (1986)	56
	Philippines (1986)	55
1970s	Chile (1970, 1973)	38
1960s	Vietnam (1963)	32
	Brazil (1964)	31
	Dominican Republic (1962)	29
	Cuba (1960-65)	27
1950s	Guatemala (1954)	23
	Iran (1954)	20

This category could have incorporated plots such as those against Congo President Patrice Lumumba (1961), Indonesian President Sukarno (1966), and Cambodian Prince Sihanouk (1970), but alleged U.S. participation was tangential and/or inconclusive compared with the cited examples.[12]

---

[12] U.S. Congress, Senate, *Alleged Assassination Plots Involving Foreign Leaders*, An Interim Report of the Select Committee to Study Governmental Operations with respect to Intelligence Activities, 94th Congress, 1st Session, Washington, U.S. GPO, November 20, 1975, p. 4, 13-70; Kissinger, Henry A., *White House Years*, Boston, Little, Brown and Co., 1979, p. 457-468; Hersh, Seymour, *The Price of Power: Kissinger in the Nixon White House*, New York, Summit Books, 1983, p. 184-202.

Common Characteristics

Unlike U.S. supported insurgencies and resistance movements, each coup was instigated by a special interest group. Official U.S. dissatisfaction with every incumbent was on public display, but any direct collaboration between U.S. and indigenous schemes was invariably covert. There were no widespread uprisings or prolonged operations. No doctrine addresses U.S. support for coups, which often depend most on the idiosyncracies of pivotal players. The basic objective, to replace the party in power, nevertheless was achieved in 8 of 10 instances. Failures transpired in Cuba and Panama.

All 10 coups conducted with U.S. complicity erupted well after World War II. Eight took place in tropical parts of Latin America (Map 3), but geographic influences on their conduct were negligible, because key actions occurred in cities. Combat operations by indigenous forces were brief and small-scale (even surgical) or nonexistent.

Rare threats of U.S. force produced no positive results. A carrier task force dispatched toward Brazil in March 1964 to expedite the demise of President Joao Goulart's government aborted that mission before arrival, then explained its presence as a training exercise.[13] Demonstrations never made Panama's Noriega knuckle under; U.S. troops on site during the unsuccessful coup in October 1989 did not deter swift reprisals.[14]

U.S. military formations never participated actively in any cited coup. Political and economic sanctions, the primary substitute, provided substantial leverage in eight cases (Vietnam, Cuba, and Panama were exceptions). They made it virtually impossible for Ferdinand Marcos (Philippines), Jean-Claude Duvalier (Haiti), and Mohammed Mussaddiq (Iran) to cope with internal problems and retain control of their respective countries. U.S. security assistance

---

[13] Parker, Phyllis R., *Brazil and the Quiet Intervention*, 1964, Austin, Tx, University of Texas Press, 1979, 147 p.; David, Steven R., *Third World Coups d'Etat and International Security*, Baltimore, Md., Johns Hopkins University Press, 1987, p. 49-51.

[14] Pertman, Adam, "U.S. Shows Its Might to Press Noriega," *Boston Globe*, August 17, 1989, p. 1; "Panama Says U.S. Is Planning to Invade," *Washington Times*, August 28, 1989, p. 10; Pear, Robert, "U.S. Now Says Noriega Can Stay If He Steps Aside," *New York Times*, August 16, 1989, p. 9; Corddry, Charles W., "U.S. to Send 1,300 Troops to Panama," *Baltimore Sun*, April 2, 1988, p. 1; Englberg, Stephen, "Bush Aides Admit a U.S. Role in Coup and Bad Handling," *New York Times*, October 6, 1989, p. 1.

in contrast sometimes helped consolidate or sustain success, but never helped achieve it.[15]

Actions confined primarily to political warfare accomplished the ultimate mission twice. Behind-the-scenes operations very nearly boomeranged before CIA's last-minute manipulation of mobs in Teheran helped topple Iran's left-leaning Prime Minister Mussaddiq and placed Shah Mohammed Reza Pahlavi back on the Peacock Throne, after brief exile in Italy.[16] The first attempt to unseat Chile's President Salvadore Allende (1970) failed, but continuing U.S. efforts, which emphasized dirty tricks such as bribes, disinformation, and covert funds for opposition parties, contributed to his downfall three years later (September 1973).[17]

Psychological operations, which often were useful, proved decisive once. CIA actions engineered to oust President Arbenz Guzmán from Guatemala in 1954 were a masterpiece of deception that caused his followers to capitulate when faced with armed forces far less capable than they were led to believe. Ends and means matched in cost-effective ways, armed conflict was short and conclusive, casualties were few. [18]

Three cited coups culminated in actual or attempted assassinations. Senior U.S. officials condoned and may have encouraged the first, against

---

[15] See, for example, Niksch, Larry A., *Philippines under Aquino*, Issue Brief 86104, Washington, Congressional Research Service, July 3, 1986, 14 p.; Abbott, Elizabeth, *Haiti: The Duvaliers and Their Legacy*, New York, McGraw-Hill, 1988, p. 296-330 passim; Galdi, Theodor W. and Robert D. Shuey, *U.S. Economic Sanctions Against Specific Foreign Countries*, p. 86-89, 141-142, 144-145; Roosevelt, Kermit, *Countercoup: The Struggle for the Control of Iran*, N.Y., McGraw-Hill, 1979, 217 p.

[16] Rubin, Barry, *Paved with Good Intentions: The American Experience in Iran*, NY, Oxford University Press, 1980, 426 p.; Roosevelt, Kermit, *Countercoup: The Struggle for Control of Iran*, p. 169-197.

[17] U.S. Congress, Senate, *Covert Action in Chile, 1963-1973*, Staff Report of the Select Committee to Study Governmental Operations with Respect to Intelligence Activities, 94th Congress, 1st Session, Washington, U.S. GPO, December 18, 1975, 62 p.; U.S. Congress, House, *United States and Chile During the Allende Years, 1970-1973*, Hearings before the Subcommittee on Inter-American Affairs of the Committee of Foreign Affairs, 94th Congress, 1st Session Washington, U.S. GPO, 1975, 677 p.

[18] Schlesinger, Stephen and Steven Kinzer, *Bitter Fruit*, Garden City, NY, Doubleday Anchor Books, 1983, 320 p.; Freemantle, Brian, *CIA*, NY, Stein and Day, 1983 p. 169-170; *Facts on File*, June 15-24, 1954, p. 206 and June 25-July 1, 1954, p. 213.

dictatorial President Rafael Trujillo (Dominican Republic, May 31, 1961).[19] The violent death of South Vietnam's President No Dinh Diem during the course of a U.S.-encouraged coup two years later (November 2, 1963) may have been spontaneous,[20] but unfulfilled contracts on the life of Cuban Chief of State Fidel Castro during the period 1960-65 were calculated, according to congressional findings.[21]

Culminating Comments

Whether any of the coups d'etat cited strengthened U.S. politico-military positions is debatable, because pluses and minuses seldom were cleancut, even when friendly governments superseded anti-U.S. leftists. Short-term benefits often became long-term liabilities. Regional results sometimes bore little resemblance to those that obtained in the targeted country or in the United States (Figure 8).

Covert U.S. actions that helped displace President Salvador Allende, for example, disrupted long-standing democratic traditions in Chile. Army Commander-in-Chief René Schneider, a strict constitutionalist who abhorred military coups, was mortally wounded when he resisted abduction.[22] The military junta that eventually relieved Allende's duly elected regime repressed all opposition and paved the way for the dictatorship of General Augusto Pinochet Ugarte, who crushed local critics.[23] Eighteen months and nine governmental flip-flops in the midst of war elapsed after the murder of Vietnam's President Diem before Air Vice Marshall Nguyen Cao Ky seized control in June 1965. General Nguyen Van Thieu (Ky was his running mate) finally won a presidential election with 35% of the vote in September 1967; 10 civilian candidates who split the remaining 65% declared fraud. Neither

---

[19] U.S. Congress, Senate, *Alleged Assassination Plots Involving Foreign Leaders*, p. 191-216, 262-263, 270-272.

[20] *Ibid.*, p. 217-223, 261-262.

[21] *Ibid.*, p. 71-180, 267-270, 274-279.

[22] *Ibid.*, p. 5, 225-254, 272.

[23] Falcoff, Mark, Arturo Valenzuela, and Susan Kaufman Purcell, *Chile: Prospects for Democracy*, NY, Council on Foreign Relations, 1988, 80 p.; Browning, D. Lea, Laura Trejo, and Marcel Zwamborn, *Chile: The Plebiscite and Beyond*, Washington, International Human Rights Law Group, February 1989, 120 p.

the United States nor South Vietnam profited much from protracted instability in such circumstances.[24] Every other case is somewhat equivocal.

Coups d'etat, perhaps more than any other type LIC, demand exceptional foresight.[25] U.S leaders fortunately should be able to think future problems through and plot several successive moves on the international "chessboard" before they decide to participate, because preparation times in most cases are measured in months. Bare bones doctrine, perhaps in the form of a checklist, might help U.S. officials pick the proper option. Reasonably reliable intelligence concerning likely successors, their attitudes toward the United States, and their expected programs is imperative. So is reasonable appreciation for congressional and public opinion, at home and abroad.

---

[24] Karnow, Stanley, *Vietnam: A History*, NY, Viking Press, 1983, p. 270-422 passim; Asprey, Robert B., *War in the Shadows*, Vol. II, p. 1152-54, 1192-94, 1215.

[25] Kirkpatrick, Jeanne, "The Coup Game," *Washington Post*, October 16, 1989, p. A19; Luttwak, Edward, *Coup d'Etat*, NY, Alfred A. Knopf, 1969, 209 p.

FIGURE 8

COUP D'ETAT WINNERS AND LOSERS
Incumbents Compared with Replacements

	Incumbents	Replacements
Panama (1989)		
Name	Noriega	Coup failed
Political Office	None	
Civil/Military Status	Military	
Accession to Power	Intrigue	
Power Base	Armed forces	
Political Bias	Ambivalent	
Alignment	Anti U.S.	
Philippines (1986)		
Name	Marcos	Aquino
Political Office	President	President
Civil/Military Status	Civilian	Civilian
Accession to Power	Elected	Elected
Power Base	Political machine	Popular support
Political Bias	Right	Center
Alignment	Pro U.S.	Neutral
Haiti (1986)		
Name	Duvalier	Namphy
Political Office	President	President
Civil/Military Status	Civilian	Military
Accession to Power	Rigged referendum	Coup
Power Base	Tonton Macoute	Security Forces
Political Bias	Right	Right
Alignment	Neutral	Neutral
Chile (1973)		
Name	Allende	Pinochet
Political Office	President	President
Civil/Military Status	Civilian	Military
Accession to Power	Election	Coup
Power Base	Popular support	Security forces
Political Bias	Left	Right
Alignment	Anti U.S.	Anti Communist

Figure 8 (Con't)

	Incumbents	Replacements
Brazil (1964)		
Name	Goulart	Branco
Political Office	President	President
Civil/Military Status	Civilian	Military
Accession to Power	Vice Presidency	Coup
Power Base	Underdeveloped	Armed Forces
Political Bias	Left	Right
Alignment	Anti U.S.	Pro U.S.
Vietnam (1963)		
Name	Diem	Thieu
Political Office	President	President
Civil/Military Status	Civilian	Military
Accession to Power	Mandate	Rigged election
Power Base	Catholics, Northerners	Armed forces
Political Bias	Right	Right
Alignment	Pro U.S.	Pro U.S.
Dominican Rebublic (1961)		
Name	Trujillo	Bosch
Political Office	President	President
Civil/Military Status	Military	Civilian
Accession to Power	Seizure	Elected
Power Base	Armed Forces	Armed forces
Political Bias	Right	Left
Alignment	Pro U.S.	Anti U.S.
Cuba (1960-65)		
Name	Castro	None
Political Office	President	
Civil/Military Status	Military	
Accession to Power	Revolution	
Power Base	Popular Support	
Political Bias	Left	
Alignment	Anti U.S.	

Figure 8 (Con't)

	Incumbents	Replacements
Guatemala (1954)		
Name	Arbenz	Armas
Political Office	President	President
Civil/Military Status	Civilian	Military
Accession to Power	Elected	Coup
Power Base	Popular Support	Armed Forces
Political Bias	Left	Right
Alignment	Anti U.S.	Pro U.S.
Iran (1953)		
Name	Mussaddiq	Pahlavi
Political Office	Prime Minister	Shah
Civil/Military Status	Civilian	Civilian
Accession to Power	Appointed	Dynastic
Power Base	Popular support	Security forces
Political Bias	Left	Right
Alignment	Anti U.S.	Pro U.S.

COUNTERINSURGENCIES

Eleven counterinsurgencies selected for study are grouped below in chronological order, according to the decade during which they started. Two remain active:

		Annex A-B Case Numbers
1980s	Philippines (1984-)	54
	El Salvador (1980-)	47
1970s		
1960s	Thailand (1965-85)	35
	Guatemala (1965-74)	34
	Zaire (1960-64)	30
1950s	Laos (1955-65)	25
	Vietnam (1955-65)	24
1940s	Indochina (1946-54)	17
	Philippines (1946-55)	16
	Greece (1946-49)	15
1930s		
1920s		
1910-19		
1899-1909	Philippines (1899-1913)	1

Vietnam and Laos (1955-65) were parts of a regional struggle to unify former French Indochina under Vietnamese rule. This survey treats them separately to emphasize differences.

Common Characteristics

The 10 counterinsurgency cases that post-dated World War II display many more similarities than differences, despite wide dispersion in time and space. East Asia was the focus for 60%. Another 20% took place in Central America. Tropical lands were most popular; China and Greece were exceptions. The latter also was the only highly developed country (Map 4).

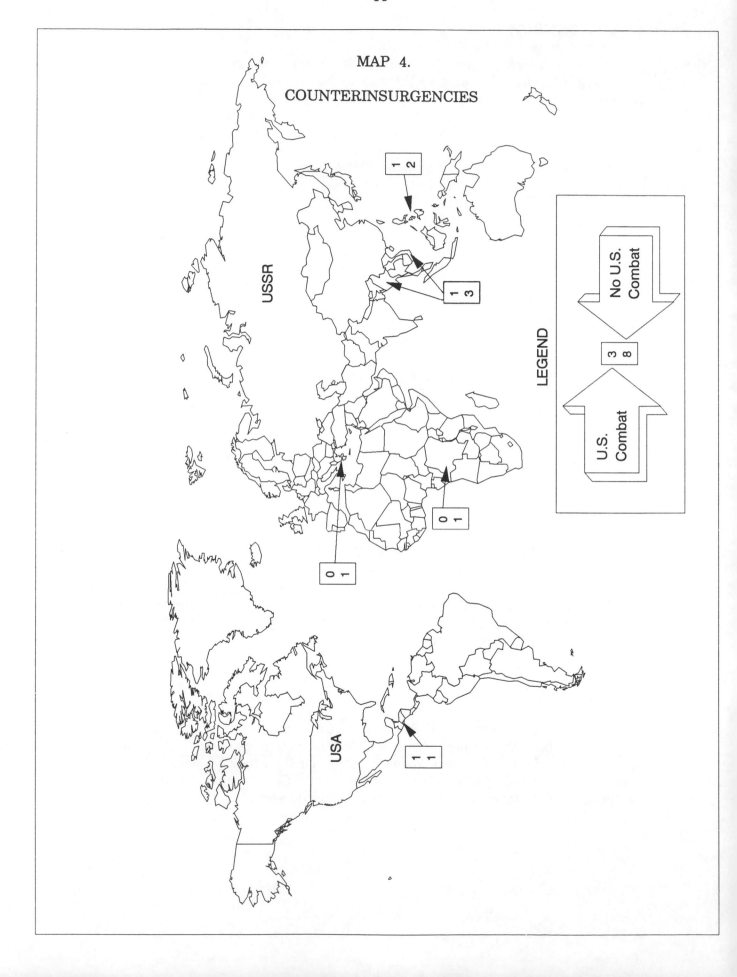

MAP 4.

COUNTERINSURGENCIES

Foreign internal defense (FID), America's paramount counterinsurgency role, tends to be a protracted process. U.S. participation in four of the post-World War II conflicts lingered longer than 10 years (El Salvador, Thailand 1965 to 1985, and Vietnam/Laos from 1955 to 1965). Five more exceeded five years. The shortest, in Greece, was 3 years plus 8 months.

Communists and their sympathizers were among U.S. opponents in every counterinsurgency since 1946. Containment, to prevent the expansion of communist influence and preserve the balance of power, was a major U.S. objective. Nation building, a concomitant aim, sought to create or strengthen popular support for friendly foreign governments, even in Greece, which had long been a democratic state.[26] Political, economic, legal, social, and technological programs comprised the core. "Do-it-yourself" policies put the onus on U.S. allies in all anti-communist counterinsurgencies, other than Vietnam after the U.S. ground combat buildup began in 1965 (Iadrang Valley, the first big battle, occurred in mid-November).[27] Military assistance to U.S. friends even so was important in every instance. Sanctions were inapplicable against insurgents, but occasionally increased pressures on outside supporters.

U.S. armed forces began to develop counterinsurgency doctrine in the 1920s. The prototype document, a Marine Corps manual published in 1940, dealt mainly with military aspects, especially small unit tactics and logistics.[28] The U.S. Army Center for Special Warfare further focused and refined doctrine during the 1950s and early 1960s, with meticulous attention to civil-military relationships.[29] The gulf between theory and practice, however, remained large, partly because serious students of the subject were scarce, even in the Defense Department, and few of them had much influence on high level decisionmaking. U.S. clients often performed less well than expected as a result.

Seven counterinsurgencies minimized U.S. military activity. U.S. on-the-spot advisors, training teams, and support forces, such as airlift, supply, and maintenance, were most prominent in Greece, the Philippines (1946-53), Vietnam and Laos (1955-65), Zaire, Thailand, and El Salvador.

---

[26] Roubatis, Yiannis P. *Tangled Webs: The U.S. in Greece, 1947-1967*, N.Y. Pella Publishing Co., 1987, p. 31-90.

[27] *The Pentagon Papers: As Published By the New York Times*, N.Y., Quadrangle Books, 1971, p. 392-427, 470-496.

[28] *Small Wars Manual*, Washington, U.S. GPO, 1940, 511 p.

[29] The U.S. Army Psychological Warfare Center, established in 1952, was successively redesignated the Special Warfare Center (1957), John F. Kennedy Center for Special Warfare (1964), JFK Center for Military Assistance (1969), and JFK Special Warfare Center and School (1986).

Significant Differences

Scatterguns might have dispensed causes of the 11 insurgencies and resistance movements that this country countered. Stimuli were more complex than the following summary suggests, but main motivations nevertheless are identifiable. Deep-seated dissatisfaction with the way governments served the people clearly led the list. Ideology often underlay other causes, but contrary to U.S. belief was elemental only once (Greece):

Reform	Anti-colonial Resistance	Reunification	Separatism	Ideology
Phillipines (1946-53) Guatemala (1965-74) Thailand (1965-85) El Salvador (1979-) Philippines (1984-)	Philippines (1899-1913) Indochina (1946-54)	Vietnam (1955-65) Laos (1955-65)	Zaire (1960-64)	Greece (1946-49)

Extensive U.S. armed combat connected with counterinsurgency was limited to three cases, the last of which terminated 16 years ago: Philippines (1899-1913); Vietnam (1964-65); and Guatemala (1965-74). Invaders from beyond friendly borders posed significant problems only once, when North Vietnam employed forces in South Vietnam, Laos, and Cambodia. Three more cases, however, featured extensive logistic support to U.S. opponents from privileged sanctuaries (Greece, Zaire, and El Salvador).

U.S. assistance for France during its futile struggle to defeat the Viet Minh (1946-54)[30] and attempts to preserve a free and independent government in the Philippines (1984-)[31] were atypical FIDs, because both featured remote control. U.S. representatives on site were few and their roles were restricted.

---

[30] U.S. Congress, Senate, *The U.S. Government and the Vietnam War*, Part I, p. 1-227; *The Pentagon Papers*, p. 1-67; Asprey, Robert B., *War In the Shadows*, Vol. II, p. 735 - 803.

[31] Steinberg, David Joel, *The Philippines: A Singular and Plural Place*, Boulder, CO, Westview Press, 1982, p. 99-130; Niksch, Larry A., *Philippines Under Aquino*, Issue Brief IB 86104, Washington, Congressional Research Service, March 27, 1990, 13 p.

Aguinaldo's revolt followed by Moro uprising in the Philippines (1899-1913) probably was the first and last of its kind.[32] America no longer has "imperial" holdings. Puerto Rican dissidents who insist on independence pose the only potentially analogous threat. Guam and the Virgin Islands are comparatively quiescent.

Culminating Comments

Few U.S. counterinsurgencies constitute unqualified successes. One recent study, for example, concludes that in Greece and the Philippines (1946-53), two of the most auspicious, "the American program per se was irrelevant" for many reasons.[33] All 11 U.S. efforts could be called unprofessional, if that overstatement were correct but, in fact, only three were unqualified failures: Indochina (1946-54); Vietnam and Laos (1955-65). U.S. assistance was insufficient in the first instance and frequently inappropriate in the others. Overall results were most favorable in the Philippines (1899-1913) and Greece. The rest fit somewhere on a scale between fully satisfactory and unsatisfactory or, like El Salvador and the Philippines (1984-) remain uncertain.

U.S. counterinsurgency experience since World War II furnishes three potentially useful lessons that might improve future performance:

- The United States can help friends help themselves most effectively only when counterinsurgency principles and practices are in consonance and U.S. assistance suits the situation.

- Assistance to countries unwilling to reform rarely is wise, because desired results almost always are delayed and may be unobtainable.

---

[32] Gates, John Morgan, *Schoolbooks and Krags: The United States Army in the Philippines, 1899-1902*, Westport, CT, Greenwood Press, 1973, 315 p.; Merriman, Howard M., "The Philippines (1899-1902)," in *Challenge and Response in Internal Conflict*, Ed. by D. M. Condit and Bert H. Cooper, Jr., et al., Vol. I, Washington, Center for Research in Social Systems, American University, February, 1968, p. 91-114; Dupuy, R. Ernest and William H. Baumer, *The Little Wars of the United States*, N.Y., Hawthorn Books, 1968, p. 65-93; Sarkesian, Sam C., *America's Forgotten Wars: The Counterrevolutionary Past and Lessons for the Future*, Westport, CT, Greenwood Press, 1984, p. 165-177.

[33] Shafer, D. Michael, *Deadly Paradigms: The Failure of U.S. Counterinsurgency Policy*, Princeton, N.J., Princeton University Press, 1988, p. 238-239.

• Patience is one prerequisite for success, since CI operations invariably are lengthy.[34]

COMBATTING TERRORISM

U.S. experience combatting transnational terrorism is scant compared with most other classes of low-intensity conflict. Only three lengthy LICs against renegade states, punctuated by periodic eruptions, are represented. None preceded 1970. Two radiated from the Middle East, the other from neighboring north Africa:

	Annex A-B Case Numbers
Syria (1979 -)	46
Iran (1979 -)	45
Libya (1970 -)	37

Senior U.S. officials also have accused North Korea, Cuba, and Nicaragua of sponsoring and/or supporting transnational terrorism as a matter of state policy. The Soviet Union allegedly participated as well, although William J. Casey, speaking as Director of Central Intelligence, conceded that, "to give the devil his due, we have seen only indirect evidence," because all such alleged activities are covert or clandestine, and thus hard to prove.[35] Low-intensity conflicts with all four of those suspect countries therefore are covered elsewhere in this report.

---

[34] "A thoroughly methodical approach. . .encourages a steamroller outlook which provides the people with faith in ultimate victory" by counterinsurgents. "By preparing for a long haul, the government may achieve victory quicker than expected. By seeking quick military victories. . it will certainly get a long haul for which neither it nor the people may be prepared." Thompson, Robert, *Defeating Communist Insurgency*, NY, Praeger, 1966, p. 58.

[35] Weinraub, Bernard, "President Accuses 5 'Outlaw' states of World Terror," *New York Times*, July 9, 1985, p. 1; Sterling, Clare, *the Terror Network: The Secret War of International Terrorism*, N.Y., Holt, Rinehart, and Winston/Reader's Digest, 1981, 357 p.; Casey, William J., "The International Linkages -- What Do We Know?," in *Hydra of Carnage: International Linkages of Terrorism*, Ed. by Uri Ra'anan et al, Lexington, MA, Lexington Books, 1986, p. 8-9.

Common Characteristics

No transnational terrorists have yet attacked important targets in the United States (some consider President Kennedy's assassination a salient exception). U.S. citizens and property overseas, however, have repeatedly been targeted.[36]

U.S. tormenters typically projected power far beyond their borders to conceal the true source of skulduggery. Hostage-taking by Ayatollah Khomeini's henchmen in Teheran was the single exception. Assassinations, abductions, bombings, and aircraft hijacking were favorite tactics.[37]

Successful anti/counterterrorism depends on timely, accurate human intelligence (HUMINT). More often than not, however, deficiencies prevented positive identification of perpetrators and their whereabouts. CIA, for example, reportedly had no agents in Teheran to answer critical questions when U.S. hostage rescue planning began in November 1979.[38] Reliable information is still especially sparse concerning hostages that pro-Iran groups presumably have held in Lebanon since 1984.[39]

Persistent doctrinal disputes make it difficult to get U.S.interagency or interdepartmental players all operating in consonance at the same time.[40] Of-

---

[36] Wootten, James P. *Terrorist Incidents Involving U.S. Citizens or Property 1981-1989: A Chronology*, Issue Brief IB86096, Washington, Congressional Research Service, March 26, 1990, 15 p.

[37] Sample sources include Mark, Clyde R., *U.S. Embassy in Beirut: The Bombing of Sept. 20, 1984*, Issue Brief IB84133, Washington, Congressional Research Service, February 11 1985, 20 p.; *Hijacking*, Washington, Department of Defense News Summary, September 30, 1985, 10 p.; Browne, Marjorie Ann and Ellen C. Collier, *Foreign Airport Security: Diplomatic Framework and U.S. Policy*, Issue Brief IB85162, Washington, Congressional Research Service, March 4, 1987, 15 p.

[38] Beckwith, Charlie A. and Donald Knox, *Delta Force*, N.Y., Harcourt Brace Jovanovich, 1983, p. 192, 199-200.

[39] Mark, Clyde R., *Lebanon: The Remaining U.S. Hostages*, Issue Brief IB85183, Washington, Congressional Research Service, April 10, 1990, 15 p.

[40] Collins, John M., *Green Berets, SEALs, and Spetsnaz*, p. 57-62. Problems described therein persist.

ficial policy, for example, promises no concessions to terrorists.[41] U.S. officials nevertheless sold or approved the sale of weapons to hostile Iran, which they hoped would intercede on U.S. behalf with pro-Iran hostage holders in Lebanon. Executive Order 12333, which forbids assassination (an ill-defined term) as a facet of national policy, never was intended to protect terrorists, but does so as presently interpreted.[42] Whether political and economic sanctions impress terrorists and sponsoring states in desired ways is disputable.[43]

Significant Differences

U.S. anti/counterterror tactics have been quite dissimilar, despite the small sample. Orthodox and unorthodox operations variously accentuated active and passive options. Violence varied remarkably, even when armed forces were the chosen implement.

The U.S. LIC with Libya has been in progress since 1970.[44] Proven and alleged provocations that peaked with the terrorist bombing of a night club in Berlin, Germany finally triggered a U.S. retaliatory air strike against five target areas near Tripoli and Benghazi on April 15, 1986. More than 100 aircraft, including 16 F-111 bombers from bases in Great Britain and 14 A-6 carrier-based fighter-bombers from the Mediterranean, participated in that 11-minute raid, which remains one of a kind. No other U.S. counterterror action similarly employed conventional air power to punish the perpetator. That

---

[41] *The United States Government Antiterrorism Program: Summary Report*, Washington, Executive Committee on Terrorism for the Special Coordination Committee, National Security Council, June 1979, 22 p.; *Public Report of the Vice President's Task Force on Combatting Terrorism*, Washington, U.S. GPO, February 1986, 34 p.; *International Terrorism: The Taking of U.S. Citizens Hostage*, Washington, Dept. of State, May 6, 1986, 3 p.

[42] Paragraph 2.11, Section 401, Title 50, United States Code, Annotated, *Executive Order 12333*, December 4, 1981; *Assassination*, Draft Memorandum of Law, Washington, Office of the Judge Advocate General, Dept. of the Army, undated (1989), 8 p.; Barclay, Glen St. J., "Selective Assassination An Answer To the Terrorist's Trade, *Pacific Defense Reporter*, February 1987, p. 87; Beecher, William, "Considering Assassination," *Boston Globe*, December 14, 1984, p. 23.

[43] "How Do Boycotts Work? Let Me Count the Ways . . . ," *Counterterrorism*, June 29, 1987, p. 4.

[44] Mark, Clyde R., *Libya: U.S. Relations*, Issue Brief IB86040, Washington, Congressional Research Service, May 26, 1987, 21 p.

particular action accomplished its purpose, which was to deter Libyan terorism, but lessons learned await additional demonstrations, because identical procedures might backfire disastrously under indistinguishable circumstances.[45]

Three U.S. hostage rescue missions in dissimilar environments demonstrate needs for diversified forces and skills.

Four U.S. Navy Tomcats on October 11, 1985 intercepted an Egyptian airliner enroute to Tunis and forced it to land at Sigonella, Sicily with Palestinian Liberation Front (PLF) terrorists on board after they hijacked the cruise ship *Achille Lauro* and subsequently surrendered to authorities in Cairo. Repercussions of that politically sensitive operation temporarily strained U.S. international relations, first with President Mubarak in Cairo, who returned the felons to PLO custody, then with the Italian Government, which released the apparent ringleader without trial.[46]

The abortive Desert One raid on April 24, 1980 to rescue U.S. hostages in Tehran was supposed to clandestinely infiltrate a highly skilled heliborne force into hostile territory, then airlift captives to safety. It failed. Iran voluntarily released all captives on January 20, 1981, after 444 days imprisonment. Whether U.S. political and economic sanctions contributed is dubious,[47] but they probably reduced Iran's military capabilities during its subsequent war with Iraq.

---

[45] *Ibid.*, p. 9-10; Turndorf, David, "The U.S. Raid on Libya: A Forceful Response to Terrorism," *Brooklyn Journal of International Law*, Vol. 14, No. 1, 1988, p. 187-221; Cordesman, Anthony, "After the Raid: The Emerging Lessons from the U.S. Attack on Libya," *Armed Forces*, August 1986, p. 355-360; Zilian, Frederick, Jr., "The U.S. Raid on Libya -- and NATO," *Orbis*, Fall 1986, p. 499-524.

[46] The PLF is a radical splinter group of the Palestinian Liberation Organization (PLO). Wilson, George C., "Weinberger Tells How Hijackers Were Intercepted," *Washington Post*, October 11, 1985, p. 18; Keller, Bill, "U.S. Plans Were Made on Open Line," *New York Times*, October 15, 1985, p. 10; Kifner, John, "U.S. Aide Bids Mubarak End Divisions," *New York Times*, October 22, 1985, p. 10; Pichirallo, Joe and Howard Kurtz, "Federal Counts Filed Against 4 Italy Holds," *Washington Post*, October 15, 1985, p. 1.

[47] Beckwith, Charlie and Donald Knox, *Delta Force*, p. 187-300; *Rescue Mission Report* (Holloway Report), unpublished monograph, Washington, Dept. of Defense, August 1980, 78 p.; Ryan, Paul B., *The Iranian Rescue Mission: Why It Failed*, Annapolis, Md, Naval Institute Press, 1985, 185 p.; Carter, Jimmy, *Keeping Faith: Memoirs of a President*, NY, Bantam Books, 1983, p. 431-535; Vance, Cyrus, *Hard Choices: Critical Years in America's Foreign Policy*, NY, Simon and Schuster, 1983, p. 373-83, 398-412.

Unsuccessful attempts to free Americans incarcerated in Lebanon thus far reflect HUMINT failures that make hostage rescue missions impractical.[48] U.S. counterterror tactics meanwhile rely primarily on political and economic incentives, employed as "carrots and sticks" against Iran and Syria, although the influence on the jailers is conjectural. Progress in any event was imperceptible until April-May 1990, when two U.S. prisoners were released.

U.S. antiterror specialists also have found it difficult to develop fool proof defenses. Truck bombs in Beirut badly damaged the U.S. Embassy (April 18, 1983), its Annex (September 20, 1984) and, in between, obliterated a Marine barrack (October 23, 1983). Casualties totalled 327 dead and 283 injured. Steps to strengthen security followed each terrorist attack, but no reliable formula is yet forthcoming.[49]

Culminating Comments

Transnational terrorists have tested U.S. countercapabilities only slightly. Prognoses seem premature, because the cases are remarkably different and none is closed. The Tripoli-Benghazi raid could be called an unqualified success, but no U.S. official knows for sure why Qadhafi chose not to retaliate later, perhaps with untraceable terrorist attacks. The *Achille Lauro* affair, also well implemented, soured somewhat because key culprits had to be tried in absentia and the rest received relatively lenient sentences.[50] All other U.S. operations were seriously flawed.

Nevertheless, it is possible to venture a few lessons learned from such scant experience, all of which emphasize fundamentals:

- Consistent success will remain elusive until senior U.S. decisionmakers settle conceptual disputes and lift the most debilitating legal limitations.

---

[48] Mark, Clyde R., *Lebanon: The Remaining Hostages*, Issue Brief IB85183 Washington, Congressional Research Service, May 4, 1990, 15 p. ; Livingstone, Neil and David Halevy, "Operation Betrayal," *Soldier of Fortune*, October 1989, p. 66-71.

[49] *Report of the DOD Commission on Beirut International Airport Terrorist Act*, October 23, 1983 (the Long Report), Washington, Department of Defense, December 20, 1983, 141 p.; Mark, Clyde R., *Marine Security in Beirut: A Comparison of the House Armed Services and Long Commission Reports*, Washington, Congressional Research Service, January 6, 1984, 13 p. and *U.S. Embassy in Beirut*, p. 1-4, 18.

[50] *Facts on File Yearbook*, NY, Facts on File Publications, 1986, p. 29, 518-519.

- Flexible anti/counterterrorism plans, programs, and operations are imperative, given diversified requirements that never are quite alike.

- A professional core of HUMINT and covert operations specialists under competent control could open important options that currently are closed to the United States.

- An ounce of prevention almost always is worth a pound of cure.

CONVENTIONAL OPERATIONS

Twenty low-intensity conflicts under consideration featured the employment of U.S. conventional armed forces in situations that sometimes were unconventional, but nevertheless different than those heretofore described. Subcategories include punitive expeditions, protective expeditions, peacemaking, and rescue operations not related to counterterrorism:

	Annex A-B Case Numbers
Punitive Expeditions	
Panama (1989-90)	60
Grenada (1983)	53
Libya (1981, 86)	37
Mexico (1914-17)	7
Protective Expeditions	
Persian Gulf (1987-88)	59
China (1953-60)	21
China (1912-41)	6
China (1900)	2
Peacemaking	
Lebanon (1984)	52
Dominican Republic (1965-66)	33
Lebanon (1958)	26
Korea (1953)	22
Nicaragua (1926-33)	10
Dominican Republic (1916-24)	9
Haiti (1915-34)	8
Cuba (1906-09)	5
Colombia/Panama (1901-14)	3
Rescue Mission	
Mayaguez (1975)	42
Zaire (1964)	30
Morocco (1904)	4

Common Characteristics

U.S. armed combat in 7 of the 20 LICs listed above was brief (a few months or more). Some lasted much longer, but fighting was sporadic. Nine cases predated World War II. No case currently is active. The following table omits five countries. No U.S. combat occurred during rescue missions in Morocco and Zaire; combat in Cuba, Lebanon (1958), and Korea was confined to incidents.

Armed Combat		
Less than 1 year	1-5 years	More than 5 years
Panama (1989-90) Lebanon (1984) Grenada (1983) Mayaguez (1975) Libya (1981, 86) Dominican Republic (1965) China (1900)	Persian Gulf (1987-88) Mexico (1914-17)	China (1953-60) Nicaragua (1926-33) Domincian Republic (1916-24) Haiti (1915-34) China (1912-41) Colombia/Panama (1901-14)

Nine cases occurred in Latin America. Five center on East Asia; three of them were in China (1900, 1912-41, 1953-60). The rest were equally distributed between Africa and the Middle East:

Far East	Latin America	Mid East
N. Korea (1953-) Cambodia (1975) China (1953-60) China (1912-41) China (1900)	Panama (1989-90) Grenada (1983) Dominican Republic (1965) Nicaragua (1926-33) Dominican Republic (1916-24) Haiti (1915-34) Mexico (1914-17) Cuba (1906-09) Colombia/Panama (1901-14)	Persian Gulf (1987-88) Lebanon (1984) Lebanon (1958)
		Africa
		Libya (1981, 86) Zaire (1964) Morocco (1904)

Significant Differences

Punitive expeditions, protective expeditions, peacemaking, and conventional rescue operations, unlike all other LIC types, invariably involve U.S. armed combat. Beyond that, however, they have little in common. Subsequent discussion therefore addresses each of those subcategories separately.

Punitive Expeditions

Punitive expeditions against Panama (1989-90), Libya (1970), and Mexico (1914-17) were unilateral U.S. operations. Allied participation in Grenada was perfunctory. No U.S. opponent possessed a strong military establishment. Three of the four were in Central America or the Caribbean within easy reach of the Continental United States.

U.S. armed forces accomplished assigned missions fast and effectively, if not efficiently,[51] except for incursions into Mexico, which lasted almost three years. Casualties in each case were few. U.S. forces never seized or held foreign territory permanently. They departed as soon as it seemed prudent to do so (two years elapsed before post-war Grenada stabilized sufficiently).

Land power alone stopped Pancho Villa's raids north of the Rio Grande.[52] Naval air power sufficed for armed clashes with Libyan interceptors over the Gulf of Sidra (1981, 86).[53] Land-sea-air power collectively implemented Operation Urgent Fury in Grenada and Operation Just Cause in Panama.[54]

---

[51] The Grenada incursion attracted most criticism, of which the following citations are indicative. Lind, William S., *The Grenada Operation*, Report to the Congressional Military Reform Caucus, Washington, April 5, 1984, 5 p.; "JCS Replies to Criticism of Grenada Operation," *Army*, August 1984, p. 28-33, 36-37; Schemmer, Benjamin F., "JCS Reply to Congressional Reform Caucus' Critique of the Grenada Rescue Operation," *Armed Forces Journal*, July 1984, p.12-14, 18, 99.

[52] Dupuy, "R. Ernest and William H. Baumer, *The Little Wars of the United States*, p.123-143; Davis, Harold E., "Mexico (1916-1917), in *Challenge and Response in Internal Conflict*, Vol. III, April 1968, p. 129-153; Sarkesian, Sam C., *America's Forgotten Wars*, p. 183-194.

[53] Mark, Clyde R., *Libya : U.S. Relations*, Issue Brief IB86040, Washington, Congressional Research Service, May 26, 1987, p. 7-9.

[54] "Panama : Operation Just Cause," *Current News*, Special Edition, Part I, No. 1827 and Part II, No. 1828, Washington, Dept. of Defense, February 19, 1990, 142 p. total.

Special operations forces (SOF) in the latter two cases performed missions for which conventional contingents were poorly qualified.[55]

Protective Expeditions

U.S. protective expeditions include three in China: one episode during the Boxer Rebellion (1900)[56]; gunboat diplomacy designed to keep Chinese rivers and coastal waters open for U.S. commerce (1912-41)[57]; defense of Formosa and other islands close to mainland China (1953-60).[58] Escort service in the Persian Gulf (1987-88) makes four.[59]

All cases accentuate U.S. armed combat, but otherwise bear little resemblance to punitive expeditions described in the previous section. Without exception, they were defensive operations in remote locations. Naval power was paramount or very important in every instance. Conventional forces performed most U.S. missions. SOF undertook a few highly specialized tasks

---

[55] Bolger, Daniel P., "Special Operations and the Grenada Campaign," *Parameters*, December 1988, p.49-61; Capaccio, Tony, "Green Berets Fill in the Void in Panama" and "U.S. Commando Units Were Stars in Panama," *Defense Week*, February 5, 1990, p. 1, 12-13, 16

[56] O'Conner, Richard, *The Spirit Soldiers: A Historical Narrative of the Boxer Rebellion*, NY, G.P. Putnam's Sons, 1973, 379 p.; Tan, Chester, "China (1898-1901)," in *Challenge and Response in Internal Conflict*, Vol I, p.1-27; Dupuy, R. Ernest and William H. Baumer, *The Little Wars of the United States*, P. 100-122.

[57] Cole, Bernard D., *Gunboats and Marines: The United States Navy in China*, 1925-28, Newark, NJ, University of Delaware Press, 1983, 229 p.; Perry, Hamilton D., *The Panay Incident*, NY, McMillan Co., 1969, 295 p.; McKenna, Richard, *Sand Pebbles*, NY, Harper and Row, 1962, 597 p.; Tolley, Kemp, *Yangtze Patrol*, Annapolis, MD., U.S. Naval Institute Press, 1971, 329 p.

[58] *China: The Great Contemporary Issues*, NY, NY times/Arno Press, 1972, p. 216-229, 306-320; George, Alexander L. and Richard Smoke, *Deterrence in American Foreign Policy*, NY, Columbia University Press, 1974, p.226-294, 363-389; Gurtov, Melvin, "The Taiwan Strait Crisis Revisited: Politics and Foreign Policy in Chinese Motives," *Modern China*, January 1976, p. 49-103.

[59] Congressional Research Service, Washington: Laipson, Ellen B. (coordinator), *Persian Gulf: Overview of Issues*, Issue Brief IB87229, November 25, 1988, 13 p.; O'Rourke, Ronald, *Persian Gulf: U.S. Military Operations*, Issue Brief IB87145, January 19, 1989, 14 p.; Mark, Clyde R., *Persian Gulf and the War Powers Debate: Review of Events*, Issue Brief 87207, February 6, 1989, 15 p.

only in the Persian Gulf.[60] Allies were key players in every case, and provided preponderant power during the Boxer Rebellion.

<u>Peacemaking</u>

Peacemaking operations, as opposed to peacekeeping, employ coercive rather than persuasive means to prevent armed combat between third party belligerents. Nine cases make this the largest class within the LIC category called "Conventional Operations:" Colombia/Panama (1901-14); Cuba (1906-09); Haiti (1915-34); Dominican Republic (1916-24); Nicaragua (1926-33); North Korea (1953-); Lebanon (1958); Dominican Republic (1965-66); and Lebanon (1984).

Five cases on that list are among the least relevant in this day and age. All were protracted U.S. "police actions" in Latin America, justified by treaty rights, Theodore Roosevelt's so-called "Corollary" to the Monroe Doctrine, and/or requests by the indigenous government. The last of that lot ended 57 years ago (see Annex A for amplification).

The deployment of U.S. combat forces in Lebanon (July-October 1958), designed to prevent foreign and domestic foes from toppling the government, was initiated at President Chamoun's request. Unlike other U.S. peacemaking, it was crisp and conclusive, with only four U.S. fatalities (one from enemy fire). It also was the largest, most complex American contingency during the dozen years between mid-intensity conflicts in Korea and Vietnam. No other U.S. force of comparable size was employed in the Middle East until Persian Gulf problems erupted three decades later.[61]

Peacemaking in Korea (1953-) already has lasted 37 years, and no end is in sight. A January 1968 North Korean raid on Republic of Korea (ROK) President Park's residence, numerous infiltration tunnels that penetrate ROK territory, and the infamous "tree trimming incident" near Panmunjom in

---

[60] Capaccio, Tony, "DOD Details Commandos' Gulf Role," *Defense Week*, February 21, 1989, p. 16 and "Night Stalking Kiowas Stopped Iranian Mischief," June 19, 1989, p. 16.

[61] Riskin, Steven M., *Lebanon: Operational Aspects of U.S. Deployment of Forces, 1958*, Washington, Congressional Research Service, August 3, 1982, 11 p.; Blechman, Barry M. and Stephen S. Kaplan, *Force Without War*, p. 225-257; Shulimson, Jack, *Marines in Lebanon, 1958*, Washington, Historical Branch, G-3 Division, HQ. U.S. Marine Corps, 1966, 50 p.; Spiller, Roger J., *"Not War, But Like War": The American Intervention in Lebanon*, Leavenworth Papers No. 3, Ft. Leavenworth, KA, Combat Studies Institute, U.S. Army Command and General Staff College, January 1981, 58 p.; Said, Abdul Aziz, "Lebanon (1958)," in *Challenge and Response in Internal Conflict*, Vol. II, March 1967, p. 431-455.

August 1976 typify continuing altercations along the Demilitarized Zone (DMZ).[62] How many U.S. armed forces of what kind are needed on site to help ROK counterparts forestall another war with North Korea is uncertain. The Nixon Doctrine, for example, justified withdrawals in 1971. The Carter Administration planned, but did not implement, large additional drawdowns later in that decade.[63] Whether renewed demands for reductions will succeed or fail depends primarily on the perceived deterrent value of a strong U.S. presence and budgetary pressures.

The Lebanon peace*keeping* mission (1982-84) culminated in a peace*making* disaster with many negative repercussions (see subsequent section entitled "Nonviolent Conflicts" for details).

Rescue Operations

Three of the four U.S. rescue operations unrelated to counterterrorism involved U.S. naval vessels, but otherwise were dissimilar.

The first, in Morocco (1904), retrieved an American citizen and his stepson abducted and held for ransom by a brigand named Raisuli. The American man-of-war *Brooklyn* stood off Tangier to show that we meant business, but Washington held the Moorish government responsible for the safe release of both captives ("Perdicaris alive or Raisuli dead" is the way Secretary of State John Hay put it). That end was achieved after slightly more than a month, without landing Marines, despite contrary advice from the U.S. Consul-General.[64]

---

[62] Bermudez, Joseph S., *North Korean Special Forces*, Coulsdon, Surrey, Jane's Publishing Co., 1988, p. 32-33; *Facts on File Yearbook*, 1968, p. 17 and 1976, p. 618, 625, 641; Schemmer, Benjamin F., "North Korea Buries Its Aircraft, Guns, Submarines, and Radars Inside Granite," *Armed Forces Journal*, August 1984, p. 95-97.

[63] U.S. Congress, Senate, *U.S. Troop Withdrawal from the Republic of Korea*, A Report to the Committee on Foreign Relations, 95th Congress, 2nd Session, Washington, U.S. GPO, 1978, 85 p.; Niksch, Larry A., *Korea: U.S. Troop Withdrawal and the Question of Northeast Asia Stability*, Issue Brief IB79053, Washington, Congressional Research Service, May 14, 1979, 29 p.; U.S. Congress, Senate, *Korea: U.S. Troop Withdrawal Program*, Report of the Pacific Study Group to the Committee on Armed Services, 96th Congress, 1st Session Washington, U.S. GPO, 1979, 11 p.

[64] "Morocco: Abduction of Ion Perdicaris by Bandits," *Foreign Relations of the United States*, Washington, Dept. of State, 1904, p. 496-504.

Case two involved U.S. airlift for Belgian paratroopers who hoped to rescue hostages held by insurgents near Stanleyville in Zaire. Many were saved; many were not.[65]

A "non-rescue" incident occurred on January 23, 1968, when North Korea seized the USS *Pueblo* crammed with state-of-the-art electronic intelligence (ELINT) instruments. Bureaucratic U.S. bungling between noon and 8 pm on that date prevented decisive counteractions. Subsequent diplomacy and demonstrations were useless. North Korea returned the crew after 11 months, but retained the ship, which was a treasure trove. The entire affair, combined with budding U.S. failure in Vietnam, reinforced widely held views that the United States was becoming a "paper tiger."[66]

Case four, the *Mayaguez* rescue mission (May 1975), took place when Cambodia extended its territorial waters 90 miles into the Gulf of Thailand, then commandeered a U.S. merchant ship well within that limit. U.S. passivity during the *Pueblo* affair consciously affected behavior following the *Mayaguez* affront. U.S. leaders, most of whom (rightly or wrongly) believed that America's credibility and self-respect were at stake, decided to mass and apply multicapable armed forces quickly. Rescuers retrieved the ship and crew, but the entire affair remains a contentious topic 15 years later.[67]

NONVIOLENT CONFLICTS

Nonviolence characterized U.S. participation in 12 low-intensity conflicts categorized as posturing, hands off support for friends, hands off opposition to foes, and peacekeeping (the following table shows two of them twice-- USSR and Sinai, a subset of Israel). U.S. armed forces figured prominently in four cases: U.S.-Soviet confrontations; Jordan; and both peacekeeping missions. Security assistance and/or sanctions were the main U.S. implements in most others.

---

[65] Wagoner, Fred E., *Dragon Rouge: The Rescue of Hostages in the Congo*, Washington, National Defense University Press, 1980, 219 p.

[66] Liston, Robert A., *The Pueblo Surrender: A Covert Action by the National Security Agency*, NY, M. Evans and Co., 1988, 294 p.; Gallery, Daniel V., *The Pueblo Incident*, NY, Doubleday & Co., 1970, 174 p.

[67] Bolger, Daniel P., *Americans at War: An Era of Violent Peace, 1975-1986*, Novato, CA, Presidio Press, 1988, p. 19-98; Head, Richard G. et al, *Crisis Resolution: Presidential Decision Making in the Mayaguez and Korean Confrontations*, Boulder CO, Westview Press, 1978, p. 101-48; U.S. Congress, House, *Seizure of the Mayaguez*, Hearings Before the Committee on International Relations, Parts I-III, 94th Congress, 1st Session, Washington, U.S. GPO, 1975, 325 p; Part IV, 1976, 162 p.

	Annex A-B Case Numbers
Posturing	
Jordan (1970)	36
USSR (1961, 1962)	18
Hands Off Support	
Falkland Islands (1982)	51
Israel (1948-)	19
Hands Off Opposition	
Cambodia (1975-78)	43
Cyprus (1974-78)	41
OPEC (1974-75)	40
Libya (1970-)	37
South Africa (1960-)	28
Cuba (1965-)	27
USSR (1946-)	18
China (1945-49)	14
Peacekeeping	
Lebanon (1982-84)	52
Sinai (1976-)	19

Common Characteristics

Most conflicts in this class minimized physical risks to U.S. security. Political and economic implements almost always took precedence over military power, even when U.S. armed forces deployed in large numbers (the Cuban Missile Crisis of 1962 was the most notable exception).

Hands off opposition accounted for more than half of the 12 cases, which comprise two groups when divided according to duration. The five longest (15 years or more) all are still active. The rest lasted five years or less--the Jordanian crisis of 1970 spanned just one month; the Falkland Island conflict terminated in slightly more than two.

Significant Differences

U.S. nonviolent LICs in the main share few features. Five cases happened in the Middle East. Distribution by time and place otherwise was disparate. Each subcategory consequently deserves individual treatment.

Posturing

Shows of force, which attempt to impress opponents in required ways from standoff positions, keep crises from escalating and/or encourage deescalation, if they succeed. Naval power is often employed for such purposes, as exemplified by repeated U.S. surges in the Indian Ocean since 1971.[68] This subsection concentrates on combined arms posturing connected with two totally different U.S. low-intensity conflicts: Soviet Union, 1961 and 1962; Jordan, 1970.

The first major U.S.-Soviet confrontation occurred in August, 1961, when the German Democratic Republic began to build a wall between East and West Berlin, which is more than 100 miles from the nearest NATO territory. President Kennedy rapidly reinforced the U.S. Berlin Brigade and temporarily mobilized sizable reserves in response. Neither gesture appreciably altered the local military balance, which lopsidedly favored Communist forces, but both symbolized U.S. will to resist armed aggression. America's strategic nuclear weapons remained a reasonably credible backstop for deterrent (some suggest warfighting) purposes at that time.[69]

"Brinksmanship" was much riskier when episode two, the Cuban missile crisis, erupted a mere 14 months later (October 1962), because Soviet nuclear systems by then could strike many more targets in the United States. U.S. conventional military power, however, sufficed in the peculiar circumstances that pertained after President Kennedy told Khrushchev to cease installing medium-range ballistic missiles and bombs on Cuban bases, render them inoperable, and remove all posthaste. Soviet rather than U.S. armed forces were at the end of long and tenuous logistic links. The greatest U.S. short-notice military surge in history marshalled many divisions and air wings,

---

[68] U.S. Congress, House, *Means of Measuring Naval Power with Special Reference to U.S. and Soviet Activities in the Indian Ocean*, Subcommittee on the Near East and South Asia of the Committee on Foreign Affairs, 93rd Congress, 2nd Session, Washington, U.S. GPO, May 12, 1974, 16 p., McCain, John, "The Importance of Carriers in an Era of Changing Strategic Priorities," *Congressional Record*, November 9, 1989, p. S15384-S15394.

[69] For background, see Schick, James M., *The Berlin Crisis, 1958-62*, Philadelphia, PA, University of Pennsylvania Press, 1971, 236 p.; Blechman, Barry M. and Steven S. Kaplan, *Force Without War*, p. 343-439.

were at the end of long and tenuous logistic links. The greatest U.S. short-notice military surge in history marshalled many divisions and air wings, ready to invade Cuba, if ordered. The U.S. Navy dominated the Caribbean and adjacent waters. Khrushchev acquiesced.[70]

Conditions during the Jordanian crisis of 1970 were far more complicated. Military power, despite its visibility, was subordinate to subtleties. Eight players took the field or coached from the sidelines. U.S. military posturing during that period buttressed political ploys designed to preserve Jordan's independence without a regional (perhaps global) explosion. Neither the State Department nor the Department of Defense quashed rumors that U.S. forces were about to invade. On the contrary, they openly publicized or leaked reports of Sixth Fleet maneuvering in the eastern Mediterranean, paratroop alerts, and other activities as a form of psychological warfare (psywar). How much (even whether) U.S. "wild card" shows of force influenced the outcome is uncertain, but they demonstrated determination. The crisis was resolved without serious escalation.[71]

Hands Off Support

The record includes only two cases of "hands off" U.S. support for friends, discounting insurgencies, resistance movements, and counterinsurgencies that previous sections address (Afghanistan, Angola, Cambodia; Indochina, Philippines twice).

The Falkland Islands/Malvinas conflict (1982) was little noted and not long remembered in the United States. Satellite intelligence, otherwise unob-

[70] Kennedy, John F., *Public Papers of the Presidents, 1962*, Washington, U.S. GPO, 1963, p. 806-11, 812, 813-15, 821; Garthoff, Raymond L., *Reflections on the Cuban Missile Crises*, Washington, Brookings Institution, 1989, 236 p.; Yarmolinsky, Adam, "Department of Defense Operations During the Cuban Missile Crisis," a report to the President on February 13, 1963, Ed. by Dan Caldwell, *Naval War College Review*, July-August 1979, p. 83-99; Kennedy, Robert F. *Thirteen Days: A Memoir of the Cuban Missile Crisis*, NY, W. W. Norton and Co., 1969, 224 p.

[71] Kissinger, Henry A., *The White House Years*, p. 594-631; Hersh, Seymour M., *The Price of Power*, p. 234-249; Blechman, Barry M. and Stephen S. Kaplan, *Force Without War*, p. 257-288.

tainable by our British allies, diplomatic backing, and some logistic support, were America's main contributions.[72]

The Arab-Israeli feud (1948-) conversely is among the longest and most important on the list of 60 U.S. LICs. The United States is not tied to Israel by treaty, but a special relationship has nevertheless persisted more than 40 years, through three major wars (1956, 1967, 1973) and endless lesser collisions.[73] U.S. diplomatic support has been steadfast in the United Nations and elsewhere. Grants and loans since the 1973 war amount to almost 20% of all U.S. foreign aid over the last 17 years. American military aid currently covers half of Israel's defense budget. U.S. economic aid helped shrink that country's inflation from 445% to 16% between 1985 and 1987.[74] Such connections remain strong.

Hands Off Opposition

Eight cases under consideration constitute hands off opposition to countries whose policies and operations were inimical to U.S. security interests and/or otherwise provoked adverse U.S. responses: futile attempts to prevent a communist takeover in China (1946-49); the U.S.-Soviet Cold War, except for eruptions between 1946 and 1968; South Africa (1960-); Cuba (1965); most U.S. dealing with Libya (1970-); the war of words with OPEC

---

[72] *Perspectives on Negotiation: Four Case Studies and Interpretations*, Ed. by Dianne B. Bendahmane and John W. McDonald, Jr., Washington, Foreign Service Institute, Dept. of State, 1986, p. 51-97; "Ex-Navy Chief Says U.S. Aid Crucial in Falklands War," *Philadelphia Inquirer*, May 30, 1988, p. 3; Guilmartin, John F., *The South Atlantic War: Lessons and Analytical Guideposts, A Military Historian's Perspective*, paper presented at the Southwest National Security Conference, Southern Methodist University, TX, April 15, 1983, 33 p.

[73] Overviews and assorted examples are available in Laipson, Ellen B., *Israeli-American Relations*, Issue Brief IB 82008, Washington, Congressional Research Service, October 11, 1989, 16 p.; Green, Stephen, *Taking Sides: America's Secret Relations with a Militant Israel*, NY, William Morrow, 1984, 370 p.; Sheehan, Edward R. F., *The Arabs, Israelis, and Kissinger: A Secret History of American Diplomacy in the Middle East*, NY, Reader's Digest Press, 1976, 287 p.; Safran, Nadav, *Israel: The Embattled Ally*, Cambridge, MA, Belknap Press of Harvard University Press, 1978, 633 p.

[74] Mark, Clyde R., *United States Aid to Israel, 1949-1989*, unpublished memorandum, Washington, Congressional Research Service, November 26, 1989, 3 p.; U.S. Congress, Senate, *Foreign Assistance and Related Programs Appropriations for Fiscal Year 1989*, Part 5, Hearings Before a Subcommittee on Appropriations, 100th Congress, 2nd Session, Washington, U.S. GPO, 1988, p. 247-250.

(1974-75); and Cambodia when Khmer Rouge were in control (1975-78). A few merit amplification to indicate diversity.

The first two U.S.-Soviet episodes are particularly noteworthy, because they transpired while the United States possessed a monopoly of strategic nuclear weapons. U.S. leaders took no direct advantage of that potential leverage, although its deterrent value doubtless restricted Soviet initiatives. The UN Security Council, with the United States as its most potent member, induced Stalin to withdraw troops from Iranian Azerbaijan in 1946, when they overstayed their welcome after World War II.[75] A massive and sustained airlift, the greatest ever, circumvented the Soviet blockade of Berlin in 1948-49 without resort to armed convoys or dangerous escalation.[76]

Hands off opposition, however, was unworkable when Khrushchev crushed the 1956 uprising in Hungary, a so-called "satellite state." U.S. nuclear superiority, while still indisputable, was starting to dissipate (Bear bombers, the first Soviet intercontinental delivery system, began to deploy that year). Neither the United States nor its NATO partners possessed enough offensive striking power in Europe to penetrate Soviet-occupied territory without running unacceptable risks.[77] The strategic nuclear balance was worse and the theater balance no better when Brezhnev quashed the Czech rebellion of 1968. U.S. diplomacy and economic pressures in the absence of sufficient military power failed to impress him.[78] Independence movements in the Baltic states currently create similar problems for President Bush.[79]

---

[75] Campbell, John C., *The United States in World Affairs, 1945-1947*, NY, Harper and Brothers, 1947, p. 85-91, 102-110; *The United States and the United Nations*, Report Series 7, Washington, GPO, 1947, p. 33-34; Irani, Robert G., *The Azerbaijani Crisis, 1945-46: An Options Analysis of U.S. Policy*, thesis, University of Maryland, 1973, 495 p.

[76] Tusa, Ann and John, *The Berlin Airlift*, NY Atheneum, 1988, 445 p.; Shlaim, Avi, *The United States and the Berlin Blockade, 1948-49: A Study in Crisis Decision-Making*, Berkeley, CA, University of California Press, 1983, 463 p.

[77] *The Hungarian Revolution*, Ed. by Melvin J. Lasky, London, Martin Secker & Warburg, 1957, 318 p.; Meray, Tibor, *Thirteen Days that Shook the Kremlin*, NY, Praeger, 1959, 290 p.

[78] Shawcross, William, *Dubcek*, NY, Simon and Schuster, 1970, 317 p.; Schwartz, Harry, *Prague's 200 Days: The Struggle for Democracy in Czechoslovakia*, NY, Praeger, 1969, 274 p.

[79] Bite, Vita, *The Baltic Republics' Push for Independence: Implications for U.S. Policy*, Issue Brief IB90075, Washington, Congressional Research Service, April 19, 1990, 15 p.

U.S. hands off opposition to South Africa's repressive apartheid policies and nuclear weapon programs has taken place in a totally different context for more than a quarter century. That country, in contrast to the Soviet Union, has never threatened U.S. security interests. American military power has never been applicable. U.S. officials instead have relied entirely on diplomatic pressures, variable arms embargoes implemented unilaterally and through the U.N., export-import impositions, and assorted other economic sanctions. How well such actions have served U.S. purposes is quite controversial. Apartheid essentially remains in place, despite emendations and expectations. South Africa's nuclear weapons programs, never acknowledged, apparently persist.[80]

The hands off LIC connected with Cyprus (1974-78) was a rarity for two reasons: the object of U.S. displeasure was a NATO member, not an enemy; Congress not the Administration, instigated and sustained all actions. The ruling military junta in Athens, which hoped to merge Cyprus with Greece, started a chain reaction when it backed a successful coup against the government of that independent, non-aligned island. Turkey intervened militarily twice, first to protect its Cypriot minorities, then to ensure their territorial integrity. Congress, urged by a few persuasive members, responded with an embargo on arms to Turkey. The Executive Branch, weakened by Watergate, objected futilely. All parties concerned experienced strained relations as a result, even after the embargo ended completely in September 1978.[81]

U.S. posturing in 1974-75 to prevent OPEC from "strangling" the industrialized world, was truly a "war of words." The operation was preemptive, because the Arab oil embargo of 1973-74 had subsided, petroleum prices had stabilized at reasonable levels, and OPEC leaders displayed no interest in further economic conflict. The President, Secretary of State, and Secretary of Defense nevertheless intimated that U.S. armed forces might be used to keep oil lines open, if the necessity should arise. OPEC members

---

[80] Branaman, Brenda M., *South Africa: U.S. Policy After Sanctions*, Issue Brief IB87128, Washington, Congressional Research Service, January 19, 1990, 14 p.; Galdi, Theodor W. and Robert D. Shuey. *U.S. Economic Sanctions Imposed Against Specific Foreign Countries*, p. 179-191; *South Africa: Time Running Out*, Report of the Study Commission on U.S. Policy Toward Southern Africa, Berkeley, CA, University of California Press, 1981, p. 340-365.

[81] U.S. Congress, House, *Congressional-Executive Relations and the Turkish Arms Embargo*, Report Prepared for the Committee on Foreign Affairs, Congress and Foreign Policy Series No. 3, Washington, U.S. GPO, June 1981, 60 p.; *Perspectives on Negotiation*, Ed. by Dianne B. Bendahmane and John W. McDonald, Jr., p. 99-152.

received that message loud and clear, but there is no evidence they would have shown greater restraint if it had never been sent.[82]

Peacekeeping

The United States has participated in major peacekeeping operations only twice, both times as part of multinational forces in the Middle East. The first effort failed, for several reasons. The second so far is successful.

U.S. Marines in Lebanon (1982-84) inadvertently violated a prerequisite for peace*keepers* (as opposed to peace*makers*) when they became embroiled in military operations that compromised their neutrality. Disaster befell when terrorists destroyed their Beirut headquarters, killing 241 occupants and wounding 112 others. Contributing factors included instructions subject to assorted interpretations, faulty intelligence, inflexible rules of engagement, unsatisfactory security procedures, and a flawed chain of command.[83] U.S. forces withdrew soon thereafter.

Sinai peacekeeping missions interposed between Israelis and Egyptians conversely have gone well since 1976, albeit in less volatile situations. A small U.S. Sinai Support Mission/Field Mission of 200 civilians oversaw activities at selected Egyptian and Israeli installations on that peninsula until 1982, when the United States formed the Multinational Force and Observers (MFO) with members from 11 countries to handle expanded responsibilities. Authorized strength is 2,600 military and 34 civilians. No serious incidents have occurred during their tenure.[84]

Even so, further thought on the subject may be advisable. Peacekeeping demands forces organized, trained, equipped, and psychologically suited for

---

[82] Official U.S. statements are reproduced and military options are discussed in detail in U.S. Congress, House, *Oil Fields as Military Objectives: A Feasibility Study*, a report prepared for the Special Subcommittee on Investigations of the Committee on International Relations, 94th Congress, 1st Session, Washington, U.S. GPO, August 21, 1975, 111 p.

[83] *Report of the DOD Commission on Beirut International Airport Terrorist Act*, October 23, 1983, 141 p.; Shuger, Scott, "What America Hasn't Learned From Its Greatest Peacekeeping Disaster," *Washingtonian Monthly*, October 1989, p. 40-46.

[84] *United States Sinai Support Mission*, Report to the Congress, Washington, The White House, May 26, 1982, 67 p.; Browne, Marjorie Ann, *The Future of International Peacekeeping: The UN/Non-UN Option*, Research Report, Washington, National War College, March 1984, p. 21-23, 50-51; Homan, Cornelis, "MFO: Peacekeeping in the Middle East," *Military Review*, September 1983, p. 2-13.

onerous duty. Army paratroopers and Marines, designed foremost to seize and retain initiative in stressful situations, especially offensive armed combat, may not be as appropriate as less elite troops.[85]

Narco Conflict

International narco conflict, the latest form of U.S. LIC, is closely related to counterterrorism in many respects.[86] Producers, processors, transporters, and distributors of illegal drugs all are targets. Interception is least difficult during stages one and two, before merchandise scatters to multiple markets.

Turkey, a notable opium poppy producer, ceased to be a serious problem in 1974, when the United States began buying its crop. Bolivia's leaders, some of whom allegedly were drug traffickers, devoted greater attention to narcotics control after the United States imposed political and economic sanctions (1980-86).[87] Success, however, has been elusive in the Golden Triangle (Burma, Laos, northern Thailand), the Golden Crescent (Iran, Afghanistan, Pakistan), and Peru, where U.S. officials, indigenous governments, or both lack much leverage.

The U.S. war against illegal drug dealers in foreign countries started to concentrate on processors as well as producers about 1986, particularly in Colombia. Related roles and missions of U.S. armed services became content-

---

[85] Wise, James C., "How Not to Fight: Putting Together a U.S. Army Force for a UN Peacekeeping Operation," *Military Review*, December 1977, p. 20-31; Segal, David R., "Peacekeeping, Warfighting, and Professionalism: Attitude, Organization and Change Among Combat Soldiers on Constabulary Duty," *Journal of Political and Military Sociology*, Fall 1985, p. 167-181; Segal, David R. et al., "Paratroopers as Peacekeepers," *Armed Forces and Society*, Summer 1984, p. 487-506.

[86] U.S. steps to combat narcotics during the first half of this century did not constitute low-intensity conflict as construed herein, but nevertheless are instructive. See, for example, Kagan, Daniel, "How America Lost Its First Drug War," *Insight*, November 20, 1989, p. 8-17.

[87] Galdi, Theodor and Robert D. Shuey, *U.S. Economic Sanctions Imposed Against Specific Foreign Countries: 1979 to the Present*, p. 23-27.

ious issues in 1989. Policies appertaining thereto are still taking shape.[88]

Only two conclusions concerning this type LIC seem certain: the conflict will be protracted, no matter what strategies and force postures prevail; the outcome is unpredictable (see Annexes A-B, cases 48 and 58, for further discussion).

---

[88] *National Drug Control Strategy*, Washington, The White House, U.S. GPO, September 1989, 154 p.; Perl, Raphael F., *Drug Control: International Policy and Options*, Issue Brief IB88093, Washington, Congressional Research Service, November 7, 1989, 15 p.; "Military Role in the Drug War, *Current News*, Special Edition, Washington, Dept. of Defense, No. 1798, August 3, 1989, 46 p., No. 1807, October 18, 1989, 71 p., No. 1846, May 1990, 37 p. ; U.S. Congress, House, *Drugs and Latin America: Economic and Political Impact and U.S. Policy Options*, Report of the Committee on Narcotics Abuse and Control, 100th Congress, 1st Session, Washington, U.S. GPO, 1989, 135 p.

U.S. LIC PERFORMANCE

U.S. Twentieth Century LIC performance summarized herein has been spotty, as the tables below and Figures 9 and 10 at the end of this section indicate. The absence of strong opposing views expressed publicly is the principal criterion for unqualified success and failure. The remainder receive mixed reviews, even if the United States achieved all basic objectives. U.S. influence on outcomes was questionable in some cases. Assorted qualifiers, such as unhappy side effects and high costs, kept others out of the "success" column. Entries for active conflicts indicate the U.S. record as of May 1990:

	Resolved Conflicts	Active Conflicts	Grand Total
Success	15	3	18
Failure	9	1	10
Inconclusive	22	10	32
	46	14	60

Crises listed as subsets under six lengthy LICs reflect a somewhat less favorable record. More than half terminated in failure:

	Resolved Conflicts	Active Conflicts	Grand Total
Success	2	1	3
Failure	8	1	9
Inconclusive	5	0	5
	15	2	17

SUCCESSES

The United States has done reasonably well with three long-standing and still active LICs against the Soviet Union (1946-), North Korea (1953-), and Afghanistan (1980-). The catalog of U.S. successes nevertheless is not quite as sanguine as statistics suggest. The first 8 of 18 total (44%) seem anachronistic or nearly so, because such cases are unlikely to reoccur (see Figure 9). Clear-cut success since then has been especially elusive in connection with anti/counterterrorism, narco conflict, and coups. Approximately 40% of all conventional operations, a U.S. specialty, turned out well, compared with less than a quarter of nonviolent LICs (Figure 11). Only three crises ended successfully, according to majority opinion: Azerbaijan (1946); Berlin blockade (1948); and the raid on Tripoli, Libya (1986). The United Nations contributed as much or more than the United States in Azerbaijan.

FAILURES

Nine undisputable failures among 46 completed cases at first seems respectable. All, however, occurred after World War II, which reduces the postwar ratio to 9 of 33 (27%). Two of those disappointments had serious national and international repercussions for the United States: Vietnam (1955-65) and Lebanon (1982-84). *The Pueblo*, Desert One, and Lebanese hostage crises, plus abortive coups in Panama, swell the list of highly visible embarrassments.

MIXED OPINION

The mixed opinion category includes 32 of the 60 LIC cases surveyed, because observers view consequences from different perspectives. Pro-Israel factions, for example, applaud U.S. support that ensures the existence of that besieged state; consequent problems with Arab countries cause others to object. The U.S.-instigated coup against Arbenz Guzmán in Guatemala (1954) was a short-term success, but a long-term failure, because U.S. counterinsurgency efforts soon were required to keep his successor in office. Sanctions that tormented the Sandinistas simultaneously tightened their ties with Moscow. Most Americans see the Cuban missile crisis as an obvious U.S. victory. Skeptics concur with Khrushchev, who contends that removing MRBMs was a small price to pay for what he hoped would be a perpetually Communist Cuba.[1]

A few mixed opinions for past LICs eventually may shift to unqualified success or failure, after additional information and time for reflection become available. All 14 active conflicts are subject to similar reappraisal.

[1] Khrushchev, Nikita S., *Khrushchev Remembers*, Ed. and translated by Strobe Talbott, Boston, Little, Brown, and Co., 1970, p. 504.

Figure 9

U.S. LIC SCORECARD

	Resolved Conflicts			Active Conflicts		
	Success[1]	Mixed Opinion[2]	Failure[1]	Mainly Success[1]	Mixed Opinion[2]	Mainly Failure[1]
1. Philippines (1899-1913)	x					
2. China (1900)	x					
3. Colombia/Panama (1901-14)	x					
4. Morocco (1904)		x				
5. Cuba (1906-09)	x					
6. China (1912-41)	x					
7. Mexico (1914-17)		x				
8. Haiti (1915-34)		x				
9. Dominican Republic (1916-24)		x				
10. Nicaragua (1926-33)		x				
11. Philippines (1942-45)	x					
12. Burma (1942-45)	x					
13. France (1944)	x					
14. China (1945-49)			x			
15. Greece (1946-49)	x					
16. Philippines (1946-55)		x				
17. Indochina (1946-54)			x			
18. U.S.S.R. (1946 -)[3]				x		
a. Azerbaijan (1946)	x					
b. Berlin Blockade (1948)	x					
c. Hungary (1956)			x			
d. Berlin Wall (1961)			x			
e. Cuban Missile Crisis (1962)		x				
f. Czechoslovakia (1968)			x			
19. Israel vs. Arabs (1948 -)[3]					x	
a. War (1956)		x				
b. War (1967)		x				
c. War (1973)		x				
d. Sinai (1976 -)				x		
20. Iran (1951-53)	x					
21. China (1953-79)	x					
22. North Korea (1953 -)[3]				x		
Pueblo (1968)			x			
23. Guatemala (1953-54)		x				
24. Vietnam (1955-65)			x			
25. Laos (1955-65)			x			
26. Lebanon (1958)	x					
27. Cuba (1960 -)[3]						x
a. Anti-Castro Acts (1960-65)			x			
b. Bay of Pigs (1961)			x			
28. South Africa (1960 -)					x	
29. Dominican Republic (1960-62)		x				
30. Zaire (1960-64)		x				

Figure 9 (cont.)

U.S. LIC SCORECARD

	Resolved Conflicts			Active Conflicts		
	Success [1]	Mixed Opinion [2]	Failure [1]	Mainly Success [1]	Mixed Opinion [2]	Mainly Failure [1]
31. Brazil (1961-64)		x				
32. Vietnam (1963)		x				
33. Dominican Republic (1965-66)		x				
34. Guatemala (1965-74)			x			
35. Thailand (1965-85)		x				
36. Jordan (1970)		x				
37. Libya (1970 -) [3]					x	
a. Gulf of Sidra (1981, 86)		x				
b. Tripoli Raid (1986)	x					
38. Chile (1970-73)		x				
39. Iraq (1972-75)			x			
40. OPEC (1974-75)		x				
41. Cyprus (1974-78)			x			
42. Mayaguez (1975)		x				
43. Cambodia (1975 -)						x
44. Nicaragua (1978-79)		x				
45. Iran (1979 -)					x	
a. Desert One (1980)			x			
b. Lebanese Hostages (1984-)			x			
46. Syria (1979 -)					x	
47. El Salvador (1979 -)					x	
48. Bolivia (1980-86)	x					
49. Afghanistan (1980 -)				x		
50. Nicaragua (1981-90)		x				
51. Falkland Islands (1982)		x				
52. Lebanon (1982-84)			x			
53. Grenada (1983)		x				
54. Philippines (1984 -)					x	
55. Philippines (1985-86)	x					
56. Haiti (1985-86)			x			
57. Angola (1986 -)					x	
58. Narco Conflict (1986 -)					x	
59. Persian Gulf (1987-88)	x					
60. Panama (1987-90)		x				
Totals	15	22	9	3	10	1

1. Maintstream consensus that disregards radical views.
2. No mainstream consensus.
3. Subordinate entries, which do not count in totals above, are:
    Resolved conflicts, success 3, mixed opinion 5, failure 8.
    Active conflicts, success 1, mixed opinion 0, failure 0.

Figure 10

U.S. LIC SCORECARD
By Type Conflict

	Insurgency, Resistance	Coups d'Etat	Counter-Insurgency	Combatting Terrorism	Conventional Operations [1]	Nonviolent Operations [2]
1. Philippines (1899-1913)			S			
2. China (1900)					S	
3. Colombia/Panama (1901-14)					S	
4. Morocco (1904)					M	
5. Cuba (1906-09)					S	
6. China (1912-41)					S	
7. Mexico (1914-17)					M	
8. Haiti (1915-34)					M	
9. Dominican Republic (1916-24)					M	
10. Nicaragua (1926-33)					M	
11. Philippines (1942-45)	S					
12. Burma (1942-45)	S					
13. France (1944)	S					
14. China (1945-49)						F
15. Greece (1946-49)			S			
16. Philippines (1946-55)			M			
17. Indochina (1946-54)			F			
18. U.S.S.R. (1946 -)						S
a. Azerbaijan (1946)						S
b. Berlin Blockade (1948)						S
c. Hungary (1956)						F
d. Berlin Wall (1961)						F
e. Cuban Missiles Crisis (1962)						M
f. Czechoslovakia (1968)						F
19. Israel vs. Arabs (1948 -)						M
a. War (1956)						M
b. War (1967)						M
c. War (1973)						M
d. Sinai (1976 -)						S [1]
20. Iran (1951-53)			S			
21. China (1953-79)					S	
22. North Korea (1953 -)					S	
Pueblo (1968)						F [2]
23. Guatemala (1953-54)		M				
24. Vietnam (1955-65)			F			
25. Laos (1955-65)			F			
26. Lebanon (1958)					S	
27. Cuba (1960 -)	F	F [1]				F
a. Anti-Castro Acts (1960-65)		F [1]				
b. Bay of Pigs (1961)	F					
28. South Africa (1960 -)						M
29. Dominican Republic (1960-62)		M				
30. Zaire (1960-64)			M		M [1]	

Figure 10 (cont.)

U.S. LIC SCORECARD
By Type Conflict

	Insurgency, Resistance	Coups d'Etat	Counter Insurgency	Combatting Terrorism	Conventional Operations [1]	Nonviolent Operations [2]
31. Brazil (1961-64)		M				
32. Vietnam (1963)		M				
33. Dominican Republic (1965-66)					M	
34. Guatemala (1965-74)			F			
35. Thailand (1965-85)			M			
36. Jordan (1970)						M
37. Libya (1970 -)				S	M [1]	M
a. Gulf of Sidra (1981,86)				M		
b. Tripoli Raid (1986)				S		
38. Chile (1970-73)			M			
39. Iraq (1972-75)	F					
40. OPEC (1974-75)						M
41. Cyprus (1974-78)						F
42. Mayaguez (1975)					M	
43. Cambodia (1975 -)	M					M [1]
44. Nicaragua (1978-79)	M					
45. Iran (1979 -)				M		
a. Desert One (1980)				F		
b. Lebanese Hostages (1984-)				F		
46. Syria (1979 -)				M		
47. El Salvador (1979 -)			M			
48. Bolivia (1980-86)						S
49. Afghanistan (1980 -)	S					
50. Nicaragua (1981-90)	M					
51. Falkland Islands (1982)						M
52. Lebanon (1982-84)						F
53. Grenada (1983)					M	
54. Philippines (1984 -)			M			
55. Philippines (1985-86)		S				
56. Haiti (1985-86)		F				
57. Angola (1986 -)	M					
58. Narco Conflict (1986 -)				M		
59. Persian Gulf (1987-88)					S	
60. Panama (1987-90)		F			M	
Totals	S 4 / F 2 / M 4	S 2 / F 3 / M 5	S 2 / F 4 / M 5	S 1 / F 0 / M 3	S 8 / F 0 / M 11	S 3 / F 4 / M 7

NOTE: S is success. F is failure. M is mixed opinion.

1. The grand total is 68, because cases 29, 43, 52, and 60 count in two categories; cases 26 and 37 count in three.

2. Episodes indicated do not count in totals.

U.S. PROBLEMS AND PROSPECTS

Many lessons that emerge from this lengthy review of U.S. low-intensity conflict experience are equally applicable to MIC and HIC. Agreed goals, perceptive threat appraisals, flexible plans, appropriate programs, competent operators, and team play, for example, almost always promote success and reduce prospects of failure.[1]

LIC-specific findings herein identify patterns and trends that likely will influence future U.S. performance.[2]

IMPORTANT LIC PATTERNS

U.S. exposure to Twentieth Century LICs reveals several fundamental patterns (constants, as opposed to variables). Factor four is the only one that shows signs of change:

- Extreme diversification
- Cultural shock
- Fixation on armed force
- Concentration on communism
- Preeminence of manpower
- Unique deterrent techniques
- Low utility of multilateral alliances
- Public opinion misconceptions

Extreme Diversification

Diversity is the dominant feature of low-intensity conflict, which constitutes seven discrete types in this report. The list includes 15, if subcategories count separately.

---

[1] For fundamentals, see Collins, John M, *U.S. Defense Planning: A Critique*, Boulder, CO, Westview Press, 1982, p. 3-12.

[2] Various other views include Secretary Weinberger's National Press Club Speech," *Current News*, Special Edition, No. 1244, Washington, Dept. of Defense, January 8, 1985, 92 p. ;Schultz, George P. "Power and Diplomacy in the 1980s," *Department of State Bulletin*, May 1984, p. 12-15 and "Terrorism in the Modern World," *Department of State Bulletin*, December 1984, p. 16-17; Huntington, Samuel P., "Playing to Win," *The National Interest*, Spring 1986, p. 13, 15-16; Engelhardt, Michael J., "America Can Win Sometimes: U.S. Success and Failure in Small Wars," *Conflict Quarterly*, Winter 1989, p. 20-35.

LIC causes, outcomes, and consequences commonly were more complex and less predictable than mid- and high-intensity conflicts. No U.S. LIC was a declared war. U.S. national interests were seldom clean-cut. Some LICs emphasized violence, others avoided it. Durations varied from days to decades. Coups depended primarily on covert operations. Posturing to impress opponents relied mainly on overt maneuvers. Individuals adroit at sabotage, subversion, and other specialized offensive activities proved much better suited for unconventional warfare (UW) than for foreign internal defense (FID). Hostage rescue teams bore little resemblance to peacekeeping contingents. Foreign language proficiency, cross-cultural understanding, tact, and persuasive skills were critically important whenever on-site U.S. personnel helped friends help themselves, but much less so when America's role was hands off support from afar. U.S. political and economic power played widely varied roles.

Each type LIC, in short, demanded tailor-made objectives, doctrines, task organizations, implements, and training to cope with particular threats in specialized circumstances. Capabilities designed to deal equally well with every future variety thus will deal acceptably well with few or none.

Cultural Shock

All 60 U.S. LICs judged by this survey occurred in remote locations. Only special operations in Mexico, France during World War II, and crises later along Europe's Iron Curtain transpired on familiar territory. Non-Western cultures that were strange to most Americans predominated elsewhere, with the possible exception of South Africa.

Language barriers repeatedly posed problems at important times and places. British recipients of U.S. satellite intelligence during the Falkland Islands fracas were the only U.S. associates who spoke English as their native tongue. Many bilingual U.S. Hispanics are well versed in Spanish, the most widespread language of Latin America, and Spanish is popular in U.S. schools, but few LIC specialists are fluent and fewer still speak Portuguese. The vernacular for U.S. friends in most cases was truly foreign. Arabic, Farsi, Chinese, Korean, Tagalog, Thai, and Vietnamese were among the most exotic. Requirements continue, because U.S. spokesmen (especially advisers) cannot communicate well unless they are conversant, and many foreigners are resentful when forced to confer in English.[3]

---

[3] Bruton, James K. and Wayne D. Zajac, "Cultural Interaction: The Forgotten Dimension of Low-Intensity Conflict," *Special Warfare*, April 1988, p. 29-33; Blaufarb, Douglas S., "Economic/Security Assistance and Special Operations," a chapter in *Special Operations in U.S. Strategy*, Ed. by Frank R. Barnett, B. Hugh Tovar, and Richard H. Shultz, Washington, National Defense University Press, 1984, p. 206-208, 216-217, and discussants p. 224-227; Dascal, Steven E., "The Insurgency Threat and Ways to Deflect It," *Military Review*, January 1986, p. 36.

Fixation on Armed Force

Most U.S. officials tend to emphasize military and technological aspects of low-intensity conflict.[4] Psychological operations fare less well.[5] There is no doctrine for political and economic warfare.

Congress in 1986 directed the Department of Defense to install an Assistant Secretary for Special Operations and Low-intensity Conflict (ASD SO/LIC) and activate U.S. Special Operations Command (USSOCOM), with a four-star flag officer as Commander-in-Chief.[6] LIC-related legislation that pertains to other departments and agencies is less comprehensive or lacking.

Only the Joint Chiefs of Staff currently are developing LIC doctrine.[7] Few parallel efforts are apparent in the Department of State or elsewhere in the U.S. Government. The foundation for LIC plans, programs, and operations, which commonly require interdepartmental/interagency collaboration, thus remains unfirm. The National Security Council is just starting to explore associated problems.

Concentration on Communism

Containing communism was a basic U.S. objective in 27 of 47 LIC cases since World War II. Nationalism, however, may have been more important than ideology to many opponents, including Mao Zedong and Ho Chi Minh, who might have become U.S. friends if treated differently during their earlier days.[8] The United States frequently sacrificed democratic ideals to sustain dictators like Trujillo, Somoza, Marcos, and the Shah of Iran, simply because

---

[4] Nearly every book about low-intensity conflict centers on armed force. So do official documents of which the following is typical: *U.S. Weapons: The Low-Intensity Threat Is Not Necessarily a Low-Technology Threat*, Washington, General Accounting Office, March 1990, 24 p.

[5] See, for example, *Political Warfare and Psychological Operations: Rethinking the U.S. Approach*, Ed. by Carnes Lord and Frank R. Barnett, Washington, National Defense University Press, 1989, 242 p.

[6] Nichol, James P., *Special Operations and Low-Intensity Conflict: U.S. Progress and Problems*, Issue Brief IB90091, Washington, Congressional Research Service, May 18, 1990, 15 p.

[7] *JCS Pub 3-07: Doctrine for Joint Operations in Low Intensity Conflict*, Final Draft, Washington, Joint Chiefs of Staff, January 1990.

[8] For views on that controversial subject see Kahn, E.H. Jr., *The China Hands: America's Foreign Service Officers and What Befell Them*, NY, Viking, 1975, 337 p.; Kahin, George McT and John W. Lewis, *The United States in Vietnam*, NY, Dial Press, 1967, 465 p.

they were anticommunists. Whether that pattern will dissipate in response to reduced communist appeal and Soviet influence in developing countries remains uncertain.

Preeminence of Manpower

Highly qualified manpower in most cases proved more beneficial than hyper-expensive high technology, whether U.S. roles were military or nonmilitary, hands on or hands off. Vietnam's General Vo Nguyen Giap, who emerged victorious first over France, then over the United States, reached a similar conclusion after he captured Saigon and saw the computerized command center. "No wonder we won," he quipped. "The other side couldn't think."[9]

Sun Tzu, circa 500 B.C., wrote: "foreknowledge cannot be elicited from spirits, nor from gods, nor by analogy with past events, nor from calculations. It must be obtained from men who know the enemy situation."[10] Signal intelligence (SIGINT), electronic intelligence (ELINT), communications intelligence (COMINT), and photographic intelligence (PHOTINT) furnish U.S. LIC specialists with invaluable information about enemy activities, but experience in this century indicates that human intelligence (HUMINT) is the sine qua non. Covert and clandestine collection means are critically important when needs exist to ascertain the temper of potential insurgents, locate terrorist hideouts, retrieve hostages, predict the outcome of coups, target individuals, or conduct surgical strikes against small groups concealed in cities, to cite just a few common HUMINT requirements.[11]

Unique Deterrent Techniques

Deterrent concepts designed to discourage LICs generally depend more on "carrots" and less on "sticks" than those connected with mid- and high-intensity conflicts, but the proper prescription varies considerably from type to type. Political, economic, social, legal, even military reforms, for example,

---

[9] Reliably reported by sources who wish to remain anonymous.

[10] Sun Tzu, *The Art of War*, NY, Oxford University Press, 1963, p. 144-145.

[11] McCarter, James, *A Short Course in the Secret War*, NY, Dell Publishing Co., 1988, 265 p.; Richelson, Jeffrey, *The U.S. Intelligence Community*, 2nd Ed., Cambridge, MA, Ballinger Publishing Co., 1989, p. 233-249; Molnar, Andrew R. et al., *Human Factors Considerations of Undergrounds in Insurgencies*, Washington, Special Operations Research Office, American University, November 1963, p. 235-239; Thompson, Robert, *Defeating Communist Insurgency*, London, Chatto & Windus, 1966, p. 85, 86-87, 94.

often prevent or reverse insurgencies and forestall coups.[12] Promise of punishment rather than reward conversely puts teeth into shows of force. No one yet has devised reliable ways to deter suicidal terrorists, who scorn worldly goods and welcome death. Inflammatory rhetoric by senior officials in fact may provoke rather than repress transnational terrorists, particularly if they bluff repeatedly.[13]

Low Utility of Multilateral Alliances

Collective security, a pillar of U.S. policy for much of this century, worked well during both World Wars. Multilateral alliances were politically and militarily useful throughout the mid-intensity conflict in Korea and, except for Vietnam (1965-72), subsequently helped prevent large-scale armed aggression by any adversary against the United States and its allies.

Multilateral alliances, however, have seldom embellished U.S. LIC capabilities. The Organization of American States (OAS) occasionally created the appearance of a united front in Latin America, but its contributions otherwise have been modest. Neither the Southeast Asia Treaty Organization (SEATO) nor its individual members responded when low-intensity conflict began to bubble in Laos and Vietnam. The Central Treaty Organization (CENTO) proved impotent in the Middle East. The North Atlantic Treaty Organization (NATO) was powerless when crises arose along its periphery (Hungary, 1956; Berlin, 1961; Czechoslovakia, 1968). Some members helped keep Persian Gulf sea lanes open in 1987-88, but all save Portugal refused overflight rights for U.S. transport aircraft during the 1973 Arab-Israeli war. Multinational participation in U.S. sponsored sanctions has seldom been strong or sustained.

Public Opinion Misconceptions

Widespread opposition to the Vietnam War began about 1967, well after conflict escalated from low to mid intensity. Many observers thereupon drew the doubtful conclusion that U.S. support will be difficult (perhaps impossible) to muster during future protracted LICs. Public opposition in the United States and/or elsewhere, however, may make nonmilitary courses seem preferable to armed force, covert action seem more suitable than open

---

[12] *Field Circular (FC) 100-20: Low-Intensity Conflict*, Ft. Leavenworth, Kansas, U.S. Army Command and General Staff College, July 16, 1986, p. 3-1 through 3-20; *Field Manual (FM) 100-20/Air Force Pamphlet (AFP) 3-20, Military Operations in Low-Intensity Conflict*, Washington, Depts. of the Army and Air Force, December 5, 1989, Chapter 2 and Appendix E.

[13] See text and end notes in Collins, John M., *Green Berets, SEALs, and Spetsnaz*, New York, Pergamon-Brassey's, 1986, p. 59-60, 80-81.

operations, and otherwise influence initial U.S. LIC options in the future as in the past.

Adverse U.S. opinion actually influenced few outcomes covered by this survey. The Iran-Contra scandal and 1983 bombing in Beirut were prominent exceptions. Public disapproval of imbroglios such as the Bay of Pigs and the Desert One raid in Iran appeared after those episodes were over. International opinion was even less consequential. Rancor in Latin America, for example, rarely altered U.S. LIC operations appreciably. Smoldering resentment, however, occasionally contributed to recurrent conflicts, especially in Central America and Iran.

IMPORTANT LIC TRENDS

LIC trends, unlike patterns, are vectored variables. Four are clearly evident. The first two, beyond U.S. control. seem solidly entrenched and probably will strengthen. The future vigor and direction of trends three and four depend entirely on decisions that senior U.S. officials take:

- LIC importance increases
- LIC complexity increases
- U.S. initiatives increase
- Congressional influence increases

LIC Importance Increases

Low-intensity conflicts can help "have not" nations and subnational groups compete with advanced societies on favorable terms. Population explosions coupled with rising expectations in less developed regions of the world encourage eruptions. Political competition multiplies resultant problems.[14]

Industrialized nations may conduct low-intensity conflicts with political and economic "weapons" as one way to achieve objectives without the risk of shooting wars that could escalate out of control. Transnational terrorism and narco conflict both could expand on short notice.

---

[14] *Supporting U.S. Strategy for Third World Conflict*, Report by the Regional Conflict Working Group Submitted to the Commission on Integrated Long-Term Strategy, Washington, U.S. GPO, June 1988, p. 4-15; Steven Metz, "An American Strategy for Low-Intensity Conflict," *Strategic Review*, Fall 1989, p. 10-12.

LIC Complexity Increases

Low-intensity conflict, the most diversified form of warfare, became increasingly complex after World War II. Comparatively simple missions, such as gunboat diplomacy inside China and security operations in Latin American protectorates, terminated 50 years ago. Anti/counterterrorism and drug interdiction, their latest replacements, are orders of magnitude more complicated.

Communists, once seen as the main culprit, now have strong competition. Islamic fundamentalists see the United States as a foe, and act accordingly. Drug barons are another opponent. De facto proxies, once a rarity, complicate matters for friends as well as foes whenever they pursue policies at cross purposes with patrons. Television and satellite communications permit users to manipulate public opinion in countries where the most rapid communication until recently was word of mouth.

The proliferation of high-tech hardware and better training among backward nations and subnational groups already makes low-intensity combat a sporty proposition. The Pentagon once could dispatch a corporal's guard to conquer Third World miscreants, but no more. Military balances consequently require reassessment in many cases.[15]

U.S. Initiatives Increase

The Reagan Doctrine, promulgated informally in 1981, revised long-standing U.S. containment policies for competition with the Soviet Union, and approached low-intensity conflict in less cautious ways that were reminiscent of freewheeling before World War II. Rollback became the basic objective of U.S. support for resistance movements.[16] Initiatives also were evident in Grenada, the Persian Gulf, Panama, and Andean states afflicted by drug cartels.

---

[15] *U.S. Weapons: The Low-Intensity Threat is Not Necessarily a Low-Technology Threat*, 24 p. ; Baker Caleb, "Sophisticated Weapons in Third World Pose Threat to U.S. Army," *Defense News*, October 16, 1989, p. 8.

[16] Turner, Robert F., "International Law, the Reagan Doctrine, and World Peace: Going Back to the Future," *Washington Quarterly*, Autumn 1988, p. 119-136; Copson, Raymond W. and Richard P. Cronin, *"Reagan Doctrine": Assisting Anti-Marxist Guerrillas*, Issue Brief IB86113, Washington, Congressional Research Service, May 1, 1987, 17 p.

Congressional Influence Increases

Congress has increasingly influenced U.S. LIC plans and operations since the Vietnam War. Two trends are particularly important.

The War Powers Resolution (Public Law 93-148) of 1973 which passed despite President Nixon's veto, circumscribes the President's authority to introduce U.S. armed forces "into hostilities, or into situations where imminent involvement in hostilities is clearly indicated," without a declaration of war or specific statutory authorization. The Resolution further requires the President to withdraw U.S. forces after 60 days, unless Congress extends that time. A 30-day extension is permissible, if the President certifies that faster withdrawal would endanger U.S. units. Those provisions hypothetically applied to several cases in this study, but the Supreme Court has never ruled on constitutionality and they have not been put to serious test. Nevertheless, they constrain U.S. courses of action.[17]

Congress essentially left covert actions to the Executive Branch until 1974. The Hughes-Ryan Amendment, which started to tighten screws, forbade CIA to expend foreign assistance funds for any purpose "other than activities intended solely for obtaining necessary intelligence, unless and until the President finds that each such operation is important to the security of the United States and reports, in a timely fashion . . . to the appropriate committees of the Congress . . . ." The Oversight Act of 1980 refined requirements, after which covert action issues lay relatively dormant until the Iran-Contra scandal revived controversies that remain unresolved.[18]

---

[17] U.S. Congress, House, *The War Powers Resolution: Relevant Documents*, Correspondence, Reports, Subcommittee on Arms Control, International Security, and Science of the Committee on Foreign Affairs, 100th Congress, 2d Session, Washington, U.S. GPO, May 1988, 108 p.; Collier, Ellen C., *The War Powers Resolution: Fifteen Years of Experience*, Washington, Congressional Research Service, August 3, 1988, 50 p.; Clark, Robert D., Andrew M. Egeland, Jr., and David B. Sanford, *The War Powers Resolution*, Washington, National Defense University, 1985, 78 p.

[18] U.S. Congress, Senate, *Intelligence Authorization Act for FY 1990-91*, Report No. 101-174, Select Committee on Intelligence, 101st Congress, 1st Session, September 18, 1989, p. 6-9, 18-33; Grimmett, Richard F., *Covert Actions: Congressional Oversight*, Issue Brief IB87208, Washington, Congressional Research Service, March 23, 1989, 14 p.; Lowenthal, Mark M., *Intelligence Operations: Covert Action*, Issue Brief IB80020, Washington, Congressional Research Service, December 12, 1980, 17 p.

OPTIONS FOR IMPROVEMENTS

U.S. low-intensity conflict experience explored in foregoing pages indicates considerable latitude for reformation. This section, attuned to LIC patterns, trends, and persistent U.S. problems, identifies strategically significant courses of action that could strengthen LIC constituencies, structures, intelligence collection plans, capabilities, and programs.

STRENGTHEN STRUCTURES

U.S. low-intensity conflict command/control structures are weakest at the top. Corrective options could include a small group of full-time LIC professionals reporting to the National Security Council through the Assistant to the President for National Security Affairs. Such an element would be well suited to coordinate international-interdepartmental-interagency LIC activities, routinely connect the Executive Branch with Congress in related regards, develop planning/programming guidance, ensure compliance, and act as a clearinghouse for creative ideas.

Nearly all subordinate LIC structures currently belong to DOD and CIA. Parallel institutions are especially desirable in the State Department, given the primacy of political, diplomatic, and economic power in nonviolent conflicts and their importance otherwise.

U.S. military LIC communities live in worlds well removed from the rest of DOD and civilian counterparts. Closer links that increase appreciation for collective strengths, weaknesses, and synergism would be beneficial. The infant Center for Low Intensity Conflict (CLIC) at Langley AFB, Virginia is designed to improve performance in that regard, but will lack much clout unless the Joint Chiefs of Staff assume direct supervision and assign higher priorities to CLIC projects. Tighter ties between service colleges and special operations centers that serve the Army, Navy, and Air Force also would help. The Marine Corps has no comparable facilities.

Most LIC types benefit from international cooperation. New or revised U.S. alliances with low-intensity conflict rather than Soviet containment in mind might be productive.

STRENGTHEN CONSTITUENCIES

The U.S. national security establishment could better deter and, if necessary, deal with LICs, if influential constituencies made low-intensity conflict proficiency a high priority. Champions, however, are in short supply.

The President, Secretary of State, Secretary of Defense, Joint Chiefs of Staff, Director of Central Intelligence, congressional leaders, and their principal advisers are most important, because each has sweeping responsibilities coupled with authority to squelch adversarial subordinates, promote advocates, and convert apathetic employees.

Persuasion is the key to sustained and sincere support. Prestigious LIC spokesmen, with access to officials cited above, could start the process. Retired generals, admirals, and ambassadors are among them. Writings, radio/television programs, and conferences are other forums that might be influential. Military schools/colleges, the State Department's Foreign Service Institute, civilian universities, and think tanks could initiate longer-term programs that emphasize understanding of low-intensity conflict and required capabilities.

Industrial proponents, also essential, demand incentives that stimulate profits as well as fervor.[1] Military-industrial magnates, who make most money on super-expensive aircraft, armored vehicles, and ships, may never display much enthusiasm, because "big ticket" items in the low-intensity conflict field are scarce. There is, however, a potentially large market for corporations, as well as small companies, in esoteric contracts that include inexpensive space-based surveillance systems compatible with man-packed clandestine communications equipment; plastic pistols; portable bombs; pop-up barriers; anti-intrusion devices; shallow-draft boats; closed circuit SCUBA; and instruments to assist tortureless interrogations. Industrial interest nevertheless will likely remain low until manufacturers are convinced that they can make a good living by combining low-cost hardware with high-volume sales.[2]

---

[1] Capaccio, Tony, "Companies Prepare for Low-Intensity Conflict," *Defense Week*, December 18, 1989, p. 3, 14.; Biddle, Wayne, "It Must be Simple and Reliable: Special Report on the Technology of Terrorism," *Discover*, June 1986, p. 22-31.

[2] Bahnsen, Peter F., "Protracted Warfare and the Role of Technology," a chapter in *Guerrilla Warfare and Counterinsurgency*, Ed. by Richard H. Shultz et al., Lexington, Mass., Lexington Books, 1988, p. 201-210.

STRENGTHEN HUMINT

Low-intensity conflict plans and operations founded on faulty intelligence usually fail. Instruments supplement, but cannot replace, agents skilled at clandestine intelligence collection.

Critical requirements consequently exist for a corps of area-oriented human intelligence (HUMINT) professionals able to blend into particular environments. Some should be generalists, other exceedingly specialized (not many, for example, possess abilities to penetrate transnational terrorist cells or narcotic cartels). Proficiency in local dialects and familiarity with local personalities and customs are merely starting points. Competence depends on basic attributes, plus training, which is a protracted process.[3]

STRENGTHEN PLANS

U.S. "small war" strategies often suffer from symptoms that Marshal Maurice Comte de Saxe described in *Mes Rêveries* (1732) 250-years ago: ". . . in default of knowing what should be done, they do what they know."

Long-standing doctrines for unconventional warfare and foreign internal defense require refinement. What criteria, for example, should shape decisions to support particular clients: compatible aims and policies (especially human rights)?; regional and world opinion?; prospects of success?; cost? Persistent disputes about the best way to combat transnational terrorism include the proper role of force, fixed versus flexible policies, the advisability of active defense, and limits of passive defense.[4] U.S. strategic planners additionally need to develop LIC doctrines where little or no pioneering has yet been done. Subconventional deterrence, coups d'etat, and drug interdiction, as well as skillful use of security assistance and sanctions, are prime candidates.

Objective net assessments could help U.S. officials identify critical LIC threats, prioritize them according to imminence, intensity, and implications for U.S. security, then concentrate on the top few by type and by region, taking conflict causes into account along with symptoms. Clear requirements would emerge as a result: how many military units of what kinds in what states of readiness; what weapons and equipment in what quantities; what area specialization and language training; how much economic and military assistance in what sequence at what pace.

---

[3] Dulles, Allen, *The Craft of Intelligence*, NY, Harper & Row, 1963, p. 55-65; *Intelligence Requirements for the 1980s: Clandestine Collection*, Ed. by Roy Godson, Washington, National Strategy Information Center, 1982, 232 p.; Felix, Christopher, *A Short Course in the Secret War*, NY, Dell, 1963, 265 p.

[4] For discussion, see Collins, John M., *Green Berets, SEALS, and Spetsnaz*, NY, Pergamon-Brassey's, 1986, p. 56-62, and notes 84-110, p. 140-143.

STRENGTHEN PROGRAMS

The Chairman of the Special Operations Panel, House Armed Services Committee summarized SOF personnel requirements in terms equally applicable to low-intensity conflicts. Humans are more important than hardware, their quality is more important than quantities, skilled professionals cannot be mass-produced or created expeditiously after emergencies occur.[5] Personnel programs consequently deserve greater attention than they currently receive. Covert action and psychological operations, for example, could reduce military force requirements, increase prospects for success, and simultaneously cut costs in many circumstances, if properly conceived and implemented.

Security assistance levels are low for many beleaguered U.S. associates who, being unable to bear larger financial burdens alone, bypass or defer actions that could benefit U.S. interests as well as their own. Highly selective but consistently larger aid programs, coupled with broader distribution and better control of disposition, would conform well with congressional preference for a low U.S. military profile overseas and smaller U.S. defense budgets. The likelihood of last-minute American military involvement to salvage unacceptable situations might also diminish.[6]

Specialized weapons and equipment nevertheless are useful when nonmilitary power proves unable to handle low-intensity conflict problems unassisted. Sophisticated machines, such as clandestine infiltration/exfiltration aircraft able to fly pitch-black contours in bad weather, are most exciting, but their utility is limited to some LIC types under some circumstances. Area weapons, like artillery, aerial bombs, and napalm, normally are counterproductive, because indiscriminate violence tends to repel the very people that strategists seek to attract. State-of-the-art technology could be put to best use producing capable but low-cost implements designed for easy assembly, operation, maintenance, and repair by U.S. Third World Associates.[7]

ULTIMATE MESSAGES

You cannot make an omelet without breaking eggs. The process, however, favors finesse over force. Low-intensity conflicts most often call for a light touch, rather than heavy hands. Masterful planners and practitioners

---

[5] *Ibid.*, p. xiii.

[6] For details, see *Commitment to Freedom: Security Assistance As a U.S. Policy Instrument in the Third World*, a Paper by the Regional Conflict Working Group Submitted to the Commission on Integrated Long-Term Strategy, Washington, U.S. GPO, May 1988, p. 30-55.

[7] Bahnsen, Peter F., "Protracted Warfare and the Role of Technology," p. 201-210.

maximize the use of political, economic, social, and psychological implements whenever so doing minimizes armed combat.

Clausewitz, however, cautioned that "everything in strategy is very simple, but that does not mean everything is easy." [8] Many Americans find shadowy, amorphous LICs more distasteful than conventional military conflict. Some contend that the United States is traditionally and institutionally incapable of conducting most such wars without domestic acrimony so severe that difficulties multiply manyfold and success becomes elusive, even infeasible.

Politically sophisticated officials who are strategically and tactically proficient at all types of LIC nevertheless seem advisable, if well established trends correctly indicate that low-intensity conflicts increasingly will impinge on important U.S. interests. This survey of U.S. experience over the last 90 years hopefully will help expedite improvement.[9]

---

[8] Clausewitz, Karl von, *On War*, Ed. and Translated by Michael Howard and Peter Paret, Princeton, NJ, Princeton University Press, 1976, p. 178.

[9] For projections, see Paschall, Rod, *LIC 2010: Special Operations and Unconventional Warfare in the Next Century*, Washington, Brassey's (U.S.), 1990, 165 p.

Annex A

Case Summaries

Summaries in this annex appear chronologically as Cases 1-60, starting in 1899. Durations indicate dates of U.S. participation, although some conflicts started earlier and/or ended later.

No summary exceeds two pages. Each contains just enough information to identify where, when, how, and why the United States was involved. Selected sources in every instance provide ready access to additional facts and assorted interpretations, including those that concern complex cause-effect relationships. Most documents cited designate many more references for in-depth study.

Fifteen of the 46 resolved conflicts are categorized as success and 9 as failure, according to mainstream consensus. The remainder received mixed reviews. Outcomes for 14 active conflicts indicate their status as of August, 1990. The likelihood that they will escalate is high in some cases, moderate or low in others.

See Annex B for additional detail concerning congressional authorizations and limitations.

Appendices

CASE 1

PHILIPPINES (1899-1913)

Type Conflict	Counterinsurgency
Duration	February 1899-June 1913 (14+ years)
Participants	*U.S. Allies*: Friendly Filipinos *U.S. Adversaries*: Philippine insurgents
U.S. Purposes	*Interests*: Strategic, commercial *Objectives*: Annex Philippines; pacify occupants
Predominant U.S. Power	Military
Predominant U.S. Instrument	Force, but reforms were important
U.S. Armed Forces	*Predominant Type*: Conventional *Predominant Service*: Army *Predominant Function*: Armed combat
Public Opinion	*U.S.*: Support stronger than opposition *International*: No significant response

Context

Spain ceded the Philippine Islands to the United States for $20 million after the Spanish-American War, in accord with the Treaty of Paris (December 1898). President McKinley ordered the Secretary of War to occupy all ceded territories and install a military government. Philippine nationalists, led by General Emilio Aguinaldo, fought for independence.

A three-phase conflict ensued. U.S. conventional armed forces prevailed during Phase I (February-November 1899). Aguinaldo reverted to guerrilla warfare and often held the initiative during Phase II, which lasted a bit more than a year. Phase III commenced early in 1901. The U.S. Army, which replaced leaders and revised tactics, captured Aguinaldo in March. Political, economic, and social reforms undermined insurgent popularity. Hard fighting continued, but rebellion eventually abated. Christian parts of the Philippine archipelago were secure when President Theodore Roosevelt declared victory in July 1902. Muslim Moros, however, continued resistance for 11 more years, especially on Mindanao.

Key Congressional Actions

Congress authorized U.S. military force levels and offered financial inducements for service in the Philippines. The President governed the Philippines by explicit congressional authority after March 2, 1901.

Outcome: Success

The United States accomplished basic objectives. Strong U.S.-Philippine relationships developed and endured. The Philippines adopted many U.S. democratic institutions.

Selected Sources

Linn, Brian McAllister, *The U.S. Army and Counterinsurgency in the Philippine War, 1899-1902*, Chapel Hill, NC, University of North Carolina Press, 1989, 258 p.

Merriman, Howard M., "The Philippines (1899-1902)," in *Challenge and Response in Internal Conflict*, Ed. by D.M. Condit and Bert H. Cooper, Jr., et al, Vol. I, Washington, Center for Research in Social Systems, American University, February 1968, p. 91-114.

Gates, John Morgan, *Schoolbooks and Krags: The United States Army in the Philippines*, 1899-1902, Westport, CT, Greenwood Press, 1973, 315 p.

CASE 2

CHINA (1900)

Type Conflict	Protective expedition
Duration	June-September 1900 (3-plus months)
Participants	*U.S.. Allies*: Austria, Britain, France, Germany, Italy, Japan, and Russia in loose association
	U.S. Adversaries: Manchu regulars; Boxer irregulars
U.S. Purposes	*Interests*: Mainly commercial (Open Door)
	Objectives: Protect U.S. lives and property; restore stability
Predominant U.S. Power	Military
Predominant U.S. Instrument	Force
U.S. Armed Forces	*Predominant Type*: Conventional
	Predominant Service
	Beijing Garrison: Marine Corps
	Relief Expedition: Navy; Army
	Predominant Function: Armed combat
Public Opinion	*U.S.*: Supportive
	International: Supportive

Context

Chinese xenophobia bubbled in the late 19th Century, when foreigners rode roughshod over hapless inhabitants. Leased territories, spheres of influence, other concessions, and serious talk about partition undercut China's economy and compromised its sovereignty.

The "Fists of Righteous Harmony," a huge secret society colloquially called "Boxers," employed violence to extirpate Chinese Christians and foreign influence, beginning in 1898. Governing Manchus sought to suppress or conciliate that movement until early June 1900, when large-scale foreign intervention seemed imminent.

The Imperial Court reversed policy at that point, embraced the Boxers, laid siege to the Legation Quarter in Beijing, then repulsed an international relief column enroute from Tientsin. Fewer than 500 legation guards repelled repeated attacks for 55 days, until an eight-nation expeditionary force of 14,000-16,000 men (2,500 Americans) lifted the siege on August 14, after bloody battles to secure Tientsin, which also had been surrounded for almost two months. U.S. troops participated in mop up operations for a few more weeks. Most of America's China Relief Expedition returned to combat in the Philippines, whence it came, by October 1900.

Key Congressional Actions: None. Congress was not in session.

Outcome: Success

The United States achieved its short-term objectives. Instability that ensued when the Manchu Dynasty began to collapse soon thereafter was beyond U.S. control.

Selected Sources

O'Connor, Richard, *The Spirit Soldiers: A Historical Narrative of the Boxer Rebellion*, NY, G.P. Putnam's Sons, 1973, 379 p.

Tan, Chester, "China (1898-1901)," in *Challenge and Response in Internal Conflict*, Ed. by D.M. Condit and Bert H. Cooper, Jr., et al, Vol. I, Washington. Center for Research in Social Systems, American University, February 1968, p. 3-27.

CASE 3

COLOMBIA/PANAMA (1901-14)

Type Conflict	Peacemaking
Duration	14 years
Participants	*U.S. Allies*: None *U.S. Adversaries*: Colombia; anti-canal activists
U.S. Purposes	*Interests*: Commercial; strategic *Objectives*: Protect the Canal Zone; ensure internal stability
Predominant U.S. Power	Political and military
Predominant U.S. Instrument	Diplomacy and force
U.S. Armed Forces	*Predominant Type*: Conventional *Predominant Service*: Marine Corps *Predominant Function*: Internal security
Public Opinion	*U.S.*: Supportive *International*: Slight, but supportive

Context

The Hay-Pauncefore treaty of 1901 gave the United States all rights to build, operate, and fortify a canal across the Isthmus of Panama. Colombia, the possessor of that property, refused permission in August 1903. Its province of Panama, converted to an independent republic after a brief revolution two months later. The new nation leased a 10-mile-wide Canal Zone in perpetuity to the United States, which thereafter exercised control "as if it were sovereign."

U.S. Marines established a presence on the isthmus in 1901, when civil disturbances caused instability. They returned several times in 1902, prevented Colombian troops from suppressing the 1903 revolution, supervised elections in 1908 and 1912, and patrolled the Panama Canal Zone until construction was complete in 1914.

Key Congressional Actions

Congress in February 1904 ratified the Panama Canal Treaty, gave the U.S. President full power to administer the Canal Zone, and offered financial incentives for servicemen assigned to protect it.

Outcome: Success

The Panama Canal was completed without serious interference by recalcitrants and, in accord with 1977 treaties, will remain under U.S. control until the year 2000.

Selected Sources

U.S. Congress, House, *The Story of Panama*, Hearings on the Rainey Resolution Before the Committee on Foreign Affairs, 62d Congress, 2d session, Washington, U.S. GPO, 1912, 762 p., passim.

Munro, Dana G., *Intervention and Dollar Diplomacy in the Caribbean, 1900-1921*, Princeton, NJ, Princeton University Press, 1964, p. 37-64.

Martin, Charles E., "The Policy of the United States as Regards Intervention," in *Studies in History, Economics, and Public Law*, Ed. by the faculty of political science, Vol. 93, No. 2, NY, Columbia University, 1921, p. 162-173.

CASE 4

MOROCCO (1904)

Type Conflict	Conventional rescue mission
Duration	May 18 - June 24, 1904 (38 days)
Participants	*U.S.. Allies*: Moorish Government; Great Britain *U.S. Adversaries*: Berber brigands
U.S. Purposes	*Interests*: U.S. security overseas *Objectives*: Safe return of abducted U.S. citizen
Predominant U.S. Power	Politico-military
Predominant U.S. Instrument	Diplomacy; threats
U.S. Armed Forces	*Predominant Type*: Conventional *Predominant Service*: Marines *Predominant Function*: Show of force
Public Opinion	*U.S.*: Nonexistent *International*: Nonexistent

Context

Abilities to protect its citizens and property abroad are essential for any nation that aspires to world power status. The United States, which battled Barbary pirates a century before (1801-05, 1815) was tested again in a much smaller (but nevertheless important) way by another North African, the brigand Ahmed Raisuli, who abducted Ion Perdicaris and his stepson, a British subject.

The United States and Britain both dispatched warships to Tangier as evidence of resolve. Both held Moorish authorities personally responsible for the safe release of the prisoners. The U.S. consul-general at first urged Moorish officials to grant any Raisuli demand, but Secretary of State John Hay refused to guarantee concessions, give in to blackmail, or promise immunity for the crime. "Perdicaris alive or Raisuli dead" was the requirement. Negotiations nevertheless sputtered for more than a month, while Raisuli remained in his mountain redoubt. The State Department declined to land Marines. Raisuli eventually released his captives in return for $70,000 ransom.

Key Congressional Actions: None

Outcome: Mixed opinion

The United States accomplished its basic objective, but only on Raisuli's terms. U.S. military power was not an important factor. Perhaps most embarassing, Perdicaris proved to be a citizen of Greece.

Selected Sources

"Abduction of Ion Perdicaris by Bandits," *Foreign Relations of the United States*, Washington, Dept. of State, 1904, p. 496-504.

Davis, Harold E., "The Citizenship of Ion Perdicaris," *Journal of Modern History*, December 1941, p. 517-526.

Tuchman, Barbara W., "Perdicaris Alive or Raisuli Dead," *Practicing History*, NY, Ballentine Books, 1982, p. 104-117.

CASE 5

CUBA (1906-09)

Type Conflict	Peacemaking
Duration	September 1906 - January 1909 (3 years, 5 months)
Participants	*U.S.. Allies*: None *U.S. Adversaries*: None of note
U.S. Purposes	*Interests*: Stability in the Caribbean *Objectives*: Prevent disorder; install a Cuban government
Predominant U.S. Power	Politico-military
Predominant U.S. Instrument	Civilian officials, armed forces
U.S. Armed Forces	*Predominant Type*: Conventional *Predominant Service*: Army, Marines *Predominant Function*: Internal security
Public Opinion	*U.S.*: Passive to supportive, in the absence of combat *International*: Supportive

Context

U.S. military governors ruled Cuba after the Spanish-American War from January 1899 until May 1902. That country then began to function as an independent republic, but Article III of the Platt Amendment to its constitution authorized U.S. intervention, if necessary to protect "life, property, and individual liberty."

The Cuban Government requested such intervention in September 1906, when revolution arose in response to a fraudulent national election. President Theodore Roosevelt, however, expressed extreme reluctance. The Cuban President, Vice President, and designated successors thereupon resigned, leaving Cuba rudderless. U.S. Secretary of War William Howard Taft, already on site, filled the gap as Provisional Governor on September 29, with these instructions from Roosevelt: "Our business is to establish peace and order, . . .start the new government, and then leave the island." Cuba's former officials and rebels both approved. Taft, however, failed to resolve Cuba's problems peacefully. Roosevelt thereupon appointed Nebraska attorney Charles Maygood as Governor. Maygood immediately called for U.S. armed forces. A Marine brigade landed first, followed by 5,600 Army troops. Together, they disarmed belligerents, dispersed rebels, and garrisoned cities until January 28, 1909, when a duly elected Cuban government again took charge.

Key Congressional Actions

Congress approved the Platt Amendment, offered financial incentives to U.S. servicemen in Cuba, and authorized the President to reimburse the United States from Cuba's treasury to pay for intervention. Congress rescinded the Platt Amendment in 1934.

Outcome: Success

The United States achieved its short-term objectives. U.S. Marines returned to Cuba briefly in 1912 and during the so-called "Sugar Wars" (1914-1922), but even a permanent U.S. military presence might not have prevented recurring crises. Congress rescinded the Platt Amendment in 1934.

Selected Sources

Vreeland, Mildred, "Cuba (1906-1909)," in *Challenge and Response in Internal Conflict*, Ed. by D.M. Condit and Bert H. Cooper, Jr., et al, Vol. III, Washington, Center for Research in Social Systems, American University, April 1968, p. 107-127.

Munro, Dana G., *Intervention and Dollar Diplomacy in the Caribbean, 1900-1921*, Princeton, NJ, Princeton University Press, 1964, p. 125-140.

Millett, Alan R., *The Politics of Intervention: The Military Occupation of Cuba, 1906-1909*, Columbus, OH, Ohio State University, 1968, 306 p.

CASE 6

CHINA (1912-1941)

Type Conflict	Protective expedition
Duration	Thirty years
Participants	*U.S.. Allies*: None formally; some loose associations *U.S. Adversaries*: Anti-imperialists; Japan
U.S. Purposes	*Interests*: Commercial *Objectives*: Protect U.S. lives and property
Predominant U.S. Power	Military
Predominant U.S. Instrument	Gunboats; ground forces
U.S. Armed Forces	*Predominant Type*: Conventional *Predominant Services*: Navy, Marines *Predominant Function*: Shows of force; force
Public Opinion	*U.S.*: Passive *International*: Passive

Context

Several protocols between 1858 and 1901 awarded the United States, Britain, France, and Russia rights to patrol Chinese rivers and territorial waters. Overlapping spheres of influence and interference in Chinese domestic affairs were results.

U.S. naval vessels, with armed bluejackets and marines embarked, deployed to keep riverine and coastal lines of communication open. Their original mission was to ward off anti-imperialist warlords, who jeopardized American merchants and missionaries. By 1927, however, U.S. forces were caught in the midst of a civil war between Chiang Kai-shek's Kuomintang (Nationalist) government, various regional armies, and communist insurgents, led by Mao Zedong. The greatest U.S. military presence, displayed in response to endemic disorder, occurred during 1927: 5,670 servicemen ashore, 44 ships in Chinese waters. Japan, bent on replacing the Open Door with a Greater East Asia Co-Prosperity Sphere, became the primary threat to China and all foreigners therein a decade later. The *Panay*, sunk in December 1937, was the most publicized U.S. loss, but by no means the only combat action.

Key Congressional Actions

Congress ratified the 1858 treaty that first justified U.S. naval vessels in Chinese waters and appropriated funds for expeditionary forces.

Outcome: Success

The United States accomplished basic objectives over a 30-year period while limiting costs and loss of life.

Selected Sources

Tolley, Kemp, *Yangtze Patrol: The U.S. Navy in China*, Annapolis, Md., Naval Institute Press, 1971, 329 p.

Lindsay, Michael, "China (1927- 1937)" and "China (1937-1945)," in *Challenge and Response in Internal Conflict*, Ed. by D.M. Condit and Bert H. Cooper, Jr., et al, Vol. I, Washington, Center for Research in Social Systems, American University, February 1968, p. 31-68, 139-177.

CASE 7

MEXICO (1914-17)

Type Conflict	Punitive expedition
Duration	April 9, 1914 - February 5, 1917 (2 years, 10 months)
Participants	*U.S. Allies*: None *U.S. Adversaries*: Mexican Government; revolutionaries
U.S. Purposes	Interests: National prestige; border security Objectives: Command respect; punish intruders
Predominant U.S. Power	Military
Predominant U.S. Instrument	Force
U.S. Armed Forces	Predominant Type: Conventional Predominant Services: Veracruz : Multiservice Anti-Villa : Army Predominant Function: Armed Combat
Public Opinion	U.S.: Divided in 1914; supportive in 1916 International: Adverse in Latin America

Context

U.S. armed forces patrolled the Mexican border and coastal waters between 1910 and 1914, while revolution wracked that country. President Woodrow Wilson seized Vera Cruz in April 1914 when Mexican President Huerta apologized but refused a 21-gun salute to the American flag after a serious incident at Tampico. The U.S. Army and Marines occupied Vera Cruz until November 23rd.

Revolution resumed after Huerta resigned. Pancho Villa, who prevailed in the north, temporarily received U.S. support, but soon fell from favor. President Wilson first imposed an arms embargo on him, then (without consulting Congress) allowed Mexican troops in hot pursuit to transit U.S. territory. Villa's retaliatory attacks culminated in a March 9, 1916 raid on Columbus, NM. A U.S. punitive expedition that eventually totaled 12,000 men and the first U.S. aircraft in armed combat penetrated 200 miles into Mexico, but failed to find Villa. The Mexican Government, which originally granted permission for U.S. incursions, had a change of mind by mid-June.

Clashes between U.S. and Mexican Army contingents caused President Wilson to federalize the National Guard and move 150,000 troops to the Mexican border. The crisis, however, subsided and Wilson withdrew all U.S. forces by February 5, 1917, when war with Germany loomed large.

Key Congressional Actions

Congress, by joint resolution, approved U.S. military operations at Vera Cruz. It appropriated funds for the 1916 Punitive Expedition, plus U.S. forces deployed along the Mexican border.

Outcome: Mixed opinion

Vera Cruz was a military success, but a political disappointment. Latin American resentment was severe. "Blackjack" Pershing accomplished his objective, which was to disperse "the band or bands that attacked Columbus, NM." Villa escaped, but his followers scattered. No major war occurred. U.S. relations with Mexico, however, remained strained through the Hoover Administration as a direct result.

Selected Sources

Dupuy, R. Ernest and William H. Baumer, *The Little Wars of the United States*, NY, Hawthorn Books, 1968, p. 123-143.

Davis, Harold E., "Mexico (1916-1917)," in *Challenge and Response in International Conflict*, Ed. by D.M. Condit and Bert H. Cooper, Jr., Vol. III, Washington, Center for Research in Social Systems, American University, April 1968, p. 131-153.

Clendenin, Clarence C., *Blood on the Border: The United States Army and the Mexican Irregulars*, NY, McMillan, 1969, 390 p.

CASE 8

HAITI (1915-34)

Type Conflict	Peacemaking
Duration	July 28, 1915-August 15, 1934 (19 years)
Participants	*U.S. Allies*: None *U.S. Adversaries*: Disaffected populace
U.S. Purposes	*Interests*: Stability in the Caribbean *Objectives*: Forestall foreign intervention; restore stability
Predominant U.S. Power	Military
Predominant U.S. Instrument	Force; reform
U.S. Armed Forces	*Predominant Type*: Conventional *Predominant Services*: Marine Corps *Predominant Function*: Internal security
Public Opinion	*U.S.*: Some opposition; mainly apathetic *International*: Adverse in Latin America

Context

The island of Hispaniola overlooks sea lanes to and from the Panama Canal. Haiti, which occupies the western third, verged on political and economic collapse in 1915. European creditors clamored for control of Haitian customs held under lien. Some U.S. officials feared Germany might use debt collection as a pretext to establish a submarine base in that country. Mob rule catalyzed and the Monroe Doctrine justified American intervention on July 28 to protect U.S. lives and property. The ensuing occupation, sanctioned by a treaty, spanned almost two decades.

U.S. Marines put down vicious rebellions in 1915, when they won six Medals of Honor, and were awarded two more during the so-called Cacos War of 1918-20. Their administrative contribution to stability, the development of a *gendarmerie,* was less lasting than it might have been, because it initially was officered entirely by U.S. Marines, and few provisions were made for Haitians to take charge. Policymaking remained mainly in U.S. hands for the first 15 years (Haiti elected a president in 1915, but no legislature until 1930). U.S. civilian administrators improved Haiti's financial posture and, with help from Marines, used Haitian funds to institute much needed reforms. Infrastructure, especially roads, sanitation facilities, hospitals, and telecommunications sprouted. U.S. civil servants departed by 1931. The last Marines left three years later.

Key Congressional Actions

The Senate on February 28, 1916 ratified a treaty that approved U.S. intervention and authorized a constabulary "organized and officered by Americans." Congress then authorized Navy Department personnel on detail to assist Haiti indefinitely.

Outcome: Mixed opinion

The United States achieved its basic objectives. The Marine Corps preserved military lessons learned in its *Small Wars Manual*. A bitter legacy, fueled partly by racial animosities, nevertheless remained. Legal and educational systems were scarcely improved. Turmoil returned shortly after U.S. Marines departed.

Selected Sources

Monroe, Dana G., *Intervention and Dollar Diplomacy in the Caribbean, 1900-1921*, Princeton, NJ, Princeton University Press, 1964, p. 326-287.

Logan, Rayford W., "Haiti (1918-1920)," in *Challenge and Response in Internal Conflict*, Ed. by D.M. Condit and Bert H. Cooper, Jr., et al, Supplement, Washington, Center for Research in Social Systems, American University, September 1968, p. 33-57.

CASE 9

DOMINICAN REPUBLIC (1916-24)

Type Conflict	Peacemaking
Duration	May 5, 1916-September 28, 1924 (8 years, 5 months)
Participants	*U.S. Allies*: None *U.S. Adversaries*: Disaffected populace
U.S. Purposes	*Interests*: Stability in the Caribbean *Objectives*: Forestall foreign intervention; restore stability
Predominant U.S. Power	Military
Predominant U.S. Instrument	Force; reform
U.S. Armed Forces	*Predominant Type*: Conventional *Predominant Services*: Marine Corps *Predominant Function*: Internal security
Public Opinion	*U.S.*: Mainly apathetic *International*: Adverse in Latin America

Context

Circumstances in the Dominican Republic, which occupies the eastern two-thirds of Hispaniola, were similar to those in Haiti (see Case 8). Political turmoil and poverty prevailed long before the United States intervened. Germany, according to rumor, planned to satisfy European creditors, occupy Dominican custom houses to guarantee repayment, and thereby gain a Caribbean foothold. President Theodore Roosevelt, prompted in part by his corrollary to the Monroe Doctrine, set up a receivership, ratified by treaty in 1907, that was to continue until Dominican debts were paid.

International strife, however, continued. Fighting between Dominican Government forces and rivals flared in the capital. U.S. Marines, who intervened on May 6, 1916 to protect American lives and property, faced a hostile population. Organized resistance ceased by March 1917, but widespread banditry continued unabated. The U.S. military government that replaced Dominican administrators nevertheless put many reforms in motion. Marines in charge created a national guard much like the Haitian *gendarmerie* and took civic action seriously. U.S. occupation terminated two months after constitutional government recommenced on July 12, 1924.

Key Congressional Actions

The Senate on February 27, 1907 ratified the treaty that gave the United States control of Dominican finances. Congress on February 11, 1918 authorized Navy Department personnel on detail to "assist the Dominican Republic."

Outcome: Mixed opinion

The United States achieved its basic objectives and left the Dominican Republic better than before, but inhabitants bitterly resented infringements on their sovereignty. Reforms, for reasons beyond U.S. control, failed to take root. It took Dominican dictator Rafael Trujillo to restore prolonged stability (Case 28).

Selected Sources

Garbuny, Siegfried, "Dominican Republic (1916-1924)," in *Challenge and Response in Internal Conflict*, Ed. by D.M. Condit and Bert H. Cooper, Jr., et al, Supplement, Washington, Center for Research in Social Systems, American University, September 1968, p. 33-57.

Munro, Dana G., *Intervention and Dollar Diplomacy in the Caribbean, 1900-1921*, Princeton, NJ, Princeton University Press, 1964, p. 269-325.

CASE 10

NICARAGUA (1926-33)

Type Conflict	Peacemaking
Duration	November 1926 - January 1933 (6 years, 2 months)
Participants	*U.S. Allies*: None *U.S. Adversaries*: Disaffected Nicaraguans
U.S. Purposes	*Interests*: Stability in Central America *Objectives*: Terminate insurrection; strengthen government
Predominant U.S. Power	Military
Predominant U.S. Instrument	Force
U.S. Armed Forces	*Predominant Type*: Conventional *Predominant Services*: Marine Corps *Predominant Function*: Internal security
Public Opinion	U.S.: Considerable opposition International: Adverse in Latin America

Context

U.S. interference in Nicaraguan affairs dates from days when that country was considered as one possible site for an isthmian canal. A disruptive revolution in 1926 triggered the most lengthy U.S. intervention, after nominal President Diaz requested assistance. U.S. emissaries, backed by Marines, arranged a temporary settlement in May 1927 and promised to supervise a presidential election the following year.

Nicaraguan General Augusto Sandino, a presidential asperant who opposed American intervention, rebelled. The U.S. response in some respects paralleled operations in Haiti and the Dominican Republic (see Cases 8-9). Marines, for example, officered a National Guard until it became effective. Many differences, however, were significant. Armed force was the main U.S. implement. Local leaders retained more control. There was no U.S. military government. Systematic civic action programs were scarce. Sandino, popular at home and a rallying point for anti-U.S. sentiment throughout Latin America, received assistance from Mexico, Costa Rica, and Honduras for several years. He remained strong until Honduras finally deprived him of a sanctuary in 1932. He suffered severe defeats from the National Guard and agreed to negotiate after U.S. Marines withdrew in January 1933, but remained a powerful political activist until Anastasio Somoza ordered his assassination on February 21, 1934.

Key Congressional Actions

Congress on December 22, 1927 provided funds for the U.S. expeditionary force in Nicaragua, but by 1932 specifically forbid Navy appropriations "to defray the expense of sending additional Marines . . ." Resolutions to withdraw as early as 1928, however, were repeatedly rejected.

Outcome: Mixed opinion

The United States accomplished its military objectives in Nicaragua less expeditiously than on Hispaniola, and at greater cost. Political stability imposed by a dictator who controlled the National Guard was never a U.S. goal, but later was tolerated. Nicaraguan resentment is still strong in some sections.

Selected Sources

Nalty, Bernard C., "Nicaragua (1927-1933)," in *Challenge and Response in Internal Conflict*, Ed. by D.M. Condit and Bert H. Cooper, Jr., et al, Vol III, Washington, Center for Research in Social Systems, American University, April 1968, p. 157-171.

Munro, Dana G., *The United States and the Caribbean Republics, 1921-1933*, Princeton, NJ, Princeton University Press, 1974, p. 187-279.

Macaulay, Neill, *The Sandino Affair*, Chicago, Quadrangle Books, 1967, 319 p.

Millett, Richard, *Guardians of the Dynasty*, NY, Orbis Books, 1979, 284 p.

CASE 11

PHILIPPINES (1942-45)

Type Conflict	Resistance
Duration	January 1942-June 1945 (3 years, 6 months)
Participants	*U.S. Allies*: Most Philippine people; Australia *U.S. Adversaries*: Japanese armed forces; collaborators
U.S. Purposes	*Interest*: National defense *Objective*: Defeat Japan
Predominant U.S. Power	Paramilitary
Predominant U.S. Instruments	Covert actions
U.S. Armed Forces	*Predominant Type*: Special operations *Predominant Service*: Army *Predominant Function*: Unconventional Warfare
Public Opinion	*U.S.*: Supportive *International*: Allies supportive

Context

Japan attacked the Philippines on Pearl Harbor day (December 8, 1941). Resistance commenced in January 1942. At least 75 guerrilla groups eventually evolved, but few coalesced, partly because many had self-serving agendas. Communist Hukbalahaps (People's Army to Fight the Japanese), for example, savaged Philippine rivals in Central Luzon who opposed their post-war plans. Christians seldom sided with Muslim Moros on Mindanao.

First priority for all nevertheless was to expel Japan. U.S. Army officers who eluded capture after the fall of Bataan and Corregidor helped organize, equip, train, and lead some of the most effective bands. They initially were isolated, but MacArthur's General Headquarters (GHQ) began to link some of them loosely by 1943. Submarines started to supplement logistic support from local undergrounds about that time: arms, ammunition, communications equipment, medical supplies. Typical unconventional warfare (UW) missions included raids, ambushes, sabotage, and psychological operations ("I shall return" was a popular propaganda theme that bolstered Philippine morale.). Intelligence collection was General MacArthur's top priority before U.S.

liberators landed in the autumn and winter of 1944-45. Guerrilla formations thereafter conducted conventional military operations, as well as UW.

Key Congressional Actions

Resistance in the Philippines was part of World War II. Congress did not explicitly authorize forces or appropriate funds for that purpose.

Outcome: Success

Resistance fighters led and/or supported by the United States distracted Japanese armed forces in the Philippines, inflicted many casualties, increased Japanese costs, furnished critical intelligence to GHQ, and otherwise contributed to Japanese defeat.

Selected Sources

Volckmann, R.W., *We Remained: Three Years Behind the Enemy Lines in the Philippines*, NY, W.W. Norton, 1954, 244 p.

Falk, Stanley L., "The Philippines (1942-1945)," in *Challenge and Response in Internal Conflict*, Ed. by D.M. Condit and Bert H. Cooper, Jr., et al, Vol. I, Washington, Center for Research in Social Systems, American University, February 1968, p. 211-236.

CASE 12

BURMA (1942-45)

Type Conflict	Resistance
Duration	April 1942 - July 1945 (3 years, 3 months)
Participants	*U.S. Allies*: Kachins; British; Chinese *U.S. Adversaries*: Japanese armed forces; collaborators
U.S. Purposes	*Interests*: National defense *Objectives*: Defeat Japan
Predominant U.S. Power	Military; paramilitary
Predominant U.S. Instrument	Covert actions
U.S. Armed Forces	*Predominant Type*: Special operations *Predominant Services*: Army; Air Forces Predominant Function: Unconventional warfare; airlift
Public Opinion	U.S.: Supportive International: Allies supportive

Context

Most U.S. armed forces in Burma during World War II, including Merrill's Marauders, engaged primarily in conventional or semiconventional combat. OSS Detachment 101, which organized, trained, equipped, and commanded several thousand indigenous tribesmen for unconventional warfare (UW), was a prominent exception. So was the 1st Air Commando, which supported British General Orde Wingate's "Chindits" as well as U.S. forces.[1]

Burmese nationalists initially believed Japan would liberate them from British rule. Detachment 101 consequently recruited Kachin minorities. British allies, who collaborated closely, used Karens as well. Unconventional warfare missions in some respects paralleled those in the Philippines (Case 11), but differences were significant. All were in direct support of conventional military operations (51 destroyed bridges and 9 derailed trains must have helped). U.S. and allied forces also used the detachment for "eyes and ears". Tenth U.S. Air Force, for example, estimated that Detachment 101

---

[1] Colonel Philip Cochrane, 1st Air Commando, reappeared as Flip Cockran in the comic strip *Terry and the Pirates*.

designated 60-85% of its targets and assessed post-strike damage. Escape and evasion nets, another specialty, saved 574 allied fliers down in enemy territory. Resupply arrived by air and the Ledo Road, rather than by submarines. During the period May 8 to June 15, 1945, when its war was winding down, Detachment 101 (then totalling 3,200 natives) "met and routed 10,000 Japanese throughout an area of 10,000 square miles," for which it received a Presidential Distinguished Unit Citation.

Key Congressional Actions

Resistance in Burma was part of World War II. Congress did not explicitly authorize forces or appropriate funds for that purpose.

Outcome: Success

Detachment 101 distracted Japanese armed forces in Burma, inflicted many casualties, increased Japanese costs, furnished conventional forces with critical intelligence, and otherwise contributed to Japanese defeat.

Selected Sources

Peers, William R. and Dean Brelis, *Behind the Burma Road: The Story of America's Most Successful Guerrilla Force*, Boston, Little, Brown, and Co., 1963, 246 p.

Johnstone, William C., "Burma (1942-1945)," in *Challenge and Response in Internal Conflict*, Ed. by D.M. Condit and Bert H. Cooper, Jr., et al, Vol. I, Washington, Center for Research in Social Systems, American University, February 1968, p. 117-135.

Smith, E. D., *Battle for Burma*, NY, Holmes & Meier, 1979, 190 p.

CASE 13

FRANCE (1944)

Type Conflict	Resistance
Duration	January-October 1944 (10 months)
Participants	*U.S. Allies*: Free French; Britain *U.S. Adversaries*: Germans; Vichy French
U.S. Purposes	*Interests*: National Defense *Objectives*: Defeat Germany
Predominant U.S. Power	Military
Predominant U.S. Instrument	Covert actions
U.S. Armed Forces	*Predominant Type*: Special Operations *Predominant Services*: Army *Predominant Function*: Unconventional warfare
Public Opinion	*U.S.*: Supportive *International*: Allies supportive

Context

Germany defeated and occupied half of France in June 1940. Vichy puppets ruled the remainder. Charles de Gaulle, from exile in Britain, called for resistance that same month. The Free French rallied slowly but, first with British and later with U.S. assistance, became a formidable force that contributed substantially to allied landings in Normandy and southern France during the summer and fall of 1944.

Related U.S. roles date from January 1944, when French-speaking OSS agents in mufti, began to help undergrounds organize, train, and operate. Uniformed operational groups (OGs), the forerunners of U.S. Army Special Forces, performed similar functions for guerrilla bands. Three-man Jedburgh teams (named after the region where they trained in Scotland) jumped into France on or about D-Day (June 6) to coordinate resistance operations with General Eisenhower's plans. All OSS elements in the field furnished useful intelligence to higher headquarters. Results in Normandy were rewarding. Saboteurs severed roads, railways, power lines, and communication cables all over France to avoid revealing invasion sites prematurely.   German reinforcements arrived late. Retreating Germans were harassed enroute to their homeland. August landings along the Mediterranean coast benefitted in similar fashion.

Key Congressional Actions

Resistance in France was part of World War II. Congress did not explicitly authorize forces or appropriate funds for that purpose.

Outcome: Success

Resistance fighters led and/or supported by the United States distracted German forces in France, inflicted many casualties, furnished critical intelligence, and otherwise contributed to German defeat. U.S. involvement was cost-effective.

Selected Sources

MacDonald, Charles B., "France 1940-1944)," in *Challenge and Response in Internal Conflict*, Ed. by D.M. Condit and Bert H. Cooper, Jr., et al, Vol. II, Washington, Center for Research in Social Systems, American University Press, 1982, p. 27-29 and notes p. 166.

Paddock, Alfred H., Jr., *U.S. Army Special Warfare: Its Origins*, Washington, National Defense University Press, 1982, p. 27-29 and notes p. 166.

CASE 14

CHINA (1945-49)

Type Conflict	Nonviolent conflict (hands off opposition)
Duration	1945-49 (5 years)
Participants	*U.S. Allies*: Nationalist China *U.S. Adversaries*: Chinese communists; Soviet Union indirectly
U.S. Purposes	*Interests*: National defense *Objectives*: Ensure an independent, democratic China friendly to the United States; favorable balance of power in Far East
Predominant U.S. Power	Political
Predominant U.S. Instrument	Diplomacy, security assistance
U.S. Armed Forces	*Predominant Type*: Conventional *Predominant Services*: Multiservice *Predominant Function*: Military advice
Public Opinion	*U.S.*: Supportive *International*: Little influence

Context

Senior U.S. decisionmakers feared an unfavorable balance of power would develop in the Far East, if Chinese communists closely associated with the Soviet Union emerged victorious from their long-standing civil war with Chiang Kai-shek's Kuomintang. A key U.S. goal during and immediately after World War II therefore was to guarantee a free China friendly to the United States.

Some top officials in Washington cherished hopes that Chiang Kai-shek eventually could incorporate Mao Zedong's communists into the Chinese Nationalist government. Progress, however, was imperceptible, and the potential for a superpower collision seemed to increase. President Truman in December 1945 therefore appointed General Marshall as his personal emissary, empowered to intimidate and cajole both belligerents as he saw fit: promise Chiang continued U.S. patronage if he emphasized accommodation; threaten to desert him if he didn't. Marshall questioned whether a peaceful settlement was possible, but did his best until January 1947, with scant success. The situation deteriorated steadily, despite increased military assistance, until communist triumph seemed inevitable unless U.S. armed forces intervened directly. U.S. leaders, including those in Congress, declined. Political, economic, and military costs seemed excessive and the consequences uncertain. Mao proclaimed the People's Republic of China (PRC) on October 1, 1949. Chinese Nationalists retreated to Taiwan.

Key Congressional Actions

Congress authorized Navy Department personnel to assist Nationalist China in naval matters and appropriated substantial funds for security assistance.

Outcome: Failure

The United States accomplished none of its objectives. The gap between declaratory power and capabilities was huge. U.S. support for Nationalist China over a long period ensured sour relations with the People's Republic of China when Mao finally seized power (see Case 21).

Selected Sources

United States Relations with China: With Special Reference to the Period 1944-1949, Washington, Dept. of State, August 1949, p. 127-409.

Tang Tsou, *America's Failure in China, 1941-50*, Chicago, University of Chicago Press, 1963, 614 p.

Kahn, E. H., Jr., *The China Hands: America's Foreign Service Officers and What Befell Them*, NY, Viking, 1975, 337 p.

CASE 15

GREECE (1946-49)

Type Conflict	Counterinsurgency
Duration	January 1946-August 1949 (3 years, 8 months)
Participants	*U.S. Allies*: Greek Government; Britain *U.S. Adversaries*: Greek Communists, Albania, Bulgaria, Yugoslavia
U.S. Purposes	*Interests*: National security *Objectives*: Ensure an independent, democratic Greece; contain communism
Predominant U.S. Power	Economic, military
Predominant U.S. Instrument	Security assistance
U.S. Armed Forces	*Predominant Type*: Conventional *Predominant Services*: Army *Predominant Function*: Advice
Public Opinion	*U.S.*: Supportive *International*: Allies supportive

Context

Communist insurgency in Greece began before World War II ended. British forces defeated the first serious outbreak in December 1944 - January 1945, but many guerrillas melted into Greek mountains and others sought sanctuary in Albania, Yugoslavia, and Bulgaria, where they reequipped and trained. A strong underground remained in Greece to foment further rebellion in a country that bordered on bankruptcy. Greece survived with token aid until March 1947, when U.N. and British contributions terminated.

The Greek Government at that juncture requested and got a greater U.S. infusion when Congress, in response to the Truman Doctrine, appropriated funds to "support free people who are resisting attempted subjugation by armed minorities or by outside pressure." U.S. security assistance during two crucial years accounted for one-quarter of all Greek national income. It helped rebuild the war-ravaged nation, as well as its defense establishment, which the Joint U.S. Military Advisory and Planning Group, collaborating with a British Military Mission, reshaped starting in December 1947. Several factors expedited early success: an anticommunist Greek majority; its will to fight; fear that Slavic states planned to partition Macedonia and Thrace as one price for supporting Greek insurgents; resultant rebel dependence on external supplies; and finally, Tito's rift with the Cominform, which caused him to disassociate Yugoslavia from Greek guerrillas and close its border to them. Organized insurgency ceased in August 1949.

Key Congressional Actions

Congress passed the Greek-Turkish Aid Act on May 22, 1947, appropriated funds therefore on July 30, and provided for additional assistance in following years.

Outcome: Success

The massive influx of U.S. economic and military aid, coupled with recipients receptive to advice, stabilized the Greek economy and enabled Greek armed forces to increase capabilities rapidly.

Selected Sources

Lagoudakis, Charilaos G., "Greece (1946-1949)," in *Challenge and Response in Internal Conflict*, Ed. by D.M. Condit and Bert H. Cooper, Jr., et al, Vol. II, Washington, Center for Research in Social Systems, American University, March 1967, p. 499-527.

Wittner, Lawrence S., *American Intervention in Greece, 1943-1949*, NY, Columbia University Press, 1982, 445 p.

Bucci, Steven, "The Greek Civil War: What We Failed to Learn," *Special Warfare*, Summer 1989, p. 46-55.

Shafer, D. Michael, *Deadly Paradigms: The Failure of U.S. Counterinsurgency Policy*, Princeton, NJ, Princeton University Press, 1988, p. 166-204.

CASE 16

PHILIPPINES (1946-55)

Type Conflict	Counterinsurgency
Duration	January 1946-December 1955 (10 years)
Participants	*U.S. Allies*: Philippine Government
	U.S. Adversaries: Philippine insurgents
U.S. Purposes	*Interests*: National defense, democracy
	Objectives: Independent, democratic Philippines
Predominant U.S. Power	Political, economic
Predominant U.S. Instrument	Security assistance
U.S. Armed Forces	*Predominant Type*: Conventional
	Predominant Services: Army
	Predominant Function: Military advice
Public Opinion	*U.S.*: Supportive
	International: Slight

Context

Communist-instigated insurgency, planned during World War II, sprouted on Luzon in 1946. Oppressed peasants, with political, economic, and social grievances, were ripe for exploitation by Hukbalahaps (HUKs), who promised reforms the Government would not produce. Close U.S. association with Philippine policymakers who abused their authority and armed forces that terrorized the populace made America part of an expanding problem, rather than part of the solution, for several years. Corrupt Philippine officials misused U.S. security assistance funds. Conventional U.S. military advisors were ill-suited to counsel on counterinsurgency.

The turning point came in September 1950, when Ramon Magsaysay took the reins, first as Secretary of National Defense, then as President. He implemented programs that attacked causes of insurgency as well as symptoms. Military reforms protected peasants from Philippine armed forces and HUKs alike. Political reforms gave all citizens access to an honest electoral process, and concurrently recaptured their confidence. Economic reforms of immense symbolic importance began land redistribution that served common people. Civic actions of all kinds progressively improved the peasants' lot. The HUKs, who never were able to mount an ideological crusade, began to suffer defections by members who preferred Magsaysay's programs to Communist promises. The HUK revolution was virtually defunct by December 1955.

Key Congressional Actions

Congress passed several security assistance acts that authorized U.S. forces and appropriated funds for counterinsurgency efforts in the Philippines.

Outcome: Mixed opinion

The United States accomplished its main objectives, but U.S. military aid was most munificent when the worst peril had passed. The most useful U.S. advice came from Edward G. Lansdale, who was Magsaysay's confidant.

Selected Sources

Smith, Robert Ross, "The Philippines (1946-1954)," in *Challenge and Response in Internal Conflict*, Ed. by D.M Condit and Bert H. Cooper, Jr., et al., Vol. I, Washington, Center for Research in Social Systems, American University, February 1968, p. 473-507.

Shafer, D. Michael, *Deadly Paradigms: The Failure of U.S. Counterinsurgency Policy*, Princeton, NJ, Princeton University Press, 1988, p. 205-239.

Lansdale, Edward G., *In the Midst of Wars; An American's Mission to Southeast Asia*, NY, Harper & Row, 1972, p. 1-125.

CASE 17

INDOCHINA (1946-54)

Type Conflict	Counterinsurgency
Duration	January 1946-July 1954 (8 years, 7 months)
Participants	*U.S. Allies*: France *U.S. Adversaries*: Vietnamese insurgents
U.S. Purposes	*Interests*: National security; democracy *Objectives*: Contain communism; ensure free states in former Indochina
Predominant U.S. Power	Political, economic
Predominant U.S. Instrument	Security assistance
U.S. Armed Forces	*Predominant Type*: Conventional *Predominant Services*: Army, Navy *Predominant Function*: Deliver and administer military aid; evacuate civilians from N. Vietnam to S. Vietnam
Public Opinion	*U.S.*: Supportive, provided no U.S. combat *International*: Apathetic

Context

France in 1946 tried to reimpose colonial rule on a region ready for independence. The newly-proclaimed Democratic Republic of Vietnam (DRVN) refused to acquiesce. Political accommodations failed. Armed rebellion broke out before the year ended. The Soviet Union and Communist China both abetted the insurgent cause in many ways.

U.S. decisionmakers faced a dilemma. They opposed French colonialism, but also feared that communists eventually would control all of Southeast Asia unless defeated in Indochina. The "Domino Theory" clearly took precedence after the Korean War started in mid-1950. A U.S. Military Assistance Advisory Group supervised ever-increasing shipments that by 1954 totalled about 1,000 armored vehicles, 150 naval vessels of various types, 500 aircraft, and 23,000 trucks. The U.S. share of all war costs was approximately 80%, but that conventional hardware, coupled with conventional tactics, was not well suited for counterinsurgency. Direct U.S. military intervention was never a serious option, despite repeated French reversals. The final debacle came at Dien Bien Phu in May 1954. Cease-fire agreements, signed in Geneva, Switzerland, officially terminated hostilities on July 20, 1954. They also partitioned Vietnam along the 17th Parallel, pending general elections to be held in July 1956.

Key Congressional Actions

The Mutual Defense Assistance Act of 1949 instigated U.S. security assistance to recipients in Indochina. Mutual Security Acts of 1951 (amended) and 1954, along with economic appropriations, continued and expanded such programs.

Outcome: Failure

The United States accomplished none of its objectives. America after 1954 assumed regional responsibilities that France had been unable to fulfill after nearly nine years of political maneuvering and open warfare (see Case 24).

Selected Sources

U.S. Congress, Senate, *The U.S. Government and the Vietnam War: Executive and Legislative Roles and Relationships*, Part I, 1945-1961, Prepared for the Committee on Foreign Relations by the Congressional Research Service, 98th Congress, 2d Session, Washington, U.S. GPO, April 1984, 365 p.

The Pentagon Papers, as published by the New York Times, NY Quadrangle Books, 1971, p. 1-67.

Spector, Ronald H., *United States Army in Vietnam: Advice and Support, The Early Years, 1941-1960*, Washington, U.S. Army Center of Military History, 1983, 391 p.

CASE 18

USSR (1946-)

Type Conflict	Nonviolent conflict (posturing; hands off opposition)
Duration	44 years plus (still active)
Participants	*U.S. Allies*: Free World *U.S. Adversaries*: Soviet Union and its allies
U.S. Purposes	*Interests*: National security; power *Objectives*: Contain communism; deter U.S.-Soviet war; defend successfully if deterrence fails
Predominant U.S. Power	All components complementary; importance varied with circumstances
Predominant U.S. Instrument	All instruments complementary; importance varied with circumstances
U.S. Armed Forces	*Predominant Type*: Nuclear, conventional *Predominant Services*: All important *Predominant Function*: Deterrence
Public Opinion	*U.S.*: Supportive *International*: Free World supportive

Context

U.S. low-intensity conflict with the Soviet Union began before World War I ended. A mutually expedient truce prevailed during World War II, but LIC resumed immediately thereafter, and has persisted ever since. Highly publicized eruptions punctuated that continuum for the first 23 years (Azerbaijan 1946; Berlin blockade 1948; Hungary 1956; Berlin Wall 1961; Cuban missile crisis 1962; and Czechoslovakia 1968 are representative). Relations thereafter became more circumspect, but remained adversarial. Many other cases in this study were closely connected.

Both sides employed all aspects of national power and established alliance systems in attempts to achieve desired objectives without resort to armed combat, which could escalate unpredictably in ways that might benefit neither belligerent and conceivably could annihilate civilization. Political, economic, military, social, psychological, and technological components of power almost always were complementary, but relative importance depended on many variables that included opposing personalities and policies at particular times and places. Defense budgets, even so, became lavish and arsenals burgeoned. Periods of intense antagonism alternated with detente. Competition remains much like a global game of chess, except players (principals and proxies), pieces, goals, and guidelines are incessantly subject to unannounced change. Short-term setbacks sometimes lead to long-term victories, and vice versa. Whether the "Cold War" will terminate or continue (even intensify) is uncertain at this moment, although it seems to be abating in U.S. favor.

Key Congressional Actions

Congress has directly or indirectly influenced nearly every facet of U.S.-Soviet competition by authorizations, appropriations, and limitations that affect the Department of State, Department of Defense, the U.S. intelligence community, and every other official organization involved, as well as trade and financial exchange.

Outcome: Mainly success

The United States has accomplished its most important long-term objectives, despite several equivocal short-term results and some spectacular failures. We have averted or avoided war with the USSR, and communism currently is afflicted with worldwide reversals.

Escalation Potential: Cool; probability low.

Selected Sources

Gaddis, John Lewis, *Strategies of Containment: A Critical Appraisal of Postwar American National Security Policy*, NY, Oxford University Press, 1982, 432 p.

LaFeber, Walter, *America, Russia, and the Cold War*, 1945-1984, NY, Alfred A. Knopf, 1985, 348 p.

Garthoff, Raymond L., *Reflections on the Cuban Missile Crisis*, Rev. Ed., Washington, Brookings Institution, 1989, 236 p.

Kraus, Wolfgang H., "East Germany (June 1953)" and Bushkoff, Leonard, "Hungary (October-November 1956)," both in *Challenge and Response in Internal Conflict*, Ed. by D.M Condit and Bert H. Cooper, Jr., et al., Vol. II, Washington, Center for Research in Social Systems, American University, March 1967, p. 457-496, 529-578.

Tusa, Ann and John, *The Berlin Airlift*, NY, Atheneum Press, 1988, 445 p.

CASE 19

ISRAEL VS. ARABS (1948-)

Type Conflict	Nonviolent conflict (hands off support; peacekeeping)
Duration	41 years plus (still active)
Participants	*U.S. Allies*: Israel *U.S. Adversaries*: Anti-Israel nations and subnational groups
U.S. Purposes	*Interests*: Moral obligations; cultural ties *Objectives*: Preserve Israel as an independent state; promote peace
Predominant U.S. Power	Political; economic
Predominant U.S. Instrument	Diplomacy; security assistance
U.S. Armed Forces	Not applicable
Public Opinion	*U.S.*: Supportive *International*: Variable, but little support

Context

The United States and Israel have been closely linked since that country declared independence on May 14, 1948. Ties have outlasted three major Arab-Israeli wars (1956, 1967, 1973), plus innumerable lesser altercations with hostile nations and subnational groups (especially the Palestine Liberation Organization). Serious policy disputes, such as those over British-French-Israeli attacks on Eygpt in 1956, Israel's settlements in occupied territories, its 1982 invasion of Lebanon, and U.S. arms sales to neighboring Arab states, occasionally have strained relations, but none has undone America's unwritten security commitments.

Favorable pronouncements in various news media, diplomatic maneuvering in the United Nations, and security assistance on "major non-NATO ally" terms typify U.S. support that spans more than four decades. U.S. armed forces have never been needed, other than long-range airlift and sealift, even when surprise Egyptian attacks across the Suez Canal and Syrian assaults on the Golan Heights caught Israeli occupation forces napping in 1973. Israel in turn furnishes the United States with useful intelligence, some covert actions, and helps combat transnational terrorism. The United States eternally strives to promote regional peace and stability under conditions acceptable to all parties concerned. The Camp David accords of 1978 and current peacekeeping operations in the Sinai are just two parts of that process. Success, however, remains elusive, and this lengthy LIC likely will continue indefinitely.

Key Congressional Actions

Congress directly or indirectly has controlled the types, amounts, and limitations on uses of U.S. assistance to Israel since programs formally began in 1950. Joint resolutions authorize U.S. peacekeeping contingents in the Sinai.

Outcome: Mixed opinion

U.S. assistance has enabled Israel to survive as an independent state, but lasting peace with opponents, some of whom are U.S. friends, seems as dubious as ever. Whether political and economic costs to the United States have been worth it remains a contentious issue.

Escalation Potential: Hot; probability high

External military threats to Israel presently are muted, but could revive on short notice, perhaps in conjunction with an internal Palestinian Arab uprising (*Intifadah*).

Selected Sources

Dupuy, Trevor N., *Elusive Victory: The Arab-Israeli Wars, 1947-1976*, NY, Harper & Row, 1978, 669 p.

Quandt, William B., *Decade of Decisions: American Policy Toward the Arab-Israeli Conflict, 1967-1976*, Berkeley, CA, University of California Press, 1977, 313 p.

Congressional Research Service issue briefs, Washington, D.C.: Laipson, Ellen B., *Israeli-American Relations*, IB 82008, December 21, 1989, 15 p. and three by Clyde R. Mark: *U.S. Foreign Assistance Facts*, IB 85066, January 17, 1990, 15 p.; *Middle East Peace Proposals*, IB 82127, December 21, 1989, 15 p.; and *Palestine and the Palestinians*, December 21, 1989, 15 p.

CASE 20

IRAN (1951-53)

Type Conflict	Coup d'etat
Duration	April 1951-August 1953 (2 years, 4 months)
Participants	*U.S. Allies*: Britain, by 1953 *U.S. Adversaries*: Iranian nationalists; anti-American Iranians
U.S. Purposes	*Interests*: National defense; oil *Objectives*: Contain Soviet expansion; install a stable Iranian government friendly to the United States
Predominant U.S. Power	Political
Predominant U.S. Instrument	Diplomacy; covert actions
U.S. Armed Forces	Not applicable
Public Opinion	*U.S.*: Supportive *International*: Apathetic, except supportive in Britain

Context

The Anglo-Iranian Oil Company (AIOC) paid post-World War II Iran little for rights to exploit its petroleum. Muhammed Mussaddiq consequently nationalized Iran's oil industry in April 1951, shortly after he became Prime Minister. AIOC in return instigated a global boycott against Iranian oil. Political and economic chaos ensued in Iran after U.S. mediation foundered.

U.S. and British policies, previously far apart, converged by January 1953, because both feared Mussaddiq might ask Moscow for assistance. British intelligence therefore proposed and CIA perfected a plan to oust the Prime Minister. The Shah, a key participant, was to depart Teheran for a Caspian resort, leaving one directive that dismissed Mussaddiq and another that appointed General Fazlollah Zahedi as his successor. CIA would orchestrate public support for those actions to ensure success. Operation Ajax, as it was called, opened inauspiciously on August 16, 1953. Mussaddiq, forewarned, seized the Shah's messenger and took immediate countermeasures. Anti-royalist/anti-American riots, fomented mainly by communists, erupted when he publicized the plot. The Shah fled to Rome. Two days later, pro-Shah soldiers and a mob hired with CIA seed money swept the streets. Many thousands who had lost faith in Mussaddiq's leadership also began to march.

He soon went to prison, the Shah regained power, and U.S. emergency grants helped revive Iran's depleted economy. Operation Ajax served its purpose.

Key Congressional Actions

Unclassified records reflect no congressional role in Operation Ajax.

Outcome: Success

The United States accomplished its basic objectives. U.S. oil companies after 1953 participated in Iranian oil production and profits. Reasonable stability prevailed in Iran for the next 25 years. Some analysts link Operation Ajax with current anti-Americanism in Iran, but the lag between cause and effect is too great to blame its originators (see Case 45).

Selected Sources

Roosevelt, Kermit, *Countercoup: The Struggle for Control of Iran*, NY, McGraw-Hill, 1979, 217 p.

Rubin, Barry M., *Paved with Good Intentions: The American Experience and Iran*, NY, Oxford University Press, 1980, p. 54-90.

Lytle, Mark H., *The Origins of the Iranian-American Alliance, 1941-1953*, NY, Holmes & Meier, 1987, p. 192-212.

CASE 21

CHINA (1953-1979)

Type Conflict	Protective expedition; nonviolent conflict (hands off opposition)
Duration	July 1953-January 1, 1979 (25+ years)
Participants	*U.S. Allies*: Taiwan *U.S. Adversaries*: People's Republic of China; Soviet Union initially
U.S. Purposes	*Interests*: National defense *Objectives*: Contain communism; preserve the Republic of China
Predominant U.S. Power	Military until early 1960s; then political/economic
Predominant U.S. Instrument	Threats of force; then diplomacy and sanctions
U.S. Armed Forces	*Predominant Type*: Conventional *Predominant Services*: Navy *Predominant Function*: Deterrence
Public Opinion	*U.S.*: Supportive *International*: Mixed, weak

Context

Sour relations between the United States and the People's Republic of China (PRC) ensued as a direct result of U.S. support for Chiang Kai-shek during and after World War II (see Case 14). Chinese nationalists lost the civil war in 1949, retreated from the mainland to Taiwan, and there established the Republic of China with U.S. support. Close Chinese communist ties with the Soviet Union throughout the 1950s constrained U.S. options in the Far East. China, for example, remained a privileged sanctuary for 2 1/2 years, while U.S. and PRC forces fought a mid-intensity conflict in Korea. U.S.-PRC confrontations over Quemoy, Matsu, and other offshore islands started before the Korean War ended and continued thereafter. A formal U.S. defense treaty with the Republic of China in 1954 further complicated Mao's plans to "liberate" Taiwan.

The situation changed considerably in the early 1960s, when an acrimonious Sino-Soviet split demolished the myth of monolithic communism. The PRC assumed a less provocative stance toward the United States, but U.S. opposition predicated on anticommunism persisted. Armed truce best described relations until 1968. Chinese leaders at that juncture seriously began to consider conciliation, partly to help balance the burgeoning military power of an estranged Soviet Union, partly to help China fill power vacuums along its periphery as U.S. influence ebbed after the Vietnam War. The U.S.-PRC Shanghai communique of February 27, 1972 officially poured oil on troubled waters, because both sides renounced regional hegemony. Low-intensity conflict formally ceased on January 1, 1979, after several false starts, when the United States and PRC initiated normal diplomatic relations.

Key Congressional Actions

Congress appropriated security assistance funds, ratified a mutual defense treaty in 1955, and authorized the use of U.S. armed forces between 1955 and 1974 to help protect Taiwan from PRC attack. Initial Congressional support for the Vietnam War was partly to contain Communist China. Congress also applied assorted sanctions against the PRC for the full period 1950-79.

Outcome: Success

The United States accomplished its basic objective at reasonable cost (Korean war costs were connected with a mid-intensity conflict). The Republic of China remains independent and noncommunist.

Selected Sources

Sutter, Robert G., *China Watch: Toward Sino-American Reconciliation*, Baltimore, Md., Johns Hopkins University Press, 1978, 155 p.

Barnett, A. Doak, *China and the Major Powers in East Asia*, Washington, Brookings Institution, 1979, 416 p.

Dulles, Foster Rhea, *American Foreign Policy Toward Communist China, 1949-1969*, NY, Crowell, 1972, p. 149-210.

CASE 22

NORTH KOREA (1953-)

Type Conflict	Peacemaking
Duration	36 years plus (still active)
Participants	*U.S. Allies*: Republic of Korea (ROK) *U.S. Adversaries*: North Korea
U.S. Purposes	*Interests*: National defense *Objectives*: Safeguard South Korea
Predominant U.S. Power	Military
Predominant U.S. Instrument	Threats of force; security assistance
U.S. Armed Forces	*Predominant Type*: Conventional *Predominant Services*: Army *Predominant Function*: Deterrence
Public Opinion	*U.S.*: Supportive *International*: Free World supportive

Context

The Korean War, a U.S. mid-intensity conflict, terminated with an armistice signed on July 27, 1953. The United States and North Korea have been locked in a low-intensity conflict ever since. A Mutual Defense Treaty formalized U.S.-ROK security relations when it entered into force on November 17, 1954.

Deterrence has been the main mission of U.S. armed forces in Korea for the past 36 years. Army elements deployed along the Demilitarized Zone (DMZ) are the most visible symbol of U.S. resolve to defend the ROK against North Korean aggression. Two divisions served that purpose between May 1955 and March 1971, when one withdrew. U.S. tactical fighter squadrons in Korea gradually increased from two to five in partial compensation. President Carter abandoned plans to withdraw all U.S. ground forces by 1982. ROK military posture, in response to massive U.S. assistance programs, had improved immensely, but North Korea's rebuilt military machine by then had become one of the world's most formidable. Countless clashes continued to occur, of which the Blue House raid and *Pueblo* capture (both January 1968), the EC-121 shootdown (April 1969), and tree trimming incident at Panmunjom (August 1976) were merely among the most publicized. U.S. soldiers and seamen killed or wounded by North Korea since 1953 currently total 90 and 133 respectively. The Combat Infantry Badge has been authorized under certain specified conditions for the last 20 years. No signs of true peace are in sight.

Key Congressional Actions

The Senate ratified the U.S.-ROK Mutual Defense Treaty which, among other things, is the basis for U.S. armed forces in Korea. Congress continues to appropriate security assistance funds for the ROK and imposes stringent sanctions on North Korea.

Outcome: Success

The United States accomplished its basic objectives. The ROK is developing politically and economically behind the military shield that U.S. armed forces and assistance programs helped provide.

Escalation Potential: Hot; probability high

Korea currently is quiescent, but Kim Il-Sung remains intransigent and military capabilities at his disposal are immense.

Selected Sources

Bok, Lee Suk, *The Impact of U.S. Forces in Korea*, Washington, National Defense University Press, 1987, 101 p.

Olsen, Edward A., *U.S. Policy and the Two Koreas*, Boulder, Co., Westview Press, 1988, 115 p.

Congressional Research Service issue briefs, Washington, D.C.: Sutter, Robert G., *Korea-U.S. Relations: Issues for Congress*, IB89136, January 24, 1990, 12 p. ; Niksch, Larry A., *U.S. Troop Withdrawal and the Question of Northeast Asian Stability*, IB79053, May 29, 1979, 21 p.

CASE 23

GUATEMALA (1953-54)

Type Conflict	Coup d'etat
Duration	March 1953-June 1954 (16 months)
Participants	*U.S. Allies*: None *U.S. Adversaries*: Guatemalan Government
U.S. Purposes	*Interests*: Western Hemisphere security; commercial *Objectives*: Contain communism; oust Arbenz; ensure a friendly Guatemalan Government
Predominant U.S. Power	Paramilitary
Predominant U.S. Instrument	Covert actions
U.S. Armed Forces	Not applicable
Public Opinion	*U.S.*: Supportive *International*: Latin Americans generally opposed.

Context

Whether the Monroe Doctrine or the United Fruit Company prompted the United States to overthrow the democratically elected government of Guatemalan President Arbenz Guzmán still stimulates debate. Communist encroachment, however, seemed clear to President Eisenhower and his advisors even before Guatemala legally expropriated huge United Fruit holdings in March 1953. U.S. political and economic pressures to topple Arbenz mounted immediately thereafter. Operation Success (PBSUCCESS) was the upshot.

CIA set up shop at Opa-Locka, Florida following Eisenhower's decision to develop a plan, created a base in Honduras for Colonel Castillo Armas, who was Arbenz' designated successor, furnished him money, and recruited a few mercenaries who became his "liberation army." A second "rebel" camp sprouted in nearby Nicaragua. Political preparations proceeded simultaneously. U.S. Information Agency sought to convince the Organization of American States (OAS) that Communists indeed were undermining Guatemala. OAS members unanimously approved the Caracas Declaration of March 1954, which condemned communism in Latin America. Soviet arms shipments to Guatemala activated PBSUCCESS in May 1954, with anti-Arbenz propaganda. The "invasion" by 150 men and a few antiquated aircraft began on June 19, multiplied out of all proportion by clever psychological operations. Rumors ran riot, because jammers blotted out Government radios. PBSUCCESS culminated in almost bloodless victory on June 1954, when Arbenz resigned.

Key Congressional Actions

Congress affirmed support for the Caracas Declaration, but had no prior knowledge of PBSUCCESS.

Outcome: Mixed opinion

The United States accomplished its basic objectives. The United Fruit Company regained lost lands (then sold all to Del Monte in 1972), but Guatemala in the aftermath was so unstable that U.S. counterinsurgency operations ensued in the 1960s (Case 33).

Selected Sources

Schlesinger, Stephen and Steven Kinzer, *Bitter Fruit: The Untold Story of the American Coup in Guatemala*, Garden City, NY, Anchor Books, 1983, 320 p.

Immerman, Richard H., *The CIA in Guatemala: The Foreign Policy of Intervention*, Austin, TX, University of Texas Press, 1982, 291 p.

Marks, Frederick W., "The CIA and Castillo Armas in Guatemala 1954 : New Clues to an Old Puzzle," *Diplomatic History*, Winter 1990, p. 67-95.

CASE 24

VIETNAM (1955-65)

Type Conflict	Counterinsurgency
Duration	January 1955-June 1965 (10 years, 6 months)
Participants	*U.S. Allies*: Republic of Vietnam (RVN) *U.S. Adversaries*: Democratic Republic of Vietnam (DRV); Viet Cong
U.S. Purposes	*Interests*: National defense *Objectives*: Contain communism; develop and defend RVN
Predominant U.S. Power	Politico-military; economic
Predominant U.S. Instruments	Security assistance; sanctions
U.S. Armed Forces	*Predominant Type*: Conventional *Predominant Services*: Army *Predominant Function*: Military advice
Public Opinion	*U.S.*: Supportive *International*: Wide variance

Context

The Southeast Asia Treaty Organization (SEATO), formed September 1954, pledged to meet common dangers together after French Indochina fragmented (Case 17), but no member besides the United States contributed much to the defense of South Vietnam and Laos, both of which were beset by DRV-sustained insurgencies. RVN eventually became first priority, because all was lost if it fell. (See Case 25 for Laos).

Guerrilla warfare began to augment Viet Cong underground activities in 1956, after President Diem refused to hold general elections prescribed by the 1954 cease-fire agreement. Neither Diem nor his U.S. advisors diagnosed that threat correctly. A united front was obligatory, but improvident policies and incompetent officials exacerbated political, ethnic, religious, and cultural factionalism. U.S. economic aid was often misallocated. RVN armed forces prepared primarily to defend against conventional invasion. Favoritism prevented the expeditious promotion of officers who might have fostered improvement. South Vietnam and its U.S. ally were clearly losing the war when Diem was assassinated in 1963 (Case 31). The situation went from bad to worse during the next 18 months, while the search for a replacement continued. U.S. force levels and security assistance costs escalated during that period, as conflict intensity increased. U.S. combat casualties tripled between 1963 and 1964 (389 to 1,186). First the U.S. Navy, then the Air Force, Marines, and conventional Army formations joined the fray. LIC no longer typified U.S. participation after mid-1965.

Key Congressional Actions

Congress funded extensive aid programs for RVN. The Tonkin Gulf Resolution of August 10, 1964 (H.J. Res. 1145) approved the use of armed forces to assist SEATO protocol states that included RVN and Laos.

Outcome: failure

The United States accomplished none of its objectives. RVN was completely under communist control by 1975, after a costly mid-intensity conflict.

Selected Sources

Fall, Bernard B., "South Vietnam (1956 to November 1963)," in *Challenge and Response in Internal Conflict*, Ed. by D.M. Condit and Bert H. Cooper, Jr., et al., Vol. I, Washington, Center for Research in Social Systems, American University, February 1968, p. 332-375

U.S. Congress, Senate, *The U.S. Government and the Vietnam War: Executive and Legislative Roles and Relationships*, Prepared for the Committee on Foreign Relations by the Congressional Research Service, Washington, U.S. GPO, Part I, 1945-1961, April 1984, p. 259-365, Part II, 1961-1964, 424 p., and Part III, January-July 1965, December 1988, 489 p.

CASE 25

LAOS (1955-65)

Type Conflict	Counterinsurgency
Duration	January 1955-June 1965 (10 years, 6 months)
Participants	*U.S. Allies*: Royal Laotian Government (RLG); Hmong and Laotheung tribes; Thailand; France
	U.S. Adversaries: Pathet Lao; Democratic Republic of Vietnam (DRV); Soviet Union; China
U.S. Purposes	*Interests*: National defense
	Objectives: Contain communism; ensure an independent, friendly regime in Laos.
Predominant U.S. Power	Political-military; economic
Predominant U.S. Instruments	Security assistance; covert operations
U.S. Armed Forces	*Predominant Type*: Special opertions
	Predominant Services: Army; Air Force
	Predominant Function: Advise; support
Public Opinion	*U.S.*: Supportive
	International: Wide variance

Context

Geneva accords legally neutralized Laos at the end of the Indochina War in 1954 (Case 17). Efforts to unify that landlocked nation and keep it nonaligned as a buffer between North Vietnam and Thailand, however, were unsuccessful from the onset. Friendly Prince Souvana Phouma failed to establish a coalition government with "Red Prince" Souphanouvang, his half-brother, the titular head of communist Pathet Lao insurgents that meanwhile consolidated their hold on northern provinces and installed an underground in the panhandle. A coup and right-wing recouping operations erupted in 1960. Civil war, marked by great confusion and increased Soviet/Chinese/DRV support for the Pathet Lao, ensued for almost a year. Multinational negotiations in Geneva (mainly USA, USSR, China, DRV, and Laos) then culminated in a second declaration of neutrality on July 23, 1962. Communist activity nevertheless intensified and the war continued.

The Geneva accords of 1954 forbid foreign armed forces in Laos, except a small French military mission. U.S. counterinsurgency operations therefore initially emphasized economic assistance, administered by a pseudo-civilian office, with the Royal Laotian Army as recipient, because it was the nation's only organized entity. Inept U.S. aid programs, accompanied by corruption in high places, served communist propagandists well without compensatory improvements in Lao capabilities. A U.S. military mission, which flowered in 1960, organized Hmong and Laotheung tribesmen for guerrilla warfare until 1962 when, by international agreement, it withdrew (DRV troops did not). CIA thereafter assumed full responsibilty for the "secret war" in Laos, which became a mid-intensity conflict in 1965, when conventional air operations began from bases in Thailand and Vietnam. B-52 strikes against the Ho Chi Minh Trail soon followed.

Key Congressional Actions

Congress provided Laos with $300 million in military and economic aid between 1955 and 1964.

Outcome: Failure

The United States accomplished none of its objectives. Serious friction, first between U.S. and French representatives, then between CIA, the U.S. military mission, and Department of State, was one important contributing factor.

Selected Sources

Dommen, Arthur J., *Conflict in Laos: The Politics of Neutralism*, NY, Praeger, 1971, 454 p.

Robbins, Christopher, *The Ravens: The Men Who Flew in America's Secret War in Laos*, NY, Crown Publishers, 1987, 420 p. (especially p. 86-135).

Stanton, Shelby, *Green Berets at War: U.S. Army Special Forces in Southeast Asia 1956-1975*, NY, Dell Books, p. 34-52.

Fall, Bernard B., "Laos (1954-1962)," in *Challenge and Response in Internal Conflict*, Ed. by D.M. Condit and Bert H. Cooper, Jr., et al., Supplement, September 1968, p. 96-127.

CASE 26

LEBANON (1958)

Type Conflict	Peacemaking
Duration	May-October 1958 (6 months)
Participants	*U.S. Allies*: Lebanese Government *U.S. Adversaries*: Warring factions within Lebanon; United Arab Republic (UAR)
U.S. Purposes	*Interests*: National defense *Objectives*: Contain communism; contain UAR; restore stability in Lebanon
Predominant U.S. Power	Politico-military
Predominant U.S. Instrument	Diplomacy; armed force
U.S. Armed Forces	*Predominant Type*: Conventional *Predominant Services*: Multiservice *Predominant Function*: Interposition
Public Opinion	*U.S.*: Supportive *International*: Wide Variance

Context

Lebanese factionalism was the source of extreme friction in 1958. President Chamoun, a Maronite Christian, bid for a second term, despite constitutional proscriptions designed to maintain a delicate political balance in that sectarian land. Most Lebanese Muslims disapproved. They also preferred neutralism or pan-Arabism to Chamoun's pro-West foreign policies and feared that his endorsement of the Eisenhower Doctrine might invite unwanted U.S. intervention in Middle East affairs. The UAR (Egypt and Syria), with Soviet connections, shared those sentiments.

Serious strife started on May 8, 1958, when an anti-government journalist was assassinated. Anti-Chamoun propaganda (dubbed audio-visual aggression) fanned the flames until armed conflict erupted. The military phase of civil war, however, soon reached a stalemate, with Lebanese armed forces playing peacemaker among factional militias. President Eisenhower disregarded Chamoun's requests to intervene until rebels toppled Iraq's pro-West government on July 14. U.S. Marines began landing at Beirut the next day, followed shortly by Army troops, all interposed between warring factions. Main missions were to stabilize the situation in Lebanon and prevent the Iraqi revolution from spreading with Soviet and UAR help. No combat occurred. Diplomatic maneuvering that produced politically acceptable compromises ended the crisis. The new Lebanese President installed on September 23 lasted a full six-year term. All U.S. armed forces left by the end of October.

Key Congressional Actions

Congress passed the Middle East Resolution (H.J. Res. 117) on March 9, 1957. It approved the use of U.S. armed force if necessary to help any requesting country resist aggression controlled by international communism. It was never invoked per se.

Outcome: Success

The United States accomplished its basic objectives at reasonable costs and with few casualties (one fatality). Lebanon remained reasonably stable until 1975, when civil war reignited.

Selected Sources

Said, Abdul Aziz, "Lebanon (1958)," in *Challenge and Response in Internal Conflict*, Ed. by D.M. Condit and Bert H. Cooper, Jr., et al., Vol II, Washington, Center for Research in Social Systems, American University, March 1967, p. 432-455.

Quandt, William B., "Lebanon, 1958 . . . .," in *Force Without War: U.S. Armed Forces as a Political Instrument*, Ed., by Barry M. Blechman and Stephen S. Kaplan, Washington, Brookings Institution, 1978, p. 222-257.

Spiller, Roger J., *"Not War but Like War" : The American Intervention in Lebanon*, Leavenworth Papers No. 3, Combat Studies Institute, Ft. Leavenworth, KA, U.S. Army Command and General Staff College, January 1981, 58 p.

CASE 27

CUBA (1960-)

Type Conflict	Resistance; coup d'etat; followed by nonviolent conflict (hands off opposition)
Duration	30 years plus (still active)
Participants	*U.S. Allies*: Anti-communist Cubans *U.S. Adversaries*: Cuban government; Soviet Union
U.S. Purposes	*Interests*: Western hemisphere security *Objectives*: Contain communism; oust Castro; ensure a friendly Cuban government or isolate it
Predominant U.S. Power	Political; economic
Predominant U.S. Instrument	Sanctions; covert actions
U.S. Armed Forces	None. The Cuban missile crisis was primarily part of a U.S.-Soviet LIC (see Case 18).
Public Opinion	*U.S.*: Essentially supportive *International*: Great variability from time to time and place to place.

Context

Fidel Castro's insurgents seized control of Cuba in January 1959. U.S. recognition followed immediately, but diplomatic relations ceased precisely two years later, after Castro sought to spread leftist revolution through the Caribbean and Central America, established ties with the Soviet Union, and seized all U.S. private property in Cuba. Mutual animosity has typified U.S.-Cuban affairs ever since.

CIA reportedly hatched at least eight plots to assassinate Castro between 1960 and 1965. Few were implemented; those that were failed. U.S.-sponsored paramilitary operations at the Bay of Pigs set new standards of incompetence in April 1963. Subsequent U.S. opposition, which emphasized assorted political and economic sanctions, has been less direct, but scarcely more effective. Castro has openly embraced Marxism-Leninism since 1961. Symbiotic and parasitic Soviet-Cuban connections increased. Cuban combat forces have substantially augmented left-wing insurgent movements in Angola and Ethiopia. Extensive military assistance on behalf of leftists elsewhere included El Salvador, Nicaragua, and Grenada. Castro also has conducted widespread subversive campaigns in many other countries. U.S. pressures, in short, have had little positive influence on Cuban foreign policies, but Castro's influence outside his own country began to diminish in the late 1980s, especially after Gorbachev drastically reduced Soviet assistance.

Key Congressional Actions

Congress has imposed most U.S. sanctions against Cuba since 1960. Its members had no prior knowledge of the Bay of Pigs operation or assassination plots.

Outcome: Failure, thus far

The United States has accomplished none of its basic objectives, and probably encouraged closer Soviet-Cuba ties than otherwise might have ensued. U.S. sanctions have discomfited the Cuban people more than the Cuban Government.

Escalation Potential: Cool; probability low.

Selected Sources

Bonsal, Philip W., *Cuba, Castro, and the United States*, Pittsburgh, Pa., University of Pittsburgh Press, 1971, 318 p.

Smith, Wayne S., *The Closest of Enemies: A Personal and Diplomatic Account of U.S.-Cuban Relations Since 1957*, New York, W.W. Norton, 1987, 308 p.

Wyden, Peter, *The Bay of Pigs: The Untold Story*, New York, Simon and Schuster, 1979, 352 p.

U.S. Congress, Senate, *Alleged Assassination Plots Involving Foreign Leaders*, An Interim Report to the Select Committee to Study Governmental Operations with Respect to Intelligence Activities, 94th Congress, 1st Session, Washington, U.S. GPO, November 20, 1975, P. 71-180, 263-264, 267-270, 274-277.

Thomas, Hugh, *Cuba: The Pursuit of Freedom*, NY, Harper & Row, 1971, 1696 p.

CASE 28

SOUTH AFRICA (1960-)

Type Conflict	Nonviolent conflict (hands-off opposition)
Duration	30 years plus (still active)
Participants	*U.S. Allies*: Western Europe; United Nations
	U.S. Adversaries: South African Government
U.S. Purposes	*Interests*: National security; economic; human rights
	Objectives: End apartheid; avert revolution; prevent nuclear proliferation
Predominant U.S. Power	Political; economic
Predominant U.S. Instrument	Diplomacy; sanctions
U.S. Armed Forces	Not applicable
Public Opinion	*U.S.*: Supportive
	International: Western Europe supportive; otherwise variable (no strong opposition)

Context

U.S. opposition to South Africa's apartheid policies, which institutionalize white supremacy, predates the Sharpeville riots of March 1960. U.S. policies encourage reform for economic as well as moral reasons, because a leftist revolution could deprive the United States of strategic minerals. Diplomatic pressures, which continue, were the first manifestation. Arms, ammunition, material for their manufacture, military vehicles, and other items that could be used to enforce apartheid have been embargoed since October 1962. Restrictions relaxed slightly in the early 1980s, but toughened when Congress passed the Comprehensive Anti-Apartheid Act of 1986 (PL 99-440) over President Reagan's veto. The Departments of State, Transportation, and Treasury subsequently published implementing regulations that, for example, prescribe fair labor standards for U.S. firms in South Africa, terminate commercial flights between the two countries, ban various bank transactions, and prohibit new investments for specified exports and imports.

South Africa's refusal to sign the Limited Test Ban Treaty, support an African nuclear free zone, or ratify the Nuclear Non-Proliferation Treaty inspires additional U.S. sanctions, although the U.S. intelligence community has not confirmed the existence of a South African nuclear arsenal. Most

U.S. nuclear exports to that nation stopped in 1979. The Anti-Apartheid Act eliminated all exceptions in 1986 and forbade imports of South African uranium ore and oxide into the United States. Such pressures may have prevented South Africa from testing any nuclear weapon, but few other positive signs are evident.

Key Congressional Actions

Congress mandated many of the U.S. economic sanctions against South Africa. The Anti-Apartheid Act of 1986 is the most comprehensive.

Outcome: Mixed opinion

Some assert that U.S. diplomatic pressures and economic sanctions discourage the South African Government from applying increased force and encourage negotiated settlements. Skeptics are less certain.

Escalations potential: Cool; probability low

Selected Sources

Galdi, Theodor W. and Robert D. Shuey, *U.S. Economic Sanctions Imposed Against Specific Foreign Countries: 1979 to the Present*, Washington, Congressional Research Service, September 9, 1988, p. 179-191.

Congressional Research Service issue briefs, Washington, D.C., Branaman, Brenda M., *South Africa: U.S. Policy After Sanctions*, IB 87128, January 19, 1990, 14 p., and *South Africa: Recent Developments*, January 19, 1990, 15 p.; Donnelly, Warren H., *South Africa, Nuclear Weapons, and the IAEA*, December 26, 1989, 14 p.

CASE 29

DOMINICAN REPUBLIC (1960-62)

Type Conflict	Coup d'etat
Duration	August 1960-January 1962 (18 months)
Participants	*U.S. Allies*: Organization of American States (OAS) *U.S. Adversaries*: President Trujillo and supporters
U.S. Purposes	*Interests*: Western hemisphere security *Objectives*: Contain communism; install a stable, democratic Dominican Republic government
Predominant U.S. Power	Economic; military
Predominant U.S. Instrument	Sanctions; covert actions; threats of force
U.S. Armed Forces	*Predominant Type*: Conventional *Predominant Services*: Navy Predominant Mission: Shows of force
Public Opinion	*U.S.*: Supportive *International*: OAS supportive

Context

Dominican Republic President Rafael Trujillo was a right-wing dictator who senor U.S. officials tolerated for nearly 30 years. He created such serious domestic dissent, however, that U.S. leaders finally began to fear that left-wing dissidents might depose him, much as Castro drove Batista from Cuba. The Eisenhower Administration early in 1960 therefore studied optional ways to replace him. President Kennedy continued that tack.

The United States and all OAS associates broke diplomatic relations with the Dominican Republic and imposed severe economic sanctions in August 1960, after Trujillo "took out a contract" on Venezuela's President Betancourt. Trujillo, however, retained tight control. U.S. covert assistance to Dominican undergrounds started in the spring of 1961. Extreme instability persisted several months after Trujillo's assasination on May 31, 1961, as family members, close associates, and various other contenders jockeyed for power. Economic warfare and naval shows of force provided U.S. leverage, particularly during an autumn crisis when the Trujillo clan made concerted attempts to regain control. The interim council that eventually emerged served until general elections produced a new President acceptable to the

United States. U.S. and OAS sanctions lifted in January 1962. Second Fleet contingents, no longer needed, left simultaneously.

Key Congressional Actions

Congress declined to curtail U.S. sugar shipments to the Dominican Republic in 1960, but did so on March 31, 1961.

Outcome: Mixed opinion

The United States accomplished its short-term objectives, but left conditions that called for further U.S. intervention within four years (see Case 32).

Selected Sources

Slater, Jerome N., "The Dominican Republic, 1961-66," in *Force Without War: U.S. Armed Forces as a Political Instrument*, Ed. by Barry M. Blechman and Stephen S. Kaplan, Washington, Brookings Institution, 1978, p. 289-303.

U.S. Congress, Senate, *Alleged Assassination Plots Involving Foreign Leaders*, An Interim Report to the Select Committee to Study Governmental Operations with Respect to Intelligence Activities, 94th Congress, 1st Session, Washington, U.S. GPO, November 20, 1975, p. 191-215, 262-263, 270-272.

CASE 30

ZAIRE (1960-64)

Type Conflict	Counterinsurgency; conventional rescue mission
Duration	July 1960-December 1964 (4 years, 6 months)
Participants	*U.S. Allies*: Zaire Government; United Nations; Belgium *U.S. Adversaries*: Insurgents and supporters
U.S. Purposes	*Interests*: National defense; raw materials *Objectives*: Contain communism; ensure a stable, independent government in Zaire
Predominant U.S. Power	Politico-military
Predominant U.S. Instrument	Security assistance
U.S. Armed Forces	*Predominant Type*: Conventional *Predominant Services*: Air Force *Predominant Function*: Airlift
Public Opinion	*U.S.*: Negligible *International*: African states opposed

Context

Zaire was ill-prepared for self rule when Belgium granted independence on June 30, 1960. Experienced administrators and managers were scarce at every level. Few possessed college degrees. Near anarchy and military mutinies that accompanied the transition prompted Belgian intervention, partly to protect colonials, partly to support a secessionist movement in mineral rich Katanga Province. The United Nations arrived almost simultaneously and stayed four years, heavily backed by the United States, which had important economic interests in the Congo (industrial diamonds, cobalt, tantalum, and copper wire were prominent). U.S. leaders also intended to block possible Soviet and/or Chinese communist encroachments like those already evident elsewhere in Africa. UN troops finally defeated Katangan rebels in January 1963. U.S. airlift aircraft, a small military mission, and CIA elements assisted counterinsurgency efforts.

Insurgencies, some led by leftists, broke out in three other provinces even before UN contingents departed Katanga in June 1964. Rebels enjoyed assistance from and sanctuaries in Congo-Brazzaville and Burundi. The infant

Organization of African Unity proved powerless to help. One well-publicized crisis came when insurgents seized many hostages in Stanleyville (now Kisangani), including officials of the U.S. Consulate. Operation Dragon Rouge, a Belgian parachute assault from aircraft crewed by Americans, saved most, but by no means all, of them. Converging columns of government troops and mercenaries mopped up. The U.S. military mission and aircraft withdrew soon thereafter.

Key Congressional Actions

Congress exerted little influence on U.S. operations in Zaire.

Outcome: Mixed opinion

The United States accomplished its basic objectives. Financial costs associated with support of UN and Belgian intervention were modest, but political liabilities throughout Black Africa were considerable and long-lasting.

Selected Sources

Weissman, Stephen R., *American Foreign Policy in the Congo, 1960-1964*, Ithaca, NY, Cornell University Press, 1974, 325 p.

Revolt in the Congo, 1960-64, Ed. by Howard M. Epstein, NY, Facts on File, 1965, 187 p.

Wagoner, Fred E., *Dragon Rouge: The Rescue of Hostages in the Congo*, Washington, National Defense University Press, 1980, 219 p.

CASE 31

BRAZIL (1961-64)

Type Conflict	Coup d'etat
Duration	September 1961-April 1964 (2 years, 7 months)
Participants	*U.S. Allies*: Brazilian military officials *U.S. Adversaries*: President Goulart and supporters
U.S. Purposes	*Interests*: Western Hemisphere security *Objectives*: Contain communism; oust Goulart; ensure a friendly Brazilian government
Predominant U.S. Power	Politico-military; economic
Predominant U.S. Instrument	Security assistance; sanctions
U.S. Armed Forces	Navy and Air Force operations planned, but not implemented
Public Opinion	*U.S.*: Unimportant *International*: Unimportant, even in Latin America

Context

U.S. interests in Latin America intensified after Castro seized control of Cuba. President Kennedy's Alliance for Progress furnished a new focus for U.S. security assistance programs. Brazil, by far the largest country affected, was essential to success, but left-leaning Goulart caused U.S. anxieties even before he became President in September 1961. Goulart's foreign policies welcomed connections with the Communist Bloc. His domestic policies, particularly dealings with labor unions and cooperatives, also sounded anticommunist alarms among Brazilian generals, as well as U.S. officials. U.S. assistance, sanctions, and other manipulations in assorted combinations failed to "correct" his course.

Political, economic, and social crises first encouraged Goulart's adversaries to consider a coup early in 1963 (one ill-conceived effort failed the following October). Goulart drifted farther left and became increasingly radical until March, 1964, when conspirators lead by Army Chief of Staff Castelo Branco finally put feasible plans into action, with U.S. approval and support. A U.S. carrier task force steamed toward Brazil as part of Operation Brother Sam. Arms and ammunition were readied for airlift. Four tankers loaded petroleum, oil, and lubricants. A bloodless coup, however, deposed Goulart on April 4, 1964 before Brother Sam forces reached their destinations. General Branco was elected President one week later. Economic assistance to Brazil boomed immediately thereafter.

Key Congressional Actions

Congress was not involved in plans to oust President Goulart. It appropriated funds to assist Brazil, but the Executive Branch determined how they would be dispensed before and after the coup.

Outcome: Mixed opinion

The United States accomplished basic objectives. In the process, it disrupted democratic processes in Brazil and encouraged military, rather than civilian, rule.

Selected Sources

Skidmore, Thomas E., *Politics in Brazil, 1930-1964: An Experiment in Democracy*, NY, Oxford University Press, 1967, p. 205-330.

Parker, Phyllis R., *Brazil and the Quiet Intervention, 1964*, Austin, TX, University of Texas Press, 1979, 147 p.

CASE 32

VIETNAM (1963)

Type Conflict	Coup d'etat
Duration	May 8-November 2, 1963 (6 months)
Participants	*U.S. Allies*: Ambitious Vietnamese generals
	U.S. Adversaries: President Diem and supporters
U.S. Purposes	*Interests*: Stable, viable South Vietnam
	Objectives: Depose Diem; replace him with a President more amenable to essential reforms
Predominant U.S. Power	Political
Predominant U.S. Instrument	Psychological operations
U.S. Armed Forces	Not applicable
Public Opinion	*U.S.*: Slight
	International: Mainly apathetic

Context

President Diem's obdurate behavior cost him the confidence of President Kennedy and his closest advisers by the spring of 1963. His apparent dominance by brother Ngo Dinh Nhu and controversial Madame Nhu (colloquially called the "Dragon Lady") disaffected large parts of the population in the midst of a war that was not going well from U.S. standpoints (Case 24).

Brutal attacks on Buddhists by government troops in Hue triggered a domestic and international backlash on May 8, 1963. Several monks conspicuously immolated themselves in protests that shocked the world during the next three months. Diem, prompted by senior U.S. spokesmen, made public amends on August 14, but possible benefits dissipated a week later, when Nhu directed Special Forces and police to arrest Buddhist priests and sack their shrines countrywide. Disgruntled Vietnamese generals and U.S. decisionmakers at that juncture planned to replace Diem, unless he rid the nation of both Nhus and seriously sought to win the hearts and minds of his people. Powerful U.S. psychological pressures, however, were unpersuasive. The first plot to unseat Diem was stillborn on August 31, because the cabal (Vietnamese Generals Minh, Don, Kim, and Khiem) felt the time was not ripe. Diem and his brother subsequently were assassinated during a successful coup on November 1-2, 1963. Madame Nhu, who was abroad at the time, never returned to Vietnam.

Key Congressional Actions

Congress played no part in the deposal of Diem.

Outcome: Mixed opinion

The United States accomplished its basic objectives, but no well qualified replacement for President Diem was identified before the coup occurred. Communist insurgents prospered for 18 months until a reasonably acceptable successor took office.

Selected Sources

U.S. Congress, Senate, *The U.S. Government and the Vietnam War: Executive and Legislative Roles and Relationships*, Prepared for the Committee on Foreign Relations by the Congressional Research Service, 98th Congress, Second Session, Part II, 1961-1964, Washington, U.S. GPO, December 1984, p. 137-208.

U.S. Congress, Senate, *Alleged Assassination Plots Involving Foreign Leaders*, An Interim Report to the Select Committee to Study Governmental Operations with Respect to Intelligence Activities, 94th Congress, 1st Session, Washington, U.S. GPO, November 20, 1975, p. 217-223, 261-262.

CASE 33

DOMINICAN REPUBLIC (1965-66)

Type Conflict	Peacemaking
Duration	April 1965-September 1966 (18 months)
Participants	*U.S. Allies*: Dominican "loyalists"; Organization of American States (OAS) *U.S. Adversaries*: Dominican "constitutionalists"
U.S. Purposes	*Interests*: Western Hemisphere security *Objectives*: Contain communism; ensure a friendly Dominican Republic Government
Predominant U.S. Power	Politico-military
Predominant U.S. Instrument	Force; threats of force; diplomacy
U.S. Armed Forces	*Predominant Type*: Conventional *Predominant Services*: Multiservice Predominant Mission: Peacemaking
Public Opinion	*U.S.*: Mildly supportive *International*: Adverse in Latin America

Context

The Dominican Republic remained in flux after President Trujillo was assassinated in May 1961 (Case 29). Liberal Juan Bosch, his first elected successor, lasted just seven months before a military coup deposed him in September 1963. The head of a right-wing junta, prodded by U.S. officials, finally promised free elections within 18 months, but his perceived intent to circumvent that pledge, coupled with autocratic policies and poor performance, culminated in a second military coup by a small clique of self-styled "constitutionalists" on April 25, 1965.

Revolutionary fervor spread to civilians, whom the constitutionalists incited and armed. Their professed purpose was to reinstall Bosch as president. Counterattacks by "loyalist" troops at first were successful, but defections soon depleted their ranks. U.S. intervention followed on April 28, primarily to obviate any possibility that "Castro-style" revolutionaries might seize control. U.S. forces ashore totaled 23,000 by May 9, with reinforcements afloat. The main U.S. military missions were to separate the belligerents, block the constitutionalists, enforce a cease-fire, and evacuate U.S. civilians, as well as other foreign nationals. The Organization of

American States was a moderating influence and contributed to an Inter-American Peace Force during protracted negotiations in which U.S. "coercive diplomacy" was evident. A provisional government was proclaimed on September 3, 1965. Bosch was defeated decisively in June 1966, during genuinely free elections. The last U.S. contingents withdrew in September.

Key Congressional Actions

President Johnson briefed key Members of Congress before U.S. armed forces intervened. Congress did not play an important part in any subsequent developments.

Outcome: Mixed opinion

The United States accomplished basic objectives and all military missions. Adverse public opinion, especially in Latin America, imposed significant penalties. Whether U.S. operations were needed to block communism in the Dominican Republic is debatable.

Selected Sources

Slater, Jerome, *Intervention and Negotiation: The United States and the Dominican Revolution*, NY, Harper & Row, 1970, 254 p.

Lowenthal, Abraham F., *The Dominican Intervention*, Cambridge, MA, Harvard University Press, 1972, 246 p.

Palmer, Bruce, Jr., *Intervention in the Caribbean: The Dominican Crisis of 1965*, Lexington, KY, University Press of Kentucky, 1989, 226 p.

CASE 34

GUATEMALA (1965-74)

Type conflict	Counterinsurgency
Duration	Nine years
Participants	*U.S. Allies*: Guatemalan Government *U.S. Adversaries*: Insurgents
U.S. Purposes	*Interests*: Western Hemisphere security *Objectives*: Contain communism; ensure a friendly Guatemalan Government
Predominant U.S. Power	Politico-military
Predominant U.S. Instrument	Security assistance
U.S. Armed Forces	*Predominant Type*: Special operations *Predominant Services*: Army *Predominant Function*: Advice
Public Opinion	*U.S.*: Nonexistent *International*: Adverse in Latin America

Context

Extreme instability plagued Guatemala after a coup deposed President Arbenz Guzmán in 1954 (Case 23). His successor was assassinated in 1957. The Army ousted the next President in 1963. Left-wing insurgents, who gained strength during that period, posed serious problems for the following Administration, which lasted until 1966. Brutal repression in response lingered until the mid-1970s.

The Guatemalan Army and police totally controlled counterinsurgency policies and operations after 1965. Their pacification programs featured state-sponsored terrorism on a grand scale to discourage any citizen from assisting undergrounds or guerrillas. Uncivilized incarceration, torture, mutilation, and civilian death squads licensed to kill suspected communists and sympathizers were widely employed surreptitiously to conceal the source or plausibly deny responsibility. Repression eventually paid off, abetted inadvertently by U.S. military assistance and public safety programs in the form of hardware, training, and funds for Guatemala's military establishment and police. Insurgencies almost ceased by 1974, when U.S. presence declined considerably. The price in human rights was high, however, and America's reputation was tarnished. Outraged adversaries made targets of key U.S. officials (our ambassador, chief of the U.S. military mission, and naval attaché all were murdered in 1968; many more became casualties over the years).

Key Congressional Actions

Congress appropriated security assistance funds during this period, but specific allocations to Guatemala were primarily determined by the Executive Branch.

Outcome: Failure

The United States temporarily accomplished basic objectives, but the long-term legacy of ill will outweighed short-term benefits. Few observers believe that ends justified means. Operations that suppressed the symptoms of insurgency left causes intact. Rebellion revived in the 1980s.

Selected Sources

Latin America: The Struggle with Dependency and Beyond, Ed. by Ronald H. Chilcote and Joel C. Edelstein, NY, John Wiley & Sons, 1974, p. 169-219.

McClintock, Michael, *The American Connection: State Terror and Popular Resistance in Guatemala*, Vol. 2, London, Zed Books, 1985, p. 76-122.

CASE 35

THAILAND (1965-85)

Type Conflict	Counterinsurgency
Duration	August 1965-July 1985 (20 years)
Participants	*U.S. Allies*: Thai Government *U.S. Adversaries*: Thai insurgents; China; Vietnam
U.S. Purposes	*Interests*: National defense *Objectives*: Contain communism; ensure a friendly Thai Government
Predominant U.S. Power	Politico-military; economic
Predominant U.S. Instrument	Security assistance
U.S. Armed Forces	*Predominant Type*: Special operations *Predominant Services*: Army *Predominant Function*: Advice
Public Opinion	*U.S.*: Nonexistent *International*: Noncommunist Southeast Asia supportive

Context

The Communist Party of Thailand (CPT) instigated its first guerrilla operations in August 1965. Revolution spread from northeast to northwest, then headed south. Search and destroy sweeps, patterned after U.S. tactics then popular in Vietnam, proved counterproductive. The rural war took a turn for the better in 1972, when Thai strategists against U.S. advice adopted policies that paid close attention to peasant needs. Undergrounds, however, continued to grow in Bangkok and other key cities, while five civilian governments floundered for the next four years, until student uprisings finally triggered a military coup in October, 1976.

General Saiyud, the principal counterinsurgency architect, attacked causes as well as systems. He integrated civilian, police, and military efforts, with emphases in that order. Influential fellow officers initially opposed his programs, but found it increasingly difficult to quarrel with success. U.S. economic assistance provided essential resources for rural development. U.S. military materiel armed and Special Forces helped train Thai militia. Chinese and Vietnamese support for Thai insurgents conversely slowed, then virtually stopped. The first large group of guerrillas defectors, warmly welcomed and well rewarded in 1981, encouraged a series of mass surrenders over the next two years. The situation was under control by 1985, although General Saiyud (retired) warns that more nation building is needed to preclude future problems.

Key Congressional Actions

Congress appropriated funds to improve rural security and economic development in Thailand.

Outcome: Mixed opinion

The United States accomplished basic objectives, but was part of the problem more than part of the solution for several years. U.S. material aid was much more valuable than U.S. advice.

Selected Sources

Saiyud, Kerdphol, *The Struggle for Thailand: Counterinsurgency 1965-1985*, Bangkok, S. Research Center Co., 1986, 253 p.

Tanham, George K., *Trial in Thailand*, NY, Crane, Russak, 1974, 175 p.

CASE 36

JORDAN (1970)

Type Conflict	Nonviolent conflict (posturing)
Duration	September 1970 (1 month)
Participants	*U.S. Allies*: Jordan; Israel *U.S. Adversaries*: Palestinian radicals; Syria; Iraq; USSR
U.S. Purposes	*Interests*: Desirable power balance in Middle East *Objectives*: Preserve Jordan's monarchy; avoid armed intervention by Iraq, Syria, Israel, USSR; restrain radical groups
Predominant U.S. Power	Politico-military
Predominant U.S. Instrument	Diplomacy; shows of force; psyop
U.S. Armed Forces	*Predominant Type*: Conventional *Predominant Services*: Navy *Predominant Function*: Deterrence
Public Opinion	*U.S.*: Slight *International*: Slight

Context

King Hussein of Jordan during "Black September" 1970 cracked down on Palestinian radicals based in his country after they twice tried to assassinate him, then caused an international crisis when they hijacked four airliners and held the passengers hostage on Jordanian soil. Retaliation by Jordan's Army triggered a chain reaction. Iraqi troops already inside Jordan threatened to intervene, but did not. Syrian tank columns did. Israel made compensatory moves along its de facto frontiers. U.S. and Soviet intervention on behalf of respective clients seemed conceivable. It would take only one spark to ignite that tinderbox.

Three U.S. problems were paramount: retrieve the hostages unharmed; avoid uncontrolled escalation; preserve King Hussein, who would be ruined throughout the Arab world if Israel came to his rescue. Not many military options seemed attractive to the United States, which had just begun to disengage from Vietnam under intense domestic pressure. President Nixon, seeking to demonstrate U.S. resolve, settled for naval shows of force in the Eastern Mediterranean and "saber rattling" elsewhere intended to deter all adversaries. Delicate diplomacy, much of it conducted personally and in secret by Kissinger and associates, simultaneously encouraged Israel to exercise restraint. Separate communications urged the Soviets to persuade Syria that its forces should withdraw posthaste. Success in that endeavor is uncertain, but Syrian invaders nevertheless returned home on September 25 after brief but sharp battles inside Jordan. The last U.S. hostages were released four days later. The crisis was resolved, although Jordan did not eliminate the last Palestinian enclave until July 1971.

Key Congressional Actions

The Nixon Administration briefed Congress after the fact, not beforehand. Congress had no opportunity to approve, support, or constrain U.S. operations.

Outcome: Mixed opinion

The United States accomplished all basic objectives, but the extent to which U.S. maneuvering ensured success is impossible to prove.

Selected Sources

Kissinger, Henry A., *White House Years*, Boston, Little, Brown & Co., 1979, p. 594-631.

Quandt, William B., "Lebanon, 1958, and Jordan, 1970," in *Force Without War: U.S. Armed Forces as a Political Instrument*, Ed. by Barry M. Blechman and Stephen S. Kaplan, Washington, Brookings Institution, 1978, p. 257-288.

CASE 37

LIBYA (1970-)

Type Conflict
Punitive expedition; combatting terrorism; nonviolent conflict (hands off opposition)

Duration
20 years plus (still active)

Participants
U.S. Allies: Counterterrorism community
U.S. Adversaries: Libya; associated terrorist groups

U.S. Purposes
Interests: International security
Objectives: Deter transnational terrorism by Libya

Predominant U.S. Power
Politico-military; economic

Predominant U.S. Instrument
Sanctions; force

U.S. Armed Forces
Predominant Type: Conventional
Predominant Services: Navy; Air Force
Predominant Function: Deterrence

Public Opinion
U.S.: Supportive
International: Variable among U.S. allies

Context

Mu'ammar al-Qadhafi, widely regarded as irrational in foreign affairs, has ruled Libya as the "Revolutionary Leader" since September 1969, although he formally relinquished all official posts in the 1970s. Relations with the United States soured almost immediately. Qadhafi closed Wheelus Air Base in 1970, became a bitter critic of U.S. support for Israel, assisted revolutionary groups around the globe, encouraged transnational terrorism, tried to topple nieghboring governments friendly to the United States, and established close ties with the Soviet Union, which remains his primary source of military arms. The United States in response imposed a series of political and economic sanctions that became progressively more severe. They currently include an embargo on U.S. military sales to Libya; restrictions on travel and trade (President Reagan, for example, directed U.S. petroleum companies to cease operations in Libya and prohibited the importation of Libyan crude oil); and the termination of Most-Favored-Nation tariff status, as well as Export-Import Bank credits. U.S. efforts to encourage international sanctions have produced mixed results.

Several armed encounters between U.S. and Libyan armed forces occurred in 1981 and 1986, when U.S. naval aircraft violated Qadhafi's so-called "Line of Death" across the Gulf of Sidra. Libyan interceptors, patrol boats, and shore installations were damaged or destroyed on two occasions. Qadhafi has been quiescent since U.S. aircraft struck Tripoli and Benghazi on April 15, 1986, in retaliation for a Libyan-backed terrorist bombing in West Berlin, which was "the straw that broke the camel's back." Many mutual animosities nevertheless remain.

Key Congressional Actions

Most U.S. sanctions against Libya have been executive orders, but Congress, which generally has supported presidential policies in such regard, initiated some of its own. War powers issues have caused most contention.

Outcome: Mixed opinion

Libya's international behavior has been less belligerent since 1986, but basic U.S. objectives have not been satisfied. Whether U.S. sanctions have produced positive results is disputable.

Escalation Potential: Warm; probability moderate

Selected Sources

Haley, P. Edward, *Quddafi and the United States Since 1969*, New York, Praeger, 1984, 364 p.

Congressional Research Service issue briefs, Washington: Mark, Clyde, R., *Libya: U.S. Relations*, IB 86040, May 26, 1987, 21 p.; Copson, Raymond W., *Libya: U.S. Relations*, IB 81152, December 8, 1983, 31 p.

Bolger, Daniel P., *Americans at War : An Era of Violent Peace, 1975-1986*, Novato, CA, Presidio Press, 1988, p. 169-189, 383-441.

CASE 38

CHILE (1970-73)

Type Conflict	Coup d'etat
Duration	September 1970 - September 1973 (3 years)
Participants	*U.S. Allies*: None *U.S. Adversaries*: Chilean Government
U.S. Purposes	*Interests*: Western Hemisphere security; economic *Objectives*: Contain communism; ensure a friendly Chilean Government
Predominant U.S. Power	Political; economic
Predominant U.S. Instrument	Sanctions; covert operations
U.S. Armed Forces	Not applicable
Public Opinion	*U.S.*: Slight *International*: Variable, but not very influential in Latin America

Context

Salvador Allende, a Marxist, narrowly missed winning Chile's presidential election in 1958. The CIA successfully mounted massive covert activities to deny him victory in 1964. Less extensive spoiling efforts failed in September 1970, when Allende finished first. However he lacked a clear majority. More than a month remained before the Chilean Congress was to pick the winner. U.S. opposition took two tracks, neither of which worked. Track I emphasized overt and covert economic pressures, plus propaganda campaigns that equated Allende with communist control of Chile. Track II simultaneously encouraged a military coup, which General Rene Schneider, the Chilean Army commander-in-chief, staunchly opposed. Conspiracies collapsed after he was killed during attempts to kidnap him. Allende was inaugurated on November 3, 1970.

Allende seemed to reinforce U.S. fears, when he quickly recognized Cuba, expanded contacts with communist countries, nationalized U.S. interests in Chile's copper industries, and commenced socialist experiments. The United States in response supplied his political rivals with funds, covertly manipulated Chilean news media, terminated economic aid, denied credits, and urged corporations to tighten the squeeze. Consequent economic chaos that included riots and crippling strikes culminated in a military coup on September 11, 1973, during which Allende allegedly committed suicide.

General Pinochet, his successor, interrupted constitutional rule in Chile for the first time in 41 years.

Key Congressional Actions

No department or agency of the Executive Branch, including the CIA, kept Congress well informed, nor did oversight committees often seek information. Congressional interest and influence therefore was mainly after the fact.

Outcome: Mixed opinion

The United States finally accomplished basic objectives, but helped destroy Chile's democracy in the process. Pinochet almost immediately banned political parties, declared Chile's Congress in prolonged recess, instituted censorship, imprisoned political opponents, and deferred elections indefinitely.

Selected Sources

U.S. Congress, Senate, staff reports of the Select Committee to Study Government Operations with Respect to Intelligence Activities, 94th Congress, 1st Session, Washington, U.S. GPO: *Covert Action in Chile, 1963-1973*, December 18, 1975, 61 p.; and *Alleged Assassination Plots Involving Foreign Leaders*, November 20, 1975, p. 225-254.

U.S. Congress, House, *United States and Chile During the Allende Years, 1970-73*, Hearings Before the Subcommitee on InterAmerican Affairs of the Committee on Foreign Affairs, 94th Congress, 1st Session, Washington, U.S. GPO, 1975, 677 p.

Sigmund, Paul E., *The Overthrow of Allende and the Politics of Chile, 1964-1976*, Pittsburg, PA, University of Pittsburg Press, 1977, 326 p.

CASE 39

IRAQ (1972-75)

Type Conflict	Insurgency
Duration	May 1972 - June 1975 (3 years)
Participants	*U.S. Allies*: Iran; Israel; Kurdish separatists
	U.S. Adversaries: Iraq
U.S. Purposes	*Interests*: Middle East security
	Objectives: Weaken Iraq; contain Soviet Union
Predominant U.S. Power	Political
Predominant U.S. Instrument	Covert operations; military assistance
U.S. Armed Forces	Not applicable
Public Opinion	*U.S.*: None
	International: None

Context

Kurdistan overlaps five countries: Iran, Iraq, Syria, Turkey, and the Soviet Union. Kurds therein traditionally lead semi-autonomous lives, but Iraqi clans under Mulla Mustafa al-Barzani fought long and hard for complete freedom. The United States, which rejected his requests for assistance in 1971 and March 1972, acquiesced two months later, when the Shah of Iran invited a collaborative venture designed to weaken Iraq. Barzani, suspicious of the Shah's motives, accepted because he believed U.S. participation guaranteed good faith.

U.S. aid, all relayed by Iran, was so secretive that President Nixon and Kissinger reportedly circumvented the 40 Committee,[1] a sub-cabinet group whose members normally reviewed covert action proposals. Plans apparently called for $16 million, partly used to purchase Soviet and Chinese arms that Israel captured during its 1967 war with Arab states (an effort to conceal the true suppliers). The program, from U.S. standpoints, would at least help reduce Iraq's regional adventurism, particularly in the Persian Gulf, and at

---

[1] The 40 Committee, chaired by the Assistant to the President for National Security Affairs, included the Under Secretary of State for Political Affairs, the Deputy Secretary of Defense, the Chairman of the Joint Chiefs of Staff, and the Director of Central Intelligence.

best might even topple the pro-Soviet Baath government in Baghdad. A more amenable regime might reinstate oil rights that Iraq revoked in May 1972. Kurdish insurgents did sap Iraq's resources to some extent, but their fortunes reversed instantaneously when Iran and Iraq temporarily settled border disputes in 1975. Aid to Barzani ceased, Iraq mounted a counteroffensive that decimated his flock, and the United States refused assistance to thousands of refugees.

Key Congressional Actions

Congress had no knowledge of U.S. support for Iraqi Kurds until the House Select Committee on Intelligence, chaired by Congressman Otis Pike, held hearings and issued a classified report in January 1976.

Outcome: Failure

The United States discomfited Iraq momentarily, but there is no evidence that aid to Kurds helped contain the Soviet Union. The cost in human lives and suffering seems excessive in light of those results.

Selected Sources

"The CIA Report the President Doesn't Want You to Read: The Pike Papers," *Village Voice*, February 16, 1976, p. 71, 85.

Ghareeb, Edmund, *The Kurdish Question in Iraq*, Syracuse, New York, Syracuse University Press, 1981, p. 138-144, 210-212.

CASE 40

ORGANIZATION OF PETROLEUM EXPORTING COUNTRIES
(OPEC, 1974-75)

Type Conflict   Nonviolent conflict (hands-off
                                         opposition)

Duration   2 years

Participants   *U.S. Allies*: International Energy Agency
                                         (IEA)[1]
                                         U.S. Adversaries: Arab members of OPEC

U.S. Purposes   *Interests*: National security; commerce
                                         Objectives: Deter OPEC from imposing a
                                         severe oil embargo

Predominant U.S. Power   Politico-military

Predominant U.S. Instrument   Psychological warfare

U.S. Armed Forces   Not applicable

Public Opinion   *U.S.*: Little support for military action
                                         International: IEA states opposed military
                                         action.

Context

Arab members of OPEC imposed an oil embargo against the United States from mid-October 1973 to mid-March 1974 in reprisal for U.S. assistance to Israel during the 1973 Arab-Israeli conflict. That incomplete boycott, which allowed considerable leakage, merely inconvenienced America, but more stringent measures, if sustained and expanded, could have degraded U.S. security and crippled U.S. allies, whose dependence on petroleum imports greatly exceeded our own. A sharp rise in the price of oil also caused economic instability in the United States.

Senior U.S. officials sought cooperative economic countermeasures by major oil consuming nations and began to speculate openly about the advisability of U.S. military countermeasures in such event after Secretary of Defense Schlesinger made public statements in January 1974. The tempo picked up, when President Ford and Secretary of State Kissinger issued pronouncements concerning that subject. Each utterance addressed

---

[1] IEA members are the United States, European Community (minus France), Canada, Australia, New Zealand, and Japan.

hypothetical propositions and identified U.S. armed intervention as a last resort, if U.S. survival was at stake. Many at home and abroad nevertheless viewed their remarks as thinly veiled threats. Influential periodicals kept the topic alive for several months with various interpretations. A CRS report, prepared in response to congressional request, attracted serious attention throughout the Middle East. The issue subsided before 1975 ended, after which U.S. officials refrained from further talk about military retaliation.

Key Congressional Actions

Congress established a Strategic Petroleum Reserve on December 22, 1975 (P.L. 94-163) to help offset any oil embargo.

Outcome: Mixed opinion

The United States achieved its basic objective, but there is no proof that OPEC would have reimposed an oil embargo if U.S. officials had never openly intimated that military action was a valid response.

Selected Sources

U.S. Congress, House, *Oil Fields as Military Objectives: A Feasibility Study*, prepared for the Special Subcommittee on Investigations of the Committee on International Relations, 94th Congress, 1st Session, Washington, U.S. GPO, August 21, 1975, 111 p. See pages 77-82 for selected quotations by senior U.S. officials.

Tucker, Robert W., "Oil: The Issue of American Intervention," *Commentary*, January 1975, p. 21-31; Ignotus, Miles, "Seizing Arab Oil," *Harper's*, March 1975, p. 45-62. Rebuttals are found in Ravenal, Earl C., "The Oil-Grab Scenario," *New Republic*, January 18, 1975, p. 14-16; Stone, I.F., "War for Oil?" *New York Review*, February 6, 1975, p. 7-8, 10.

CASE 41

CYPRUS (1974-78)

Type Conflict	Nonviolent conflict (hands-off opposition)
Duration	July 15, 1974 - September 26, 1978 (4 years, 2 months)
Participants	*U.S. Allies*: None *U.S. Adversaries*: Turkey
U.S. Purposes	*Interests*: NATO solidarity; regional stability *Objectives*: Compel Turkey to withdraw troops from Cyprus
Predominant U.S. Power	Political; economic
Predominant U.S. Instrument	Sanctions
U.S. Armed Forces	Not applicable
Public Opinion	*U.S.*: Strong in the U.S. Greek community; otherwise slight influence *International*: Slight influence

Context

The ruling junta in Athens, bent on merging Cyprus with Greece (a NATO member) approved a coup that ousted Cypriot President Makarios on July 15, 1974 because he preferred an independent, nonaligned state. Turkey (also a NATO member) almost immediately intervened militarily to protect its minorities on the island and prevent total Greek control, reinforced in mid-August, and occupied the northern sector of Cyprus. Greece thereupon terminated military ties with NATO, which failed to prevent the or oppose the invasion.

Congress, despite objections from the Executive Branch (recently weakened by Watergate scandals), responded with an arms embargo against Turkey, ostensibly because that country violated its agreement to use U.S. arms only for defensive purposes. Sanctions were to remain in effect until steps to resolve the impasse on Cyprus showed "substantial progress." Sanctions were alleviated slightly in October 1975, but battles between Congress and two Administrations (Ford, Carter) raged for three more years before they lifted completely on September 26, 1978. Primary problems nevertheless remain unresolved. Greek Cypriots inhabit the southern two-thirds of Cyprus. Turkish Cypriots, plus 25,000-30,000 Turkish troops, populate the north. United Nations peacekeeping forces occupy a buffer zone between them. No permanent solution acceptable to both sides seems likely to end the stalemate soon.

Key Congressional Actions

Congress instigated, alleviated, and eventually ended the arms embargo against Turkey.

Outcome: Failure

The United States satisfied neither its basic security interests nor its objectives. Actions taken exacerbated strains between Congress and the Executive Branch, as well as between the United States and its NATO allies.

Selected Sources

U.S. Congress, House, *Congressional-Executive Relations and the Turkish Arms Embargo*, report prepared for the Committee on Foreign Affairs, Congress and Foreign Policy Series No. 3, Washington, U.S. GPO, June 1981, 60 p.

"Efforts to Resolve the Cyprus Dispute," in *Perspectives on Negotiation: Four Case Studies and Interpretations*, Ed. by Diane B. Bendahmane and John W. McDonald, Jr., Washington, Foreign Service Institute, Department of State, 1986, p. 99-152.

Laipson, Ellen, *Greece and Turkey: The Seven-Ten Ratio in Military Aid*, Washington, Congressional Research Service, December 26, 1989, 31 p.

CASE 42

MAYAGUEZ (1975)

Type Conflict	Conventional rescue mission
Duration	May 12-15, 1975 (4 days)
Participants	*U.S. Allies*: None *U.S. Adversaries*: Cambodia
U.S. Purposes	*Interests*: Freedom of the seas; U.S. national credibility *Objectives*: Retrieve hostages safely; deter recurrent "piracy"
Predominant U.S. Power	Military
Predominant U.S. Instrument	Force
U.S. Armed Forces	*Predominant Type*: Conventional *Predominant Services*: Navy/Marine Corps; Air Force *Predominant Function*: Combat
Public Opinion	*U.S.*: Supportive *International*: Thailand disapproves

Context

Khmer Rouge forces on May 12, 1975 commandeered the *S.S. Mayaguez*, a U.S. commercial cargo ship en route from Hong Kong to Sattahip, Thailand, when it passed through international waters that Cambodia claimed were territorial. Vietnam and Cambodia both had come under communist control the previous month. That devastating setback adversely affected U.S. credibility as a superpower. President Ford and his advisers believed that this act of "piracy" demanded a decisive response.

U.S. Pacific Command, as instructed, mounted a multiservice rescue operation within a matter of hours. Reconnaissance aircraft found the *Mayaguez*, which anchored at Koh Tang island, where the captive crew transferred to a small craft and continued toward Cambodia. U.S. forces, uncertain of hostage whereabouts, sank several Cambodian patrol boats in efforts to isolate the island. Air strikes against the Cambodian mainland were designed to prevent reinforcements from that quarter. U.S. Marines, despite Thai protests, staged in Thailand for a May 15 heliborne assault on Koh Tang, where they hoped to find the crew. Other Marines from Thailand "recaptured" the empty *Mayaguez*, which Cambodian officials had already promised to release. Cambodia also freed the crew, whom a U.S. destroyer recovered while they were returning to the *Mayaguez* aboard a Thai fishing boat. Marines on Koh Tang withdrew after dark on May 15 under heavy fire. U.S. combat casualties included 18 dead, 50 wounded, and 3 missing in action. 23 more died in a helicopter crash in Thailand.

Key Congressional Actions

President Ford briefed selected members of the Senate and House while the operation was in progress. Controversy, however, arose concerning presidential requirements to consult Congress beforehand, in accord with the War Powers Resolution.

Outcome: Mixed opinion

The United States accomplished its basic objectives. Relationships between U.S. operations and the release of ship and crew remain controversial.

Selected Topics

Head, Richard G. et al., *Crisis Resolution: Presidential Decision Making in the Mayaguez and Korean Confrontations*, Boulder, CO, Westview Press, 1978, p. 101-148, 265-276.

U.S. Congress, House, *Seizure of the Mayaguez*, Hearings Before the Committee on International Relations, Parts I-III, 94th Congress, 1st Session, Washington, U.S. GPO, 1975, 325 p. total; Party IV, 1976, 162 p.

Bolger, Daniel P., *Americans at War : An Era of Violent Peace, 1975-1986*, Novato, CA, Presidio Press, 1988, p. 19-98.

CASE 43

CAMBODIA (1975-)

Type Conflict	Nonviolent conflict (hands off opposition); resistance
Duration	15 years plus (still active)
Participants	*U.S. Allies*: Non-communist resistance groups; ASEAN* *U.S. Adversaries*: Khmer Rouge; Vietnam; China; Soviet Union
U.S. Purposes	*Interests*: National security; human rights *Objectives*: contain communism; ensure a friendly, democratic Cambodian Government
Predominant U.S. Power	Diplomatic; economic
Predominant U.S. Instrument	Sanctions; security assistance
U.S. Armed Forces	Not applicable
Public Opinion	*U.S.*: Supportive, but slight *International*: Variable

Context

Cambodia has seldom had smooth associations with the United States since it achieved independence in 1953. Prince Norodom Sihanouk sought unsuccessfully to remain nonaligned during the Vietnam War, but increasingly served U.S. adversaries and severed relations from 1965-1969. The Lon Nol government, installed in 1970, switched sides until mid-April 1975, when communist Khmer Rouge seized control and established Democratic Kampuchea (DK).

The United States immediately broke diplomatic relations and imposed sanctions during the period 1975-78, while the Khmer Rouge brutalized Cambodia and one-sixth of the population perished.** That phase of the conflict terminated in January 1979, when Vietnam, supported by the Soviet

---

* The Association of Southeast Asian Nations includes Brunei, Indonesia, Malaysia, the Philippines, Singapore, and Thailand.

** U.S. actions against the Khmer Rouge regime constituted hands off opposition, except the Mayaguez rescue mission (Appendix 42).

Union, defeated the Khmer Rouge, who are clients of China, and installed the People's Republic of Kampuchea (PRK) in Phnom Penh. U.S. sanctions thereupon shifted from the defunct DK to PRK and reinforced reasons to retain sanctions against Vietnam. Three resistance movements, whose leaders despise each other, united to rid Cambodia of the PRK and Vietnamese invaders. Khmer Rouge remnants, which are militarily the most capable, rely mainly on China for material assistance. Both non-communist groups depend on the United States and ASEAN for nonlethal aid, but receive most arms from China. U.S. dilemmas multiplied when Vietnam withdrew most of its armed forces in September 1989 because of attrition, economic problems, and diminishing Soviet support. The United States, seeking some practical way to ensure a democratic Cambodian Government without another bloodbath, terminated connections with the tripartite coalition in July 1990 and, in a major policy reversal, opened a dialogue with Vietnam. No solution, however, is in sight.

Key Congressional Actions

Congress legislated sanctions that applied to the DK, PRK, and Vietnam. It has appropriated funds for nonlethal aid to noncommunist resistance groups and for humanitarian purposes, but rejects requests for weapons and munitions. Future U.S. courses of action in Cambodia are subjects of sharp debate.

Outcome: Mixed opinion

The United States has not yet accomplished its objectives. There is no consensus concerning the effectiveness of past U.S. policies and practices or the desirability of proposals for the future.

Escalation Potential: Warm; potential moderate

Selected Sources

Chanda, Nayan, *Cambodia 1989: The Search for an Exit*, NY, Asia Society, June 1989, 35 p.

Clark, Dick and David Carpenter, *The Third Indochina War: Prospects for Peace*, Aspen, CO, Aspen Institute for Humanistic Studies, 1987, 16 p.

Congressional Research Service, Washington: Sutter, Robert G., *Cambodian Crisis: Problems of a Settlement and Policy Dilemmas for the United States*, Issue Brief IB 89020, February 14, 1990, 15 p.; Galdi, Theodor W. and Robert D. Shuey, *U.S. Economic Sanctions Imposed Against Specific Foreign Countries: 1979 to the Present*, September 9, 1988, p. 37-42, 225-230.

CASE 44

NICARAGUA (1978-79)

Type Conflict	Insurgency
Duration	January 1, 1978 - July 17, 1979 (18+ months)
Participants	*U.S. Allies*: Organization of American States (OAS) *U.S. Adversaries*: Nicaraguan Government
U.S. Purposes	*Interests*: Western Hemisphere stability; human rights *Objectives*: Install a democratic Nicaraguan Government friendly to the United States
Predominant U.S. Power	Political; economic
Predominant U.S. Instrument	Sanctions
U.S. Armed Forces	Not applicable
Public Opinion	*U.S.*: Variable *International*: Latin America supportive

Context

The Somoza dynasty in Nicaragua lasted more than 40 years. Anastasio, Jr., a pro-U.S., anti-communist West Point graduate who became president in 1967, exploited that office for personal gain even more than his father and brother had before. He allegedly lined his pockets, for example, with relief money after an earthquake ravaged Managua in 1972. Human rights violations were rampant during his regime.

Somoza's decisive decline dates from January 1978, when the assassination of La Prensa editor Pedro Joaquin Chamorro, his leading critic, triggered riots, a general strike, and calls for resignation. Sandinista insurgents, previously impotent, garnered support from many Nicaraguan people, plus sympathetic states such as Venezuela, Mexico, Costa Rica, and Panama. First the Inter-American Commission on Human Rights, then the UN General Assembly, censured atrocities they attributed to Somoza's National Guard. The United States suspended military assistance and instigated OAS mediation in 1978 to ease Somoza out of office. When those measures failed, the Carter Administration terminated all U.S. aid except humanitarian programs, recalled the U.S. military mission and Peace Corps personnel, then drastically reduced the embassy staff early in 1979. Senior

U.S. spokesmen subsequently called publicly and privately for Somoza to resign. He fled Nicaragua on July 17, 1979, assailed politically from all sides and bereft of material support, when the Sandinistas launched their final offensive from sanctuaries in Costa Rica.

Key Congressional Actions

Congress expressed intense and continuing interest, but there was no consensus. Many Members opposed Somoza. Others preferred him to leftist Sandinistas, who replaced him.

Outcome: Mixed opinion

The United States satisfied interests in human rights, but serious U.S. problems with Marxist Sandinistas cropped up almost immediately (Case 50). The wisdom of U.S. decisionmakers in this conflict remains subject to debate.

Selected Sources

Pastor, Robert A., *Condemned to Repetition: The United States and Nicaragua*, Princeton, N.J., Princeton University Press, 1987, p. 49-187.

LeoGrande, William M., "The Revolution in Nicaragua: Another Cuba?" *Foreign Affairs*, Fall 1979, p. 28-50; Fagan, Richard R., "Dateline Nicaragua: The End of the Affair," *Foreign Policy*, Fall 1979, p. 178-191.

Christian, Shirley, *Nicaragua : Revolution in the Family*, NY, Random House, 1985, p. 34-118.

CASE 45

IRAN (1979-)

Type Conflict	Combatting terrorism
Duration	11 years plus (still active)
Participants	*U.S. Allies*: Counterterrorism community *U.S. Adversaries*: Iran; associated terrorist groups
U.S. Purposes	*Interests*: International security *Objectives*: Deter transnational terrorism by Iran
Predominant U.S. Power	Politico-military; economic
Predominant U.S. Instrument	Sanctions; covert operations
U.S. Armed Forces	*Predominant Type*: Special operations *Predominant Services*: Multiservice *Predominant Function*: Hostage rescue
Public Opinion	*U.S.*: Supportive *International*: U.S. allies confused

Context

Revolutionaries toppled the Shah of Iran on January 16, 1979. The Ayatollah Khomeini, who replaced him, reviled the United States (the Great Satan), which had supported the Shah since CIA helped restore him to the Peacock Throne a quarter century earlier (see Case 20). Transnational terrorism has been one manifestation of Iranian animosity. The first instance occurred when radical "students" seized the U.S. Embassy in Teheran on November 4, 1979 and held 52 Americans hostage for 444 days. Terrorists organized, trained, equipped, financed, and/or encouraged by Iran subsequently attacked the U.S. Embassy, its annex, and a Marine barrack in Beirut; attacked U.S., French, and indigenous facilities in Kuwait (December 1983); hid U.S. and other hostages elsewhere in Lebanon; and probably sabotaged a Pan Am flight over Lockerbie, Scotland. Less flamboyant acts have been commonplace.

American countermeasures have taken place in conjunction with efforts to prevent the spread of radical religious fundamentalism to moderate Islamic nations in the Middle East. Two U.S. covert counterterror operations culminated in overt failures: the abortive attempt to retrieve hostages from Teheran in April 1980; the sale of U.S. arms to Iran (1985-86) with the expectation that Iran would expedite the return of hostages held in Lebanon (three may have been released for that reason). The United States, starting in 1979, severed diplomatic relations with Iran, terminated assistance programs, imposed severe restrictions on exports, imports, and travel, froze Iranian assets in the United States, and forbade financial transactions. The United States later led international efforts that denied Iran easy access to foreign arms during its war with Iraq. None of those sanctions has significantly deterred Iran's tendencies toward transnational terrorism. Khomeini's death in 1989 made little discernible difference until April-May 1990, when Iran apparently helped secure the release of two U.S. hostages held in Beirut.

Key Congressional Actions

Congress mandated some of the sanctions against Iran, but its members were not informed beforehand about U.S. covert operations. The Desert One raid and arms sales to Iran both became contentious issues after the fact.

Outcome: Mixed opinion

The United States has not yet accomplished its basic objective. Covert operations failed. Whether sanctions have reduced Iran's proclivities and capabilities for transnational terrorism is subject to debate.

Escalation Potential: Warm; probability moderate

Selected Sources

Stempel, John D., *Inside the Iranian Revolution*, Bloomington, IN, Indiana University Press, 1981, p. 165-262.

Beckwith, Charlie A. and Donald Knox, *Delta Force*, NY, Harcourt Brace Jovanovich, 1983, p. 187-300.

Galdi, Theodor and Robert D. Shuey, *U.S. Economic Sanctions Imposed Against Specific Foreign Countries: 1979 to the Present*, Washington, Congressional Research Service, December 1, 1987, p. 97-103.

Mark, Clyde R., *Lebanon : The Remaining Hostages*, Issue Brief IB 85183, Washington, Congressional Research Service, May 4, 1990, 15 p.

U.S. Congress, *Iran-Contra Affair*, Report of the Congressional Committees Investigating the, S. Rept. No. 100-216, H. Rept. No. 100-433, 100th Congress, 1st Session, Washington, U.S. GPO, November 1987, p. 157-281, 519-558.

CASE 46

SYRIA (1979-)

Type Conflict	Combatting terrorism
Duration	11 years, plus (still active)
Participants	*U.S. Allies*: Counterterrorism community *U.S. Adversaries*: Syria; associated terrorist groups
U.S. Purposes	*Interests*: International Security *Objectives*: Deter transnational terrorism by Syria
Predominant U.S. Power	Political; economic
Predominant U.S. Instrument	Sanctions
U.S. Armed Forces	Not applicable
Public Opinion	*U.S.*: Supportive *International*: European Community generally supportive

Context

Syria, in pursuit of Arab leadership and in consonance with anti-Israel goals, sponsored or otherwise supported transnational terrorism well before the U.S. Department of State published its first official list of culpable countries in 1979. The Abu Nidal Organization (ANO), Abu Mussa, Democratic Front for the Liberation of Palestine (DFLP), Hizballah, Kurdish Workers Party (PKK), Lebanese Armed Revolutionary Faction (LARF), Palestine Liberation Front (PLF), Popular Front for the Liberation of Palestine (PFLP), and Syrian Socialist Nationalist Party are prominent among groups that enjoy sanctuaries in Syria or Syrian occupied Lebanon. Most of them receive financial assistance, equipment, supplies, and training. Additional recipients include "outsiders" as disparate as the Armenian Liberation Organization, Japanese Red Army, and the Patami Liberation Organization of Thailand. Israel, its associates, Jordan, and Turkey have most often been targets.

The Syrian Government has tried to improve its image in recent years, but U.S. sanctions designed to deter further Syrian terrorism nevertheless remain in full effect. Exports of items that conceivably could embellish Syria's military or transnational terrorist capabilities are strictly controlled. Applications for export licenses seldom are approved. Even indirect U.S. aid is proscribed, unless the President certifies that case-by-case exceptions would serve U.S. interests better.

Key Congressional Actions

Congress and the Executive Branch have collaborated closely in imposing sanctions on Syria.

Outcome: Mixed opinion

The United States has not yet accomplished its basic objective. Whether sanctions have reduced Syria's proclivities and capabilities for transnational terrorism is subject to debate.

Escalation Potential: Warm; probability moderate

Selected Sources

Patterns of Global Terrorism: 1988, Washington, Dept. of State, March 1989, p. 46-47; *1989 Annual Foreign Policy Report to the Congress*, (January 21, 1989-January 20, 1990, Washington, Dept. of Commerce, 1989, p. 9-10, 12, 14, 16-17, 18-19, 21, 22.

Galdi, Theodor and Robert D. Shuey, *U.S. Economic Sanctions Imposed Against Specific Foreign Countries: 1979 to the Present*, Washington, Congressional Research Service, December 1, 1987, p. 199-202.

CASE 47

EL SALVADOR (1979-)

Type Conflict	Counterinsurgency
Duration	11 years plus (still active)
Participants	*U.S. Allies*: El Salvador Government; Central America, except Nicaragua *U.S. Adversaries*: Salvadoran insurgents; Soviet Union; Nicaragua; Cuba
U.S. Purposes	*Interests*: Western Hemisphere security *Objectives*: Contain communism; ensure a friendly Salvadoran Government
Predominant U.S. Power	Political-military; economic
Predominant U.S. Instrument	Security assistance
U.S. Armed Forces	*Predominant Type*: Special operations *Predominant Services*: Army *Predominant Function*: Advice; training
Public Opinion	*U.S.*: Generally supportive *International*: Latin America generally supportive

Context

El Salvador experienced a series of unstable, unelected governments from October 1979, when moderate colonels conducted a coup, until Napoleon Duarte was elected President in May 1984. Each administration, plagued by reactionaries who preferred the status quo and left-wing radicals who insisted on faster change, sought unsuccessfully to promote useful reforms. Guerrilla groups, which activated the Farabundo Marti National Liberation Front (FMLN) in 1980, overran rural areas and mounted massive urban strikes. Politically-motivated murders and other human rights abuse by both sides were commonplace. U.S. economic assistance during this period increased substantially. Congress, however, routinely reduced military aid requests and imposed tight controls over U.S. military and police training missions to discourage repressive measures by the government.

Duarte's enlightened programs, coupled with more munificent U.S. aid, ameliorated those trends temporarily. Many observers believed he had won the war, but their optimism proved premature. Duarte's party, unable to revive the economy or end the conflict despite repeated negotiations, splintered when it lost popular support. Rightists, headed by Alfredo

Cristiani, replaced him during the first peaceful transfer of power between elected civilians since El Salvador became a state in 1825. Political polarization nevertheless inspired renewed attacks by insurgents armed with new Soviet bloc weapons, some from Nicaragua. The response was increased repression, and the war continues with no early end in sight.

Key Congressional Actions

Congress controlled types and amounts of U.S. aid to El Salvador. It also closely monitored the size and activities of the U.S. military mission.

Outcome: Mixed opinion

The United States has not yet accomplished its basic objectives. Whether U.S. military aid levels have helped or hindered progress remains controversial.

Escalation Potential: Warm; probability moderate

Selected Sources

Bacevich, A.J. et al, *American Military Policy in Small Wars: The Case of El Salvador*, NY, Pergamon-Brassey's, 1988, 52 p.

Congressional Research Service, Washington: Storrs, Larry, *El Salvador Highlights, 1960-1990: A Summary of Major Turning Points in Salvadoran History and U.S. Policy*, March 13, 1990, 19 p. and *El Salvador Under Cristiani: U.S. Foreign Assistance Decisions*, Issue Brief IB 89122, February 15, 1990, 15 p.; *El Salvador, 1979-1989: A Briefing Book on U.S. Aid and the Situation in El Salvador*, April 28, 1989, 109 p. ; Wootten, James P., *El Salvador : Status of the War and the Role of U.S. Aid*, April 4, 1990, 19 p.

El Salvador : Pipeline of U.S. Military and Economic Aid : Fact Sheet for the Honorable Edward M. Kennedy, U.S. Senate, Washington, General Accounting Office, February 23, 1990, 15 p.

CASE 48

BOLIVIA (1980-86)

Type Conflict	Narco conflict
Duration	July 1980-July 1986 (6 years)
Participants	*U.S. Allies*: None *U.S. Adversaries*: Bolivian drug traffickers
U.S. Purposes	*Interests*: National security; law and order *Objectives*: Deter illegal drug trade by Bolivian officials; reduce traffic volume
Predominant U.S. Power	Political; economic
Predominant U.S. Instrument	Sanctions
U.S. Armed Forces	Not applicable
Public Opinion	*U.S.*: Supportive *International*: Supportive

Context

A military junta, charging the civilian government with "communism, Castroism, and anarchy," seized control of Bolivia in July 1980, determined to remove the "Marxist cancer." Violence and human rights violations marked the transition. The United States recalled its ambassador, suspended all aid, and withdrew the U.S. military mission. It also ceased narcotics control cooperation with Bolivia, because the new strong man and senior members of his Administration were personally profiting from cocaine traffic.

Bolivia changed chiefs of state through a coup in 1981, again in 1982, and by election in 1985. Each paid lip service to the war against drugs, but extreme instability, combined with political and economic obstacles, made progress minuscule, even after Bolivia in 1983 agreed to reduce coca production in return for U.S. aid. The International Security and Development Cooperation Act of 1985 therefore specified that Bolivia could receive up to 50% of earmarked Emergency Support Funds (ESF) and military assistance only if it legally established acceptable controls over coca production. The remainder would be forthcoming only after the U.S. President certified that Bolivia had eradicated crops as prescribed in the 1983 agreement. Congress withheld $7.2 million in 1986, when Bolivia failed to comply. U.S. stipulations subsequently relaxed and sanctions ceased, essentially because the Bolivian Government, as evidence of good faith, asked U.S. civilian and military drug interdiction teams to participate actively within its borders.

Key Congressional Actions

Congressional legislation caused Bolivia to instigate and sustain serious drug interdiction programs.

Outcome: Success

The United States accomplished its basic objectives at little cost in a reasonable time period. Drug interdiction in Bolivia continues to be a joint venture (see Case 58).

Selected Sources

Galdi, Theodor W. and Robert D. Shuey, *U.S. Economic Sanctions Imposed Against Specific Foreign Countries: 1979 to the Present*, Washington, Congressional Research Service, December 1, 1987, p. 23-27.

International Narcotics Control Strategy Report to the Committee on Foreign Relations and the Committee on Foreign Affairs, Washington, Bureau of International Narcotic Matters, Dept. of State, 1984, p. 31-37; 1985, p. 44-54; 1985 Update, p. 22-25; 1986, p. 53-67.

CASE 49

AFGHANISTAN (1980-)

Type Conflict	Resistance
Duration	10 years plus (still active)
Participants	*U.S. Allies*: *Mujahiddin*; Pakistan *U.S. Adversaries*: Afghan Government; Soviet Union
U.S. Purposes	*Interests*: National Defense *Objectives*: Contain communism; defeat Soviet aggression; ensure an Afghan Government friendly to the United States
Predominant U.S. Power	Political; economic
Predominant U.S. Instrument	Security assistance; sanctions
U.S. Armed Forces	Not applicable
Public Opinion	*U.S.*: Supportive *International*: U.S. associates supportive

Context

Insurgent attacks on the Soviet-backed Afghan Government began in April 1978. Soviet armed forces, which intervened on Christmas Eve 1979 to preserve faltering allies, fought an unsuccessful war of attrition against *Mujahiddin* resistance until the United Nations arranged an interim settlement. The Soviet rear guard withdrew on February 15, 1989. Observers who predicted that Afghan guerrillas would emerge victorious soon thereafter, however, were surprised, because the war continues with no winner in sight.

U.S. policymakers, who viewed the Soviet invasion as a possible threat to Pakistan and the Persian Gulf, took immediate countermeasures. U.S. efforts to influence the action were oblique from the beginning. Political, economic, and military sanctions against the Afghan Government were one manifestation, but diplomatic support for resistance movements, coupled with security assistance and funds for humanitarian purposes, was much more important. Material aid, channelled through Pakistan, became progressively more expansive and overt after 1983. Arms, for example, initially were limited to Soviet bloc models or facsimiles thereof. Later they included other systems, especially U.S. Stinger antiaircraft missiles. Total funding thus far reportedly approximates $2 billion. The United States did not contribute directly to the UN-brokered accords that led to Soviet departure, but both superpowers therein agreed to "refrain from any form of interference in the internal affairs" of Afghanistan or Pakistan. Conflict in Afghanistan coincidentally terminated U.S. detente with the Soviet Union, which had held since the 1960s. U.S. poitical and economic sanctions were important manifestations.

Key Congressional Actions

Congress rapidly increased the quantity and quality of U.S. assistance to Afghan resistance, starting in 1984. It also influenced aid policies after Soviet forces withdrew.

Outcome: Mainly success

The United States helped defeat Soviet aggression, which was the basic objective. Whether a non-communist Afghanistan friendly to the United States eventually will emerge as uncertain. Both superpowers still assist their clients, despite contrary guarantees in the treaty.

Escalation Potential: Cool; probably low

Selected Sources

Collins, Joseph J., *The Soviet Invasion of Afghanistan: A Case Study in the Use of Force in Soviet Foreign Policy*, Lexington, MA, Lexington Books, 1986, 195 p.

Congressional Research Service, Washington: Cronin, Richard P. and Francis T. Miko, *Afghanistan: Status, U.S. Role, and Implications of a Soviet Withdrawal*, Issue Brief IB 88049, January 6, 1989, 16 p.; Cronin, Richard P., *Afghanistan Peace Talks: An Annotated Chronology and Analysis of the United Nations-Sponsored Negotiations*, February 19, 1988, 37 p., and *Afghanistan After the Soviet Withdrawal: Contenders for Power*, March 2, 1989, 39 p.

Isby, David C., *War in a Distant Country, Afghanistan : Invasion and Resistance*, NY, Sterling Publishing Co., 1989, 128 p.

CASE 50

NICARAGUA (1981-90)

Type Conflict	Resistance
Duration	9 years
Participants	*U.S. Allies*: Contras; some Central American countries
	U.S. Adversaries: Sandinista Government; Soviet Union; Cuba
U.S. Purposes	*Interests*: Western Hemisphere security
	Objectives: Contain communism; ensure a Nicaraguan Government friendly to the United States
Predominant U.S. Power	Politico-military; economic
Predominant U.S. Instrument	Sanctions; security assistance
U.S. Armed Forces	*Predominant Type*: Special operations
	Predominant Services: Army
	Predominant Function: Advice; training
Public Opinion	*U.S.*: Divided
	International: Adverse in Central America

Context

U.S. policymakers initially sought accommodation with the Sandinistas, who deposed Somoza in 1979 (Case 44). Aid, however, shifted from the new Nicaraguan Government to Contra rivals in 1981, after Sandinista connections with the Soviet bloc and subversive activities became clear. The purposes of U.S. support, as variously professed, were to help interdict Sandinista supplies for Salvadoran insurgents, compel Sandinista reforms, overthrow the Sandinista Government, and/or promote a negotiated settlement. Whether sufficient military aid for the Contras might have achieved those aims became moot, because (except for sizable allocations in 1986) all was "non-lethal" after 1984, when CIA displeased Congress by covertly mining three Nicaraguan ports.

The infamous Iran-Contra affair ensued when frustrated officials in the National Security Council tried to outflank that injunction. U.S. sanctions against the Sandinista Government were severe. Embargoes on trade and credit, combined with Sandinista ineptitudes and war costs, caused Nicaragua's GNP to dive and inflation to soar. U.S. military shows of force in Honduras near Nicaragua's border also exerted some pressure on the Sandinistas.

Repeated efforts by Central American governments to mediate produced the first positive results in 1987 and, after several false starts, culminated with free elections on February 26, 1990. The United Nicaraguan Opposition (UNO) decisively defeated the Sandinistas, who retain a potent political machine, maintain a strong presence in the security forces and, in former President Ortega's words, vow to "rule from below." The shooting war seems over, but the contest for political control may continue.

Key Congressional Actions

Congress placed stringent controls on the type and amount of aid to the Contras, on U.S. covert activities, and authorized sanctions against the Nicaraguan Government in addition to those imposed by the Executive Branch.

Outcome: Mixed opinion

The United States may have accomplished its basic objectives (more time will tell). Whether other methods might have produced comparable results less painfully remains a controversial topic.

Selected Sources

Pastor, Robert A., *Condemned to Repetition: The United States and Nicaragua*, Princeton, NJ, Princeton University Press, 1987, p. 191-320, 348-379.

Turner, Robert F., *Nicaragua v. United States: A Look At the Facts*, NY, Pergamon-Brassey's, 1987, 159 p.

U.S. Congress, *Iran-Contra Affair*; Report of the Congressional Committees Investigating the, S. Rept. No. 100-216, H. Rept. No. 100-433, 100th Congress, 1st Session, Washington, U.S. GPO, November 1987, p. 1-153, 395-421, 483-516.

Congressional Research Service, Washington: Serafino, Nina M., *Nicaragua: Conditions and Issues for U.S. Policy*, Issue Brief IB 82115, February 21, 1990, 17 p. and *U.S. Assistance to Nicaraguan Guerrillas: Issues for Congress*, Issue Brief IB 84139, p. 5-10; Serafino, Nina M., and Maureen Taft-Morales, *Contra Aid: Summary and Chronology of Major Congressional Action, 1981-1989*, November 1, 1989, 19 p.

CASE 51

FALKLAND ISLANDS (1982)

Type Conflict	Nonviolent conflict (hands off support)
Duration	April 2 - June 14, 1982 (74 days)
Participants	*U.S. Allies*: Britain *U.S. Adversaries*: Argentina
U.S. Purposes	*Interests*: NATO solidarity; peace *Objectives*: Prevent war; prevent avoidable escalation; prevent Argentine victory
Predominant U.S. Power	Politico-military
Predominant U.S. Instrument	Diplomacy; intelligence; airlift
U.S. Armed Forces	*Predominant Type*: Conventional *Predominant Services*: Air Force *Predominant Function*: Airlift
Public Opinion	*U.S.*: Supportive *International*: Latin Americans opposed U.S. pro-Britain policies

Context

Argentina and Britain both laid claim to the Falkland Islands early in the 19th Century. Recurring controversy over sovereignty rights culminated on April 2, 1982 after 17 years of fruitless UN-instigated negotiations. Argentina's ruling junta at that juncture landed troops in the Falklands to resolve the issue, and retained them there despite a UN Security Council resolution that requested their recall. Britain, in response, dispatched a fleet toward those islands, with marines and special operations forces embarked.

U.S. Secretary of State Haig personally commenced mediation on April 7, in efforts to avert armed conflict. Diplomacy of the most delicate kind was required for two basic reasons: both belligerents were U.S. allies (Britain belonged to NATO, Argentina to the Rio Pact); U.S. ties to Britain were far tighter than those with Argentina, but success depended on impartiality. Maintenance of the *status quo ante* bellum was a U.S. objective, partly because approving Argentine actions would reward pugnacity. U.S. and international intercession nevertheless failed, partly because both sides took inflexible positions. The United States abstained when the Organization of American States (OAS) on April 28 approved Argentina's claim to sovereignty over the Falklands, and abandoned neutrality entirely on April 30, 1982. U.S. sanctions against Argentina and publicly announced support for Britain followed immediately. U.S. assistance, especially satellite photography, other intelligence, and supplies airlifted to Ascension Island contributed to the British victory on June 14, 1982. Strategic Air Command (SAC) tankers relieved British tankers of NATO duties during this conflict.

Key Congressional Actions: None

Outcome: Mixed opinion

The United States accomplished only one of its basic objectives. Whether open U.S. preference for Britain best served U.S. interests in Latin America is doubtful.

Selected Sources

Perspectives on Negotiation: Four Case Studies and Interpretations, Ed. by Diane B. Bendahmane and John W. McDonald, Jr., Washington, Foreign Service Institute, Dept. of State, 1986, p. 51-97.

Facts on File Yearbook, 1982, NY, Facts on File, Inc, 1983, p. 237-239, 261-262, 277-278, 301-303, 317-319, 337-338, 353-355, 377-380, 393-394, 416-417, 429-431.

Kinney, Douglas, *National Interest, National Honor : The Diplomacy of the Falklands Crisis*, NY, Praeger, 1989, 392 p.

Preece, Charlotte Phillips, *The Falkland/Malvinas Islands Crisis*, Issue Brief IB82052, Washington, Congressional Research Service, July 15, 1982, 25 p.

CASE 52

LEBANON (1982-84)

Type Conflict	Peacekeeping; peacemaking
Duration	August 25, 1982-February 26, 1984 (1 year, 6 months)
Participants	*U.S. Allies*: Lebanese Government; France; Italy; Britain *U.S. Adversaries*: Factions opposing the U.S.-backed Lebanese Government
U.S. Purposes	*Interests*: Peace in the Middle East *Objectives*: Facilitate conflict deescalation; facilitate control by the Lebanese Government
Predominant U.S. Power	Military
Predominant U.S. Instrument	Peacekeeping forces
U.S. Armed Forces	*Predominant Type*: Conventional *Predominant Services*: Marine Corps *Predominant Function*: Interposition
Public Opinion	*U.S.*: Positive until August 1983; then negative *International*: Variable

Context

Israeli Defense Forces (IDF) invaded Lebanon in June 1982 and, assisted by Phalangists (right-wing Christians), trapped 15,000 Palestinian and Syrian troops in West Beruit. To forestall further urban combat, the United States, France, and Italy formed a Multinational Force (MNF) as requested by the Lebanese Government, helped empty the pocket safely, and departed by mid-September.

The Lebanese President almost immediately asked the MNF to return, after the President-elect was assassinated, the IDF seized West Beruit, and massacres occurred in two refugee camps. Respective governments agreed. An augmented MNF that later included British troops temporarily restored relative tranquility when it interposed contingents between belligerents in Beirut. The tempo, however, picked up in April 1983. First, a bomb levelled the U.S. Embassy. Militia battles in the hills subsequently spilled into Beirut. They intensified during the summer, after the IDF announced intentions to pull back. U.S. positions ashore increasingly came under fire by August. U.S.

naval forces afloat returned it. *Peacemaking* replaced *peacekeeping*. The climax came on October 23, 1983, when the world's largest conventional explosion obliterated a Marine barrack in Beirut, leaving 241 dead. The last U.S. Marines withdrew from Lebanon on February 26, 1984, partly in response to immense political pressures in the United States. U.S. Sixth Fleet disengaged completely by March 30.

Key Congressional Actions

President Reagan kept Congress informed, "consistent with" the War Powers Resolution. Congress tacitly approved until casualties began to mount in mid-1983 and peacekeeping became a dubious mission. A resolution in October 1983 limited U.S. troop deployments to 18 more months.

Outcome: Failure

The United States ultimately accomplished none of its basic objectives. Questionable U.S. performance and high casualties caused a storm of controversy that adversely affected many careers and caused fundamental changes in procedure.

Selected Sources

Report of the DOD Commission on Beirut International Airport Terrorist Act, October 23, 1983 (the Long Report), Washington, Department of Defense, December 20, 1983, 141 p.; U.S. Congress, House, *Adequacy of U.S. Marine Corps Security in Beirut*, report of the Investigations Subcommittee of the Committee on Armed Services, 98th Congress, 1st Session, Washington, U.S. GPO, December 19, 1983, 78 p. and accompanying *Summary of Findings and Conclusions*, 3 p.; Mark, Clyde R., *Marine Security in Beirut: A Comparison of the House Armed Services and Long Commission Reports*, Washington, Congressional Research Service, January 6, 1984, 13 p.

Bolger, Daniel P., *Americans at War, 1975-1986: An Era of Violent Peace*, Novato, CA, Presido Press, 1988, p. 191-260.

Frank, Benis A., *U.S. Marines in Lebanon, 1982-1984*, Washington, U.S. GPO, 1988, 196 p.

CASE 53

GRENADA (1983-84)

Type Conflict	Punitive expedition
Duration	October 25, 1983-December 4, 1984 (13 months)
Participants	*U.S. Allies*: Organization of Eastern Caribbean States (OECS) *U.S. Adversaries*: Grenadian Marxists; Cuba
U.S. Purposes	*Interests*: Western Hemisphere security *Objectives*: Contain communism; ensure a friendly government on Grenada
Predominant U.S. Power	Military
Predominant U.S. Instrument	Force
U.S. Armed Forces	*Predominant Type*: Conventional *Predominant Services*: Multiservice *Predominant Function*: Armed combat; civil affairs
Public Opinion	*U.S.*: Supportive *International*: Almost universally adverse, except OECS

Context

The New Jewel Movement of pro-Cuba Marxists seized control of Grenada in March 1979, suspended the constitution, and tightened ties with the Soviet bloc. A potential base from which to foment and support revolutions in the Caribbean Basin began to take shape the following year. A major airfield, munitions storage facilities, barracks, and training camps were prominent components. U.S. relations soured until October 1983 when, in rapid succession, military radicals overthrew Grenada's government, violence prevailed, and English-speaking members of OECS invited the United States to restore law, order, and democratic rule.

Operation Urgent Fury opened on October 25, 1983, accompanied by security contingents (mainly police) from four OESC countries--Antigua, Dominica, St. Lucia, and St. Vincent--plus Barbados and Jamaica. Montserrat and St. Kitts, along with Britain, Canada, and France, refused to participate. Resistance ceased officially on November 2. Cuban prisoners of war were repatriated. Captured arms and documents were displayed. The last U.S.

combatants departed by December 1983, but 250 U.S. military personnel remained as part of a multinational occupation force to ensure a peaceful transition period. Its status changed on December 4, 1984, when a newly-elected Prime Minister requested its continued presence until Grenada could organize, equip, and train its own administrators and police. The last U.S. forces left in September 1985.

Key Congressional Actions

Congress was briefed, but not consulted, before the operation began. War powers issues arose during and after the fact.

Outcome: Mixed opinion

The United States accomplished its basic objectives with few casualties. Whether the operation was justified still generates disagreements.

Selected Sources

Bolger, Daniel P., *Americans at War, 1975-1986: An Era of Violent Peace*, Novato, CA, Presidio Press, 1988, p. 261-358.

American Intervention in Grenada: The Implications of Operation Urgent Fury, Ed. by Peter M. Dunn and Bruce W. Watson, Boulder, CO, Westview Press, 1985, 185 p.

Hanover, Janice R., *Grenada : Issues Concerning the Use of U.S. Forces*, Issue Brief IB 83170, Washington, Congressional Research Service, February 22, 1984, 25 p.

CASE 54

PHILIPPINES (1984-)

Type Conflict	Counterinsurgency; countercoup
Duration	6 years plus (still active)
Participants	*U.S. Allies*: Philippine Government
	U.S. Adversaries: Philippine insurgents; anti-government groups
U.S. Purposes	*Interests*: National defense
	Objectives: Contain communism; ensure a friendly Philippine Government
Predominant U.S. Power	Economic
Predominant U.S. Instrument	Security Assistance
U.S. Armed Forces	*Predominant Type*: Conventional
	Predominant Services: Air Force
	Predominant Function: Deterrence
Public Opinion	*U.S.*: Supportive
	International: Generally supportive

Context

The Philippines remained peaceful for more than a decade after President Ramon Magsaysay defeated the Huks in 1955 (see Case 16). Political corruption, economic crises, crumbling social structures, and human rights abuse, however, helped communist insurgents stage a comeback during President Ferdinand Marcos' second term. By 1972, he suspended the constitution, declared martial law, and imposed censorship to counter insurrections.

Senior U.S. officials, preoccupied with perceived Soviet threats, nevertheless supported Marcos until 1984, when Philippine insurgents attracted their attention with threats to evict U.S. forces from Clark AB, Subic Bay, and other linchpin facilities. Marcos, an obvious liability, departed under U.S. pressure in 1986 (Case 55). Several factors have limited U.S. foreign internal defense (FID) efforts since President Corazon Aquino replaced him. The Philippine bureaucracy requires reform before it can expedite important political and economic improvements. Serious social problems consequently continue to serve insurgent causes. Neither U.S. nor multilateral assistance has yet been adequate to reverse that trend. Philippine armed forces remain less effective than required, partly because few units are skilled at counterinsurgency, partly because of factionalism.

Recalcitrants among them have conducted four unsuccessful coups against Mrs. Aquino (U.S. military intervention probably saved her in December 1989). Meanwhile, insurgency remains entrenched and its growth, currently contained, could renew. The murder of U.S. servicemen in May 1990 during base rights negotiations is one such indication.

Key Congressional Actions

Congress boosted aid to the Philippines in 1986. Subsequent appropriations have been substantial, but below that level.

Outcome: Mixed opinion

President Aquino inherited many problems from her predecessor. Optimists emphasize subsequent progress. Pessimists stress persistent obstacles, including governmental deficiencies.

Escalation Potential: Hot; probability high

Selected Sources

Steinberg, David Joel, *The Philippines: A Singular and Plural Place*, Boulder, CO, Westview Press, 1982, p. 99-130.

U.S. Congress, Senate, *Insurgency and Counterinsurgency in the Philippines*, prepared for the Committee on Foreign Relations by the Congressional Research Service, 99th Congress, 1st Session, Washington, U.S., GPO, November 1985, 56 p., and Niksch, Larry A., *Philippines Under Aquino*, Issue Brief IB 86104, Washington, Congressional Research Service, March 27, 1990, 13 p.

CASE 55

PHILIPPINES (1985-86)

Type Conflict	Coup d'etat
Duration	January 1985-February 1986 (14 months)
Participants	*U.S. Allies*: none
	U.S. Adversaries: Marcos Government
U.S. Purposes	*Interests*: National defense
	Objectives: Encourage Marcos to institute reforms or resign
Predominant U.S. Power	Political; economic
Predominant U.S. Instrument	Diplomacy; sanctions and associated threats
U.S. Armed Forces	Not applicable
Public Opinion	*U.S.*: Supportive
	International: Generally supportive

Context

President Ferdinand Marcos was part of the problem, rather than part of the solution, while Philippine insurgents steadily gained strength (Case 54). The assassination of opposition leader Benigno Aquino, Jr. on August 21, 1983, which magnified domestic and U.S. disapproval, commenced his downfall. U.S. officials, concerned about military base rights, proceeded cautiously at first, but pressures on Marcos and overtures to Philippine reformers escalated sharply early in 1985, because low-key encouragement was unproductive. Marcos nevertheless continued to resist change, threatened U.S. base agreements, and implied plans to improve relations with the Soviet Union. Ultimately, in mid-October, Senator Paul Laxalt (who was President Reagan's personal emissary) explained U.S. requirements in blunt terms.

Marcos emerged as the official winner of an unscheduled presidential election he called on February 7, 1986, partly in response to Laxalt's advice. U.S. spokesmen, aware of widespread fraud, promised to suspend aid unless he stepped down. U.S. officials also sided publicly with the "losing" candidate, Corazon Aquino, who was backed by the Minister of Defense, Deputy Chief of Staff, many armed forces, and civilian multitudes in nonviolent rebellion. President Reagan warned Marcos against reprisals and recommended that he resign. Marcos did so on February 25, 1986, hours after his inauguration, then departed the Philippines from Clark AB aboard a U.S. military aircraft. Aquino appointed her cabinet the next day.

Key Congressional Actions

Congress and the Executive Branch collaborated closely throughout this case. Both contributed political and economic pressures that helped topple Marcos.

Outcome: Success

The United States accomplished its basic objective without undesirable repercussions. One major impediment to essential reforms was removed.

Selected Sources

Niksch, Larry A., "Congress and the Philippines," in U.S. Congress, House, *Congress and Foreign Policy, 1985-86*, Committee on Foreign Affairs, 99th Congress, Washington, U.S. GPO, 1988, p. 158-175.

Facts on File Yearbook, NY, Facts on File, Inc., 1983, p. 637-638; 1985, p. 806, 845-846, 1986, p. 66-68, 121-123; Kessler, Richard J., "Marcos and the Americans," *Foreign Policy*, Summer 1986, p. 40-57.

CASE 56

HAITI (1985-86)

Type Conflict	Coup d'etat
Duration	November 28, 1985-February 25, 1986 (3 months)
Participants	*U.S. Allies*: none *U.S. Adversaries*: Duvalier Government
U.S. Purposes	*Interests*: Western Hemisphere stability; human rights *Objectives*: Encourage Duvalier to institute reforms or resign
Predominant U.S. Power	Political; economic
Predominant U.S. Instrument	Diplomacy; sanctions
U.S. Armed Forces	Not applicable
Public Opinion	*U.S.*: Supportive, but slight *International*: Slight

Context

The 29-year Duvalier dynasty dates from 1957, when Francois "Papa Doc" was elected President. He retained control by connivance and violence until 1971, then amended the Haitian Constitution so he could name his son Jean-Claude (Baby Doc) President-for-Life. Haiti remained poverty-stricken during his reign, one of the world's poorest countries where contrasts between rich and poor were appalling. Security forces ferociously suppressed all opposition. Haitian emigrants started to flood Florida in the early 1980s. Haiti began transshipping Colombian cocaine about the same time.

Communism was never a central U.S. issue in Haiti, as in other Latin American states (see Cases 23, 27, 29, 31, 33-34, 38, 44, 47, 50, 53). Congress, however, was seriously concerned about human rights violations. In 1983, it therefore conditioned continued U.S. aid on Presidential certifications that Haiti was making concerted efforts to improve in several respects. Required assurances were forthcoming as late as October 12, 1985, but ceased after a huge rebellion blossomed the following month. U.S. aid programs never had been lavish (half the amount for the neighboring Dominican Republic) and the cutoff lasted less than a month (January 30-February 25, 1986). The squeeze on Haiti's destitute economy, coupled with U.S. diplomatic pressure, nevertheless helped topple "Baby Doc," who fled the country on February 7,

1986 aboard a U.S. military aircraft. U.S. economic assistance resumed within three weeks.

Key Congressional Actions

Congress stipulated requirements that Haiti must meet to qualify for development assistance and suspended aid when Haiti failed to comply.

Outcome: Failure

The United States accomplished its basic objective, but "Duvalierism" persists without Duvalier. Two military coups have occurred since he left. Human rights and poverty remain unimproved. Most U.S. aid has been suspended since November 1987, except for funds to non-governmental organizations (NGOs).

Selected Sources

Taft-Morales, Maureen, *Haiti: Political Developments and U.S. Policy Concerns*, Issue Brief IB 88104, Washington, Congressional Research Service, March 14, 1989, 15 p.

Abbott, Elizabeth, *Haiti: The Duvaliers and Their Legacy*, NY, McGraw-Hill, 1988, p. 266-366.

Danner, Mark, "A Reporter at Large: Beyond the Mountains," *New Yorker*, Part I, November 27, 1989, p. 55-100; Part II, December 4, 1989, p. 111-140; Part III, December 11, 1989, p. 100-131.

CASE 57

ANGOLA (1986-)

Type Conflict	Resistance
Duration	4 years plus (still active)
Participants	*U.S. Allies*: UNITA; South Africa indirectly; UN
	U.S. Adversaries: MPLA; Cuba; USSR
U.S. Purposes	*Interests*: National security; commercial
	Objectives: Contain communism; encourage a negotiated settlement
Predominant U.S. Power	Political; economic
Predominant U.S. Instrument	Diplomacy; sanctions; security assistance
U.S. Armed Forces	Not applicable
Public Opinion	*U.S.*: Nearly nonexistent
	International: Black Africa opposed

Context

Three insurgent groups sought to replace Portugese rulers well before Angola gained independence. The Marxist MPLA (Popular Movement for the Liberation of Angola), which prevailed with Soviet aid and Cuban troop support, proclaimed the People's Republic of Angola in November 1975. One rival faction soon fizzled. UNITA (National Union for the Total Independence of Angola), backed by the United States and (until recently) by South Africa, still resists.

Covert U.S. assistance to counter communist influence started in the early 1960s, but ceased while Nixon was President, partly to avoid provoking Portugal. It resumed in 1975, when Soviet/Cuban involvement burgeoned. That act alienated Black Africa, because it seemingly allied the United States with South Africa. Congressionally imposed restrictions stopped U.S. aid for the next decade, until repealed in August 1985.

The United States has never recognized the MPLA and has imposed economic sanctions against that Marxist-Leninist entity since 1986. Covert aid for UNITA reportedly includes Stinger and TOW missiles. U.S. diplomatic efforts to expedite the complete withdrawal of all foreign armed forces and Soviet military advisers from Angola produced a ceasefire in August 1988. South Africa thereafter cancelled all military aid to UNITA and withdrew its forces to Namibia. About 2/3 of the 50,000 Cuban troops in Angola have left.

The remainder are scheduled to depart by July 1, 1991 under United Nations supervision. The USA and USSR in collaboration are pressing both sides to negotiate an early settlement.

Key Congressional Actions

Congress has controlled the amount and type of U.S. aid to Angola since 1976. It formally approves the continued U.S. quest for a peaceful solution to that civil war.

Outcome: Mixed opinion

The United States has achieved neither of its basic objectives as yet, but it has helped stabilize a potentially explosive situation. Whether continued U.S. support for UNITA produces positive or negative results is controversial.

Escalation Potential: Cool; probability low

Selected Sources

Congressional Research Service, Washington: Branaman, Brenda M., *Angola/Namibia Negotiations*, Issue Brief IB 89047, February 8, 1990, 14 p.; Copson, Raymond W. and Robert B. Shepard, *Angola: Issues for the United States*, Issue Brief IB 81063, July 7, 1988, 15 p.; Copson, Raymond W., *Angola: Conflict Assessment and U.S. Policy Options*, December 8, 1986, 49 p.

U.S. Congress, House, *Angola: Should the United States Support UNITA?*, Hearings Before the Permanent Select Committee on Intelligence, 99th Congress, 2d Session, Washington, U.S. GPO, March 13, 1986, 60 p.

U.S. Congress, House, *Angola: Intervention or Negotiation*, Hearings Before the Subcommittee on Africa of the Committee on Foreign Affairs, 99th Congress, 1st Session, Washington, U.S. GPO, 1986, 200 p.

CASE 58

NARCO CONFLICT (1986-)

Type Conflict	Drug interdiction; combatting terrorism
Duration	4 years plus (still active)
Participants	*U.S. Allies*: Many governments *U.S. Adversaries*: Illegal international drug traffickers and governments that tolerate them
U.S. Purposes	*Interests*: National security; domestic tranquility *Objectives*: Greatly reduce the introduction of illegal narcotics into the United States and to U.S. associates; sever symbiotic connections between drug cartels and insurgents/transnational terrorists.
Predominant U.S. Power	Law enforcement; diplomacy
Predominant U.S. Instrument	Multifaceted collaboration with foreign officials
U.S. Armed Forces	*Predominant Type*: Conventional; special operations *Predominant Services*: Multiservice *Predominant Function*: Variable
Public Opinion	*U.S.*: Supportive *International*: Generally supportive of measures that require no U.S. troops.

Context

The United States fought and won its first great drug "war" early in this century, but narco conflict on a global scale is a new phenomenon of immensely greater magnitude. Smugglers annually saturate U.S. markets with illicit cocaine, heroin, and marijuana worth billions of dollars wholesale. Huge profits enable some cartels to raise and support private "armies," even become shadow governments. U.S. domestic tranquility and national security interests both are endangered.

U.S. drug control policies and programs increasingly seek to disrupt illegal processing, shipment, and sales by major drug trafficking organizations. Action to eradicate coca, opium, and marijuana crops in 14 countries is a favored part of that process, because it reduces drug supplies at the source. Alternative incomes for the "farmers" is an important aspect. Attempts to interdict illegal drug traffic before it enters the United States by land, sea, or air constitute a complementary step. P.L. 100-456, dated September 29, 1989, prescribes and delimits participation by U.S. armed services. Bilateral and multilateral collaboration is obligatory, with particular attention to intelligence sharing. The United States helps more than 70 Third World countries plan and implement law enforcement programs designed to disrupt drug cartels. Andean initiatives that involve Bolivia, Columbia, and Peru are central. U.S. sanctions exert pressure on selected states that tolerate the production or transshipment of illegal narcotics on their territory. A so-called "czar" was appointed in 1989 to coordinate the activities of 50-some U.S. federal departments, agencies, bureaus, and other executive entities that share drug control responsibilities.

Key Congressional Actions

Congressional legislation has increasingly influenced U.S. drug control policies and programs since 1986. Prescriptions cover virtually every aspect.

Outcome: Mixed opinion

The United States has accomplished neither of its basic objectives, but it is too early to predict the ultimate outcome. This conflict has scarcely started, and likely will be long. The proper blend of possible solutions to complex problems awaits further study and experiments.

Escalation Potential: Hot; probability high

Selected Sources

International Narcotics Control Strategy Report, Washington, Dept. of State, Bureau of International Narcotics Matters, March 1990, 401 p.; March 1989, 235 p.; March 1988, 289 p.

National Drug Control Strategy, Washington, The White House, January 1990, p. 49-72, 83-98, 111-112.

Perl, Raphael F., Washington, Congressional Research Service: *Drug Control: International Policy and Options*, Issue Brief IB 88093, March 19, 1990, 15 p. and *Congress and International Narcotics Control*, October 16, 1989, 27 p.

The Border War on Drugs, OTA-0-336, Office of Technology Assessment, Washington, U.S. GPO, March 1987, 62 p.; Reuter, Peter et al, *Sealing the Borders: the Effects of Increased Military Participation in Drug Interdiction*, Santa Monica, CA, RAND, January 1988, 155 p.

CASE 59

PERSIAN GULF (1987-88)

Type Conflict	Protective expedition
Duration	July 1987-December 1988 (1 year, 6 months)
Participants	*U.S. Allies*: Several NATO members; Japan; Australia; friendly Persian Gulf states
	U.S. Adversaries: Iran; Soviet Union indirectly
U.S. Purposes	*Interests*: National security; petroleum
	Objectives: Safeguard U.S.-flagged ships in the Persian Gulf; deter attacks against the western shore; contain communism and militant Shiite fundamentalism
Predominant U.S. Power	Naval
Predominant U.S. Instrument	Force; threats of force
U.S. Armed Forces	*Predominant Type*: Conventional
	Predominant Services: Navy
	Predominant Function: Protect U.S. ships
Public Opinion	*U.S.*: Generally supportive
	International: U.S. allies generally supportive

Context

The Iran-Iraq war erupted in September 1980. Iraq soon started to attack petroleum tankers enroute to and from Iranian ports in the northern Persian Gulf. Iran reciprocated against merchant ships headed for or away from Arab harbors on the western shore early in 1984, after Iraq extended its tanker campaigns farther south. Iran later laid antiship mines and deployed antiship missiles.

U.S. officials became increasingly concerned about the availability of Persian Gulf petroleum when the war escalated sharply in 1987 and feared that the Soviet Union might exploit unstable situations. The Reagan Administration therefore agreed when Kuwait, a prime target, requested permission to fly the U.S. flag from 11 of its tankers. The U.S. Navy started to escort those ships in July. It protected 136 convoys during the next 18 months (reflagged Kuwaiti tankers accounted for 188 of 270 ships therein). Britain, France, and Italy provided similar service for their respective merchantmen. They also participated in minesweeping operations, along with three other allies. Friendly Persian Gulf states furnished some facilities, surveillance aircraft, and/or otherwise simplified U.S. missions. Assorted U.S. special operations, a day-long naval battle in April 1988, and the accidental destruction of an Iranian airliner by the Aegis-armed cruiser *USS Vincennes* punctuated otherwise relatively routine U.S. activities. A UN-arranged cease-fire took effect on August 20, 1988. The U.S. Navy discontinued convoy escorts the following December.

Key Congressional Actions

The War Powers Resolution became a prominent congressional concern, particularly after Iraqi missiles killed 37 and wounded 21 crewmen aboard the guided missile frigate *USS Stark* on May 17, 1987, but it was never invoked. Other concerns included U.S. minesweeping deficiencies, dangers of escalation, burdensharing, and costs.

Outcome: Success

The United States accomplished its basic objectives. Only one escorted U.S. ship was attacked or struck a mine during transit. Two more merchantmen and two U.S. frigates were damaged under other circumstances.

Selected Sources

Congressional Research Service, Washington: Laipson, Ellen B. (coordinator), *Persian Gulf: Overview of Issues*, Issue Brief IB 87229, November 25, 1988, 13 p.; O'Rourke, Ronald, *Persian Gulf: U.S. Military Operations*, Issue Brief IB 87145, January 19, 1989, 14 p.; Mark, Clyde R., *Persian Gulf and the War Powers Debate: Review of Events*, Issue Brief IB 87207, February 6, 1989, 15 p.

"Gulf War" and "The Attack on the Stark," five articles in *U.S. Naval Institute Proceedings*, May 1988, p. 29-67.

Cordesman, Anthony H., "U.S. Mine Forces," *Armed Forces*, February 1988, p. 88-91.

CASE 60

PANAMA (1987-90)

Type Conflict	Coup d'etat; punitive expedition
Duration	June 9, 1987-January 3, 1990 (19 months)
Participants	*U.S. Allies*: None *U.S. Adversaries*: Panamanian Government
U.S. Purposes	*Interests*: National security; democracy *Objectives*: Remove Noriega; expedite the formation of a civilian government friendly to the United States; protect U.S. interests in Panama; contain communism
Predominant U.S. Power	Politico-military; economic
Predominant U.S. Instrument	Covert action; sanctions; force
U.S. Armed Forces	*Predominant Type*: Conventional *Predominant Services*: Army, Air Force *Predominant Function*: Combat; security
Public Opinion	*U.S.*: Supportive *International*: Mainly adverse

Context

General Manuel Noriega, who controlled the Panamanian Defense Forces (PDF) and National Guard, became de facto chief of state in 1983. Riots erupted in June 1987, when a senior military officer publicly accused him of electoral fraud, murder, and various forms of corruption, including illicit drug dealings. Noriega responded by suppressing all opposition,; tightened ties with Cuba, Nicaragua, and Libya; continued to violate civil, political, and human rights; and disained disapproval by the United States and OAS (Organization of American States).

The Reagan Administration imposed severe political and economic sanctions to encourage reforms, then reinforced U.S. military contingents in Panama to impress Noriega. Covert U.S. activities to foster dissent in the PDF and promote political competition reportedly followed in mid-1988, after passive measures failed. President Bush, who approved those policies, openly urged Panamanians to overthrow Noriega. PDF rebels did rise in 1989, but their coup was quickly crushed and repression increased. U.S. covert actions and psychological warfare continued until December 1989, when Noriega declared that a state of war existed with the United States and took provocative action against U.S. citizens in Panama. A U.S. invasion, Operation Just Cause, began before dawn on December 20, 1989 and culminated on January 3, 1990, the day U.S. officials took Noriega into custody. U.S. armed forces during the intervening two weeks neutralized the PDF and restored some semblance of order. U.S. sanctions ceased and assistance restarted. The last intervention forces left for the United States on February 13, 1990.

Key Congressional Actions

Congress imposed economic sanctions on the Noriega regime, generally approved Just Cause, and reinstated aid after he departed.

Outcome: Mixed opinion

The United States ultimately accomplished all basic objectives, but failed to foment a successful coup (which would have been less costly) and has been sharply criticized for excessive civilian casualties and property damage during Operation Just Cause. The UN and OAS condemned U.S. armed intervention.

Selected Sources

Congressional Research Service, Washington: Sullivan, Mark P., *Panamanian-U.S. Relations: Issues for Congress*, Issue Brief IB 90044, February 13, 1990, 13 p., *Panama: U.S. Policy After the May 1989 Elections*, Issue Brief IB 89106, December 16, 1989, 15 p., and *U.S. Sanctions and the State of the Panamanian Economy*, August 22, 1988, 49 p.; Galdi, Theodor W. and Robert D. Shuey, *U.S. Economic Sanctions Imposed Against Specific Foreign Countries: 1979 to the Present*, December 1, 1987, p. 155-161.

"Panama: Operation Just Cause," *Current News*, Special Edition, Part I, No. 1827 and Part II, No. 1828, Washington, Dept. of Defense, February 19, 1990, 142 p. total.

Annex B

KEY CONGRESSIONAL ACTIONS

Compiled by James P. Seevers

Congress, by Joint Resolution with presidential signature affixed, has formally declared war only five times in U.S. history: the War of 1812, Mexican War, Spanish-American War, World War I, and World War II. Congress, however, has directly or indirectly influenced most U.S. low-intensity conflicts in the Twentieth Century.

The 60 cases summarized herein amplify congressional actions cited in Annex A. Authorizations, appropriations, restraints, and other involvement, both implicit and explicit, cover such disparate topics as U.S. military force levels, legal limitations on their employment, mutual defense treaties, oversight, security assistance, and sanctions. Presentations are complete whenever practical, but many merely emphasize a few key points, because the record is lengthy, complex, or classified.

Congressional participation varied considerably, according to time period and type LIC. Presidential authority to engage in undeclared wars, for example, became a much sharper issue after the War Powers Resolution passed in 1973. Cases that featured U.S. armed force received different treatment than nonviolent conflicts, although overlaps often occurred.

Synopses of cases that predate World War II draw heavily on primary sources, especially *U.S. Statutes at Large*, congressional documents found through the *CIS U.S. Serial Set Index*, and the *Congressional Record*. Post-war cases are derived largely from the *Congressional Quarterly Almanac, U.S. Code Congressional and Administrative News*, the *Record*, and congressional hearings and reports. The most recent cases rely essentially on secondary sources.

LIST OF CONFLICTS

1. PHILIPPINES (1899-1913)

President McKinley on December 21, 1898 instructed the Secretary of War to occupy -- and extend military government to -- all ceded territory in the Philippines, using Spanish-American war powers as his authority.[1]

Congress , in an act approved March 22, 1899, authorized a Regular Army of 65,000 and 35,000 volunteers to deal with the Philippine Insurrection. Service was to terminate not later than July 1, 1901. Congress further authorized the President to enlist -- for up to six months -- units and individuals already in the Philippines, pending the arrival of replacements from the United States.[2]

Congress, in an act approved May 26, 1900, raised the pay of officers and enlisted men in the Philippines and increased the latter's retirement benefits.[3]

The President governed the Philippines by explicit congressional authority, rather than residual war powers, after March 2, 1901, "until otherwise provided by Congress." He was expressly permitted to protect the population.[4]

Congress closely monitored U.S. activities and costs throughout the Moro uprisings, in consonance with resolutions that required the President and Secretary of War to report.[5]

---

[1] *Congressional Record*, 55th Congress, 3rd Session, January 11, 1899, p. 572-73

[2] 30 Stat. 977, at 979-981; Linn, Bruce McAllister, *The U.S. Army and Counterinsurgency in the Philippine War, 1988-1902*, Chapel Hill, NC, University of North Carolina Press, 1989, p. 14.

[3] Senate Document No. 105, 58th Congress, 2nd Session, *Compilation of the Acts of Congress, Treaties and Proclamations Relating to Insular and Military Affairs from March 4, 1907 to March 3, 1903*, published in 1904.

[4] 31 Stat. 910.

[5] "Attack on Mount Dado, Letter From the Secretary of War, Pursuant to Senate Resolution No. 95....," Document No. 276, *Senate Documents*, Vol. 6, 59th Congress, 1st Session, Washington, U.S. GPO, 1906; "Cost of Occupation of Philippine Islands, Message From the President of the United States," Document No. 875, *House Documents*, Vol. 141, 62d Congress, 2nd Session, Washington, U.S. GPO, 1912.

2. CHINA (1900)

Secretary of State John Hay, in a July 3, 1900 circular note, stated that the "purpose of the President" during the Boxer Rebellion was to reopen communications with Peking, protect American lives, property and interests throughout China, and prevent the spread of disorder and its recurrence in cooperation with other powers in China.[6]

In his December 1900 message to Congress, President McKinley repeated those policy objectives, and added "the redress of wrongs." He stated that "our declared aims involved no war against the Chinese nation." [7]

Congress was not in session during U.S. operations that ensued in July-September 1900 (56th Congress, First Session ended June 7, 1900 and Second Session did not begin until December 3). A 1905 circuit court decision determined that U.S. involvement in the Boxer Rebellion was war, and held that congressional appropriation of pay for the soldiers in China approved U.S. action.[8]

3. COLOMBIA/PANAMA (1901-1914)

President Theodore Roosevelt in November 1903 ordered U.S. warships to prevent Colombia from suppressing a Panamanian revolution. He later asserted publicly that "If I had followed the precedent in such cases, I should have submitted a dignified state paper to the Congress and the debate would be going on yet. But I took the Canal Zone and let Congress debate, and while the debate goes on the canal does also." [9]

---

[6] *U.S. Foreign Relations*, 1901, Appendix "Affairs in China," p.12.

[7] *U.S. Foreign Relations*, 1900, p. xiv; *U.S. Foreign Relations*, 1901, Appendix, "Affairs in China" p. 12-13.

[8] Hamilton v. McClaughry, 136 F. 445, 451 (D. Kan. 1905); Wormuth, Francis D., and Edwin B. Firmage, *To Chain the Dog of War: The War Powers of Congress in History and Law*, Dallas, Southern Methodist University Press, 1986, p. 219-20.

[9] Senate Document No. 471, 63rd Congress, 2nd Session, *The Panama Canal and Our Relations with Colombia*, "Message of President Roosevelt of January 4, 1904," 1914, p. 20 and 29; Munro, Dana G., *Intervention and Dollar Diplomacy in the Caribbean: 1900-1921*, Princeton, NJ, Princeton University Press, 1964, p. 55-56; Speech at Berkeley, California, March 23, 1911, excerpt in *Congressional Record* 67th Congress, 1st Session, April 14, 1921, p. 234.

The Senate on February 23, 1904 ratified the November 1903 "Convention between the United States and the Republic of Panama for the construction of a ship canal to connect the waters of the Atlantic and Pacific oceans" (Hay-Bunau-Varilla Treaty). That treaty granted the United States permission to use its police, land and naval forces to protect the Canal, and provided other interventionary rights.[10]

Congress on April 23, 1904, appropriated funds to increase pay for U.S. military personnel in Panama. It raised enlisted pay again in 1905. An act approved April 28, 1904, provided the President with all "military, civil, and judicial powers as well as the power to make all rules and regulations necessary for the government of the Canal Zone." An act approved February 15, 1908, appropriated funds to repair and improve Marine barracks and officers quarters in the Canal Zone.[11]

4. MOROCCO (1904)

The Congressional Record makes no mention of this hostage rescue operation.

5. CUBA (1906-09)

Congress twice approved the Platt amendment, a provision that explicitly gave the United States the "right to intervene" in Cuban affairs. It first appeared as an amendment to the Army's 1902 appropriation bill, approved on March 2, 1901. A treaty signed May 2, 1903 and proclaimed on July 2, 1904 incorporated the entire amendment.[12]

The "unusual expenditures resulting from the sending of the army of pacification to Cuba" were made -- at least until November 30, 1906 -- out of

---

[10] 33 Stat. 2234.

[11] 33 Stat. 266; 33 Stat. 429; and Senate Document No. 204, 59th Congress, 2nd Session, "Acts Of Congress Relating to Noncontiguous Territory and Cuba and to Military Affairs" in 58th Congress, 1907 p. 115; 35 Stat. p.8 at 17.

[12] 31 Stat. 895; 33 Stat. 2248.

the "regular appropriation" supplemented by some emergency War Department funds.[13]

Congress, in an act approved June 30, 1907, authorized the President to use funds from the Cuban treasury to reimburse the United States for expenditures related to the intervention. The same act provided funds for a pay raise to 308 officers and 6,000 enlisted men serving in Cuba. It also appropriated money for the Signal Service spent "on account of the army of Cuban pacification" during Fiscal Year 1907.[14]

Congress, in an act approved February 15, 1908, again made a "deficiency" appropriation to provide funds for the Signal Service's support of the army of Cuban pacification during fiscal year 1908.[15]

6. CHINA (1912-41)

A June 18, 1858 treaty with China supplied justification for U.S. maintenance of naval vessels in Chinese waters.[16]

The September 7, 1901 "Settlement of Matters Growing Out of the Boxer Uprising" (Boxer Protocol) provided the basis of repeated U.S. military actions in China between 1912-41. The protocol allowed the United States to maintain a permanent guard in China for defense of the American legation, and to occupy "certain points" within the country to insure "open communication between the capital and the sea." The other signatory nations received similar rights in China. This agreement was not a treaty and thus not sent to the U.S. Senate for ratification.[17]

Congress, in an act approved December 22, 1927, appropriated funds "to defray the increased expenses" for the "expeditionary forces" that had already been sent to China and Nicaragua. During House floor debate on this "deficiency appropriation", Representative John C. Schafer attempted unsuccessfully to cut the funds by more than half. He argued that "When we

---

[13] *Congressional Record* 59th Congress, 2nd Session, January 9, 1907, p. 849-50 (December 14, letter from Secretary of War).

[14] 34 Stat. 1381.

[15] 35 Stat. 8 at 14.

[16] 1 Treaties, etc. (Malloy, 1910), 211; cited in 1 Hackworth 332.

[17] 1 Bevans, *Treaties and Other International Agreements of the United States of America, 1776-1949*, p. 302-329; and 1 Hackworth 332-33.

pass this deficiency to meet these obligations we are putting our stamp of approval upon the declaration of war with the citizens of Nicaragua and China, which war was not declared by Congress but by the President, the Director of the Budget, and the Secretary of the Navy, in violation of the war-making provisions of the Constitution." [18]

7. MEXICO (1914-17)

President Wilson on April 20, 1914 asked Congress to approve the use of armed force against Mexico. He qualified his request by asserting that "I could do what is necessary in the circumstances to enforce respect for our government without recourse to the Congress and yet not exceed my constitutional powers as President, but I do not wish to act in a matter possibly of so grave consequence except in close conference and cooperation with both the Senate and House." [19]

Congress on April 22, 1914 passed a joint resolution (H.J. Res 251) "justifying the employment by the President of the armed forces of the United States" against Mexico. The resolution further stated that the United States "disclaimed any purpose to make war upon Mexico." U.S. armed forces had occupied Vera Cruz the previous day, and on May 2 established a military government that remained for seven months. [20]

The Senate approved a concurrent resolution on March 17, 1916 that allowed for "the use of the armed forces of the United States for the sole purpose of apprehending and punishing the lawless band of armed men who entered the United States from Mexico on the 9th of March 1916..." (Sen Con. Res. 17). The House did not follow suit. A concurrent resolution does not have the force of law. [21]

The Secretary of War on June 27, 1916 asked Congress to appropriate additional funds for that fiscal year "to cover expenditures made and about to

---

[18] 45 Stat. 2 at 25; *Congressional Record* 70th Congress, 1st Session, December 8, 1927, p. 262.

[19] *Congressional Record* 64th Congress, 1st Session, "Address of the President," April 20, 1914, p. 6908-09.

[20] 38 Stat. 770; II Hackworth 332.

[21] *Congressional Record* 64th Congress, 1st Session, March 17, 1916, p. 4274.

be made" for the troops in Mexico and on the border, and to finish equipping the National Guard. Congress did so on July 1, 1916.[22]

8. HAITI (1915-1934)

President Theodore Roosevelt in his 1904 annual message to Congress (December 6) proclaimed that "Chronic wrong-doing, or an impotence which results in a general loosening of the ties of civilized society, may in America, as elsewhere, ultimately require intervention by some civilized nation, and in the Western Hemisphere the adherence of the United States to the Monroe Doctrine may force the United States, however reluctantly, in flagrant cases of such wrongdoing or impotence, to the exercise of an international police power." This so-called Roosevelt "Corollary" to the Monroe Doctrine became an element in the rationale for later military involvement in Haiti, the Dominican Republic, and Nicaragua.[23]

After landing American forces in Haiti on July 28, 1915, President Wilson expressed concern that "we do not have the legal authority to do what we apparently ought to do...", yet concluded that "I suppose there is nothing for it but to take the bull by the horns and restore order."[24]

A treaty providing for the "Administration of Haiti: Finances and Economic Development," signed September 16, 1915 and approved by the U.S. Senate on February 28, 1916, allowed U.S. intervention for preservation of Haitian independence and maintenance of "adequate" government (Article XIV). The treaty also established a constabulary "organized and officered by Americans" to be gradually replaced by Haitians (Article X).[25]

Congress, in an act approved June 12, 1916, authorized the President to send officers of the U.S. Navy and Marine Corps on detail to "assist Haiti." The act also allowed a small increase in Navy and Marine manpower. This law enabled implementation of Article X of the 1916 Treaty.[26]

---

[22] House Document No. 1245, 64th Congress, 1st Session, "Appropriation for Needs of Regular Troops in Mexico," ; 39 Stat. 337.

[23] *U.S. Foreign Relations* 1904, "Message of the President," p. XLIII.

[24] Wilson correspondence with Secretary of State Lansing, quoted in Munro, *Intervention and Dollar Diplomacy in the Caribbean, 1900-21*, p. 353.

[25] 8 Bevans 660.

[26] 39 Stat. 223.

9. DOMINICAN REPUBLIC (1916-24)

The United States and Dominican Republic on February 8, 1907 signed a treaty "providing for the assistance of the United States in the collection and application of the customs revenues of the Dominican Republic." The U.S. Senate approved the treaty on February 25. Article III stated that until the Dominican Republic paid off its debt bond, the government could not increase its public indebtedness without U.S. approval. This article also required U.S. approval for any increase in Dominican import duties.[27]

President Wilson on November 26, 1916 authorized the U.S. Navy to occupy the Dominican Republic and establish a military government. Accordingly, a Navy Commander on November 29 issued a proclamation that placed the country in a "state of Military Occupation" and made it "subject to Military Government and to the exercise of military law." The proclamation stated that the Dominican Republic had violated Article III of the 1907 treaty, thereby requiring U.S. intervention to enforce the treaty and maintain "domestic tranquility." [28]

Congress on February 11, 1918 authorized the President to send officers and enlisted men from the U.S. Navy and Marines on details to "assist the Dominican Republic." [29]

10. NICARAGUA (1926-33)

President Coolidge, in a January 10, 1927 message to Congress, cited "proprietary" rights to a Nicaraguan canal granted by the 1914 Bryan-Chamorro Treaty, the stability of Central America, and the protection of American lives, property, and economic interests as justifications for U.S. intervention in Nicaragua. He referred specifically to a November 15, 1926 letter from Adolfo Diaz, the nominal Nicaraguan President, requesting American assistance.[30]

Congress, in an act approved May 19, 1926, authorized the President "to detail officers and enlisted men of the United States Army, Navy, and Marine

---

[27] 35 Stat. 1880.

[28] 2 Hackworth 242 and 155; *U.S. Foreign Relations* 1917, p. 246-47.

[29] 40 Stat. 437.

[30] *Congressional Record* 69th Congress, 2nd Session, "Affairs in Nicaragua (H. Doc. No. 633)," January 10, 1927, p. 1324-26.

Corps to assist the governments of the Latin American Republics in military and naval matters." [31]

Congress, in an act approved December 22, 1927, appropriated funds "to defray the increased expenses" for the "expeditionary forces" that had already been sent to Nicaragua.[32]

The Senate Foreign Relations Committee on March 6, 1928 responded "adversely" to a proposed resolution (S.J. Res. 57) calling for the immediate withdrawal of U.S. armed forces from Nicaragua. The Committee argued that although it would "like to see our troops withdrawn from Nicaragua," the United States must not abandon its commitment to supervise the Nicaraguan election. S.J. Res 57 was not adopted, nor were several similar resolutions.[33]

Congress specified in the Navy Appropriation Act approved June 30, 1932 that "no money appropriated in this Act shall be used to defray the expense of sending additional Marines to Nicaragua to supervise an election there." [34]

11. PHILIPPINES (1942-25)

12. BURMA (1942-45)

13. FRANCE (1944)

Congress did not directly influence U.S. support for the three cited resistance movements during World War II.

14. CHINA (1945-49)

Approximately 60,000 U.S. armed forces remained in China after World War II; 50,000 additional U.S. Marines reinforced North China in October 1945. Undersecretary of State Dean Acheson, in response to a congressional

---

[31] 44 Stat. 565.

[32] *Congressional Record* 70th Congress, 1st Session, December 8, 1927, p. 261-262; 45 Stat. 2 at 25.

[33] *Withdrawal of Armed Forces from Nicaragua*, Senate Report No. 498, 70th Congress, 1st Session, March 6, 1928, 4 p.

[34] 47 Stat. 421 at 439.

inquiry, replied that U.S. contingents "in pursuance of instructions of the Joint Chiefs of Staff," were there to assist "Chinese authorities in the task of concentrating, disarming, and repatriating the Japanese in China." U.S. forces also secured Chinese Nationalist supply lines, allowed Nationalist troops to be utilized for other purposes, and helped move Nationalist forces from south to north.[35]

Members of Congress during the latter half of 1945 introduced at least seven resolutions calling for the withdrawal of U.S. troops from China. None of the resolutions passed. [36]

Congress, in an act approved July 16, 1946, authorized the President to provide naval vessels, services, training, plans and technical advice to Nationalist China, as well as to detail 100 officers and 200 enlisted men from the U.S. Navy and Marine Corps to "assist the Republic of China in naval matters." The United States also provided some non-military aid.[37]

Congress passed the China Aid Act of 1948 as part of the foreign assistance legislation for that year (approved April 3). It authorized $338 million under the provisions of the Economic Cooperation Act of 1948 and $125 million in military aid through grants on terms determined by the President.[38]

Congress, in an act approved October 6, 1949 as Nationalist China neared defeat, authorized $75 million in military aid for the "general area" of China as part of the "Mutual Defense Assistance Act of 1949." Congress, not the President, pushed for this aid. Senator William F. Knowland originally sought $175 million.[39]

---

[35] Chern, Kenneth S., *Dilemma in China: American Policy Debate*, 1945, Hamden, CT, Archon Books, 1980, p. 118; *U.S. Foreign Relations* 1945, Vol. VII, "The Far East, China," p. 577-78; *Congress and the Nation*, Vol. I, p. 161; May, Ernest, R., *The Truman Administration and China*, 1945-1949, Philadelphia, PA, J.B. Lippincott Co., 1975, p. 10-11.

[36] *Congressional Record* 79th Congress, 1st Session, index "China," p. 121; Chern, *Dilemma in China*, p. 138.

[37] *U.S. Code Congressional Service*, Public Law 512, 1946, p. 516; *Congress and the Nation*, Vol. I, p. 164-65.

[38] 62 Stat. 137 at 158; *Congress and the Nation*, Vol. I, p. 165.

[39] 63 Stat. 714 at 716; *Congress and the Nation*, Vol. 1, p. 166.

15. GREECE (1946-49)

President Truman, in his March 1947 "Truman Doctrine" speech before a joint session of Congress, requested $400 million in assistance to Greece and Turkey. Additionally, he asked Congress to authorize the "detail of American civil and military personnel to Greece and Turkey" to assist in reconstruction and supervise the use of U.S. assistance.[40]

Congress in 1947 passed the "Greek-Turkish Aid Act" (approved May 22) which met Truman's request. The Act authorized $400 million in military and economic aid to Greece (and Turkey). It also detailed "a limited number of members of the military services of the United States to assist those countries, in an advisory capacity only." According to the accompanying Senate report, the Act designated $300 million of the total for Greece. On July 30, 1947 Congress appropriated the funds as part of the "Supplemental Appropriation Act, 1948." [41]

The President on November 17, 1947 reported to Congress on "the activities and expenditure of funds" under the "Greek-Turkish Aid" Act. He stated that "the economic situation in Greece has not basically improved" since his initial request for aid. The President also indicated that "intensification of military operations in that country has necessitated a transfer of funds from the economic to the military program."[42]

Congress passed the "Greek-Turkish Aid Act of 1948" (approved April 3) as part of the foreign assistance legislation for that year. The Act authorized an additional $275 million in assistance to Greece (and Turkey). According to the accompanying House report, funds were not "earmarked" by country.[43]

Congress passed the "Mutual Defense Assistance Act of 1949" (approved October 6) which in part authorized an additional $211.37 million in military assistance for Greece and Turkey.[44]

---

[40] *U.S. Code Congressional Service*, 1947, "Greek-Turkish Aid," p. 1811; *Congress and the Nation*, Vol. I, p. 160-61.

[41] *U.S. Code Congressional Service*, 1947, Public Law 75, "Greek-Turkish Aid," p. 102; p. 1085; Public Law 271, p. 606 *Congress and the Nation*, Vol. I, p. 164.

[42] *U.S. Code Congressional Service*, 1947, "Report on Greek and Turkish Aid," p. 1877-78.

[43] 62 Stat. 137 at 157; and *Congress and the Nation*, Vol. I, p. 165; *U.S. Code Congressional Service*, 1948, p. 1402.

[44] *U.S. Code Congressional Service*, 1949, Public Law 329, p. 731; and *Congress and the Nation*, Vol. I, p. 166.

16. PHILIPPINES (1946-55)

Congress in 1946 passed the Republic of the Philippines Military Assistance Act (approved June 26) which authorized the President to provide the Philippines with military instruction and training, maintenance services for military equipment, and to transfer "arms, ammunition, and implements of war." Additionally, the Act permitted the President to detail officers and enlisted men of the U.S. Army, Navy and Marine Corps to assist the Government of the Philippines.[45]

Congress, in an act approved October 6, 1949, authorized $27,640,000 in military assistance to the Philippines, Iran, and South Korea as part of the Mutual Defense Assistance Act of 1949. The Senate report accompanying the bill asserted that "this assistance is needed to insure the ability of the Philippine Government to deal with subversive efforts now taking place in the guise of indigenous guerrilla uprisings." In 1950 Congress extended the Mutual Defense Assistance Program one year authorizing $16 million for the Philippines and Korea.[46]

Congress, in an act approved October 10, 1951, authorized additional assistance to the Philippines under the Mutual Security Act of 1951. The Senate report accompanying the bill stated that "in the Philippines, the Communist-inspired Huk guerrillas in certain areas are forcing the Government and the loyal citizenry to confine themselves largely to the cities."[47]

The United States between 1946 and 1952 obligated or authorized over $820 million in economic assistance loans and grants to the Philippines.[48]

The Senate on March 20, 1952 approved a Mutual Defense Treaty between the United States and the Philippines that had been signed on August 30, 1951.[49]

---

[45] *U.S. Code Congressional Service*, 1946, Public Law 454, p. 306.

[46] *U.S. Code Congressional Service*, 1949, Public Law 329, p. 731, 733; Senate Report No. 1068, p. 1991-2003.

[47] *U.S. Code Congressional and Administrative News*, 1951, Public Law 165, p. 517-20; Senate Report No. 703, p. 2250, 2277.

[48] *U.S. Overseas Loans and Grants and Assistance from International Organizations*, Obligations and Loan Authorizations, July 1, 1945-September 30, 1988, p. 81.

[49] *United States Treaties and other International Agreements*, Washington, Department of State, 1952, p. 3947.

17. INDOCHINA (1946-54)

President Truman on August 13, 1950 announced that "the United States has begun an economic assistance program which was developed after direct discussions with the leaders and technicians of Indochina...Military assistance is also being extended to provide the internal security for...VietNam, Laos, and Cambodia." The United States had initiated in February 1950 a financial assistance program to the French for their war in Indochina.[50]

Secretary of State John Foster Dulles testified on May 12, 1954 that in Indochina "we would not engage the United States in belligerency without the prior approval of Congress." [51]

The Administration used the "Mutual Defense Assistance act of 1949," which provided $75 million in military aid to the "general area" of China, as the statutory basis for the initial U.S. aid program to Indochina in 1950.[52]

Congress, in an act approved October 10, 1951, authorized economic and technical assistance to Indochina as part of the "Mutual Security Act of 1951."[53]

On July 16, 1953, Congress authorized, as part of the amended Mutual Security Act of 1951, $400 million "for the procurement of equipment, materials, and services..." to support armed forces of "Cambodia, Laos, and Vietnam and the forces of France located in such Associated States." Congress, in an act approved August 7, 1953, appropriated those funds, plus funds for defense support and economic/technical assistance.[54]

Congress in 1954 authorized as part of the Mutual Security Act of 1954 (approved August 26), $700 million for "support of the forces of nations in the

---

[50] *Congressional Record* 83rd Congress, 1st Session, July 1, 1953, p. 7780; and LaFeber, Walter, *America, Russia, and the Cold War: 1945-1984*, New York, Alfred A. Knopf, 1985, p. 108.

[51] *Congressional Quarterly Almanac*, 1954, p. 276.

[52] Gibbons, William Conrad, *The U.S. Government and the Vietnam War: Executive and Legislative Roles and Relationships*, Part I, 1945-1961, S. Prt. 98-185 Pt. 1, April 1984, p. 54

[53] *U.S. Code Congressional and Administrative News*, 1951, "Mutual Security Act of 1951," Public Law 165, p. 517, 519-20; Senate Report No. 703, p. 2276-77.

[54] 67 Stat. 152 at 153; 67 Stat. 478 at 479; *Congress and the Nation*, Vol. I, p. 171.

area of Southeast Asia," including direct assistance to the Associated States of Cambodia, Laos, and Vietnam.[55]

18. U.S.S.R. (1946-)

Azerbaijan (1946)

Secretary of State James Byrnes on March 5, 1946 sent a note to Moscow calling for the immediate withdrawal of all Soviet forces from the "territory of Iran." The Soviet Union did not reply, and on March 8 Byrnes sent another note requesting that the United States be informed about increased Soviet forces in Iran. Iran submitted the issue to the U.N Security Council, and the United States insisted that Azerbaijan remain on the agenda, despite Soviet opposition. Congress played no direct role.[56]

Berlin Blockade (1948)

The Truman Administration did not formally consult Congress regarding the U.S. response to the Soviet blockade of West Berlin. However, Congress strongly supported the Berlin airlift.[57]

Hungary (1956)

The United States did not intervene directly during Soviet suppression of the 1956 Hungarian revolution. President Eisenhower stated prior to the November 4 Soviet military action that the he would "offer economic assistance and would support Eastern Europe's quest for true sovereignty, but that the United States 'could not of course, carry out this policy by resort to

---

[55] 68 Stat. 832; *Congress and the Nation*, Vol. I, p. 172.

[56] *U.S. Foreign Relations* 1946, Vol. VII, p. 340-42 and 348; and Gaddis, John Lewis, *United States and the Origins of the Cold War*, NY, Columbia University Press, 1972, p. 310-12.

[57] LaFeber, Walter, *America, Russia, and the Cold War 1945-1984*, p. 78.

force.'" Congress played no direct legislative role, although interest was intense.[58]

Berlin Wall (1961)

President Kennedy, in a July 25 speech during the 1961 Berlin crisis, asserted that "in the days and months ahead, I shall not hesitate to ask the Congress for additional measures, or exercise any of the executive powers that I possess to meet this threat to peace." He indicated that the following day he would ask Congress for an additional $3.247 billion for the armed forces, a major increase in authorized military manpower, and the authority to call up the reserves. Congress complied with his request.[59]

Congress, in the "Foreign Assistance Act of 1961" (approved September 4) removed the $6.75 million limit on special aid to promote U.S. objectives in West Berlin and Germany.[60]

The 1961 Berlin Crisis was essentially over by October, but Congress the following year passed a concurrent resolution asserting U.S., French and British rights in Berlin, and stated that the United States would prevent violation of its rights by any means necessary, including armed force. (H. Con. Res. 570, October 10, 1962). A concurrent resolution does not have the force of law, but is a potentially potent expression of Congressional commitment.[61]

Cuban Missile Crisis (1962)

Senate Minority Leader Everet Dirksen and House Minority Leader Charles A. Hallek on September 7, 1962 called for a joint resolution authorizing the President to use force in Cuba. President Kennedy the same

---

[58] Smoke, Alexander L. and Smoke, Richard, *Deterrence in American Foreign Policy, Theory and Practice*, NY, Columbia University Press, 1974, p. 302.

[59] *Congressional Quarterly Almanac*, 1961, p. 927; Smoke and Smoke, *Deterrence in American Foreign Policy*, p.415-16 .

[60] *U.S. Code Congressional and Administrative News*, 1961, p. 470, 475-79 (P.L. 87-195); *Congressional Quarterly Almanac*, 1961, p. 295-96.

[61] U.S. Congress, House, *Background Information on the Use of U.S. Armed Forces in Foreign Countries*, 1975 Revision, Subcommittee on International Security and Scientific Affairs of the Committee on International Relations, 94th Congress, 1st Session, Washington, U.S. GPO, 1975, p. 44.

day requested authority to call up 150,000 reserves to deal with threats "anywhere in the free world." [62]

Congress passed a joint resolution (S.J. Res. 230, approved October 3, 1962) declaring that the United States would prevent Cuban aggression or subversion in the Western Hemisphere with armed force if necessary. The resolution also expressed congressional determination to prevent Cuba from developing an externally supported military capability that could endanger U.S. security.[63]

Congress passed a joint resolution (S.J. Res. 224, approved October 3, 1962) "authorizing the President to order units and members in the Ready Reserve to active duty for not more than twelve months." [64]

The Kennedy Administration on October 4, 1962 disclosed a plan to ban from U.S. ports ships owned by individuals transporting military goods to Cuba. Congress, in the foreign aid appropriation bill approved October 23, 1962, maintained the ban on U.S. aid to Cuba, and prohibited aid to third countries selling or giving military equipment to Cuba.[65]

President Kennedy on October 22, 1962 called 17 congressional leaders back from adjournment for a bipartisan briefing on the crisis.[66]

Czechoslovakia (1968)

The Soviet invasion of Czechoslovakia in August 1968 derailed a movement in Congress to reduce the number of U.S. troops in Europe. The Senate Foreign Relations Committee did not act on two troop reduction resolutions (S. Res. 49 and S. Res. 83). Senate Majority Leader Mike Mansfield stated that given the invasion "we had no choice but to maintain our present position," but maintained that troop reductions would be desirable once the situation in Eastern Europe stabilized.[67]

---

[62] *Congressional Quarterly Almanac*, 1962, p. 333.

[63] 76 Stat. 697.

[64] 76 Stat. 710.

[65] *Congressional Quarterly Almanac*, 1962, p. 336, 333; 76 Stat. 1163.

[66] *Congressional Quarterly Almanac*, 1962, p. 336; 77 Stat. 958.

[67] *Congress and the Nation*, Vol. II, p. 106.

Cold War

Many other congressional actions were manifest throughout the Cold War period. The North Atlantic Treaty, which formed NATO, was prominent. So were assorted sanctions, of which the citation below covers only a fraction.[68] Funds for "informational conflict", conducted in part by USIA, represent another enduring contribution.[69]

19. ISRAEL vs. ARABS (1948-)

Economic and Military Aid

U.S. economic and military assistance to Israel has been the principal form of support for that country in its ongoing struggle with its Arab neighbors. The United States obligated or authorized $25.8 billion in military and $15 billion in economic assistance (grants and loans) to Israel through 1988, frequently in the form of congressional "earmarks" found in spending measures. Between 1949-65 official U.S. aid to Israel was relatively modest (average $63 million per year) and mostly economic. Military assistance on a small scale started in 1959 (loan program) and began increasing in 1966. From 1971 onward U.S. assistance expanded substantially, averaging $2 billion per year, two-thirds in military assistance. Israel since 1976 has absorbed the largest share of the overall U.S. aid program, and by the mid-1980s averaged $3-3.5 billion per year. Some legislative highlights of U.S. aid to Israel follow.[70]

Congress on January 12, 1971, in a measure amending the Foreign Military Sales Act, expressed its sense that "the President should be supported in his position that arms will be made available and credits provided to Israel." Additionally, the Foreign Assistance Act of 1971, approved on February 7,

---

[68] Galdi, Theodor W. and Robert D. Shuey, *U.S. Economic Sanctions Imposed Against Specific Countries, 1979 to Present*, Washington, Congressional Research Service, December 1, 1989, p. 209-221.

[69] Binder, David, "As Cold War Recedes, Radio Services Face Cuts," *New York Times*, June 29, 1990, p. A6

[70] *U.S. Overseas Loans and Grants and Assistance from International Organizations*, Obligations and Loan Authorization, July 1, 1945-September 30, 1988, p. 19; Mark, Clyde R., *Israel: U.S. Foreign Assistance Facts*, Issue Brief IB 85066, Washington, Congressional Research Service, January 17, 1990, p. 3-4; and Laipson, Ellen B., *Israeli-American Relations*, Issue Brief IB 82008, Washington, Congressional Research Service, December 21, 1989, p.10-11.

1972, authorized $300 million in foreign military sales and $50 million in security supporting assistance to Israel.[71]

President Nixon on October 19, 1973, in the midst of the "Yom Kippur War," requested $2.2 billion in emergency security assistance for Israel. Congress in the Emergency Security Assistance Act of 1973 (H.R. 1108, approved December 24, 1973) provided the aid.[72]

Congress in the "Special International Security Assistance Act of 1979" (S. 1007, approved July 20, 1979) authorized $3 billion in supplemental aid to Israel, in accordance with the peace treaty signed by Israel and Egypt that year.[73]

During FY 1981-83, Congress gave economic grants to Israel, despite President Reagan's attempts to provide one-third of the assistance in the form of loans. In FY 1984 and 85, Congress provided more economic aid than the President requested.[74]

U.S. Supervision of Peace Accords

Congress in 1975 passed a joint resolution (H.J. Res 683, approved October 13) to "implement the United States proposal for the early-warning system in Sinai." The measure authorized President Ford to send civilians to Sinai to monitor the agreement signed by Egypt and Israel on September 4, 1975.[75]

Congress in 1981 passed the "Multinational Force and Observers Participation Resolution" (S.J. Res. 100, approved December 29) authorizing the President to send up to 1200 soldiers to support the Sinai peacekeeping force in accordance with the 1979 treaty.[76]

---

[71] 84 Stat. 2053 (P.L. 91-672); *U.S. Code Congressional and Administrative News*, 1972, P.L. 92-226, p. 23, 30 and 37.

[72] *U.S. Code Congressional and Administrative News*, 1973, p. 922-23 (P.L. 93-199).

[73] 93 Stat. 89 (P.L. 96-35).

[74] *Congress and the Nation*, Vol. VI, p. 195.

[75] 89 Stat. 572 (P.L. 94-110).

[76] 95 Stat. 1693 (P.L. 97-132).

20. IRAN (1951-53)

Congress apparently played no significant part in U.S. efforts to oust Iranian Prime Minister Mussaddiq.

21. CHINA (1953-79)

Offshore Islands

President Eisenhower during the 1954-55 Quemoy/Matsu crisis claimed that he would "not hesitate" to exercise his constitutional powers fully and take emergency action to "protect the rights and security of the United States." Nevertheless, he asked Congress for a resolution authorizing use of force if necessary against Communist China, because it would "clearly and publicly" establish Executive authority to take military action, thereby reducing the risk of Chinese Communist miscalculation and a major crisis.[77]

Congress in 1955 passed a Joint Resolution (H.J. Res. 159, approved January 29) authorizing the President "to employ the Armed Forces of the United States as he deems necessary for the specific purpose of securing and protecting Formosa and the Pescadores against armed attack..." The resolution was repealed in 1974.[78]

The Senate on February 9, 1955 approved a "Mutual Defense Treaty" signed by the United States and Taiwan December 2. The Treaty specifically granted the United States the right to "dispose" armed forces " in and about Taiwan and the Pescadores as may be required for their defense, as determined by mutual agreement."[79]

Sanctions Against the People's Republic of China (PRC)

The Executive Branch in 1949-50 cut off all trade with Communist China in accordance with the Trading With the Enemy Act (1917) and the Export

---

[77] "Formosa Message," *U.S. Code Congressional and Administrative News*, 1955, p. 939.

[78] *Ibid.*; Public Law 4, p. 5.

[79] *U.S. Treaties and Other International Agreements*, Vol. VI, Part 1, 1955. p. 433.

Control Act (1949). The Nixon Administration lifted the trade embargo and reduced export controls on the PRC in June 1971.[80]

Congress repeatedly opposed PRC membership in, or recognition by, the United Nations. A concurrent resolution approved July 23, 1956 (H. Con. Res. 265) expressed that sentiment. Between 1953-64 Congress passed three similar resolutions and inserted similar language in the State Department or foreign aid appropriation acts each year.[81]

U.S. Aid to Taiwan

The United States has obligated or authorized roughly $4.2 billion in military and $1.7 billion in economic assistance (grants and loans) to Taiwan since 1950.[82] Economic aid terminated in 1965.

Normalization of U.S. Relations with PRC

The joint U.S.-P.R.C. "Shanghai Communique," issued jointly on February 27, 1972 at the conclusion of President Nixon's visit, affirmed that the United States would progressively reduce its forces and military installations on Taiwan as the tension in the area diminished.[83]

Congress on September 26, 1978, within the International Security Assistance Act passed that year, declared its sense that "there should be prior consultation between the Congress and executive branch on any proposed policy changes affecting the continuation in force of the Taiwan Mutual Defense Treaty of 1954." President Carter thus surprised Congress and angered many Members when he terminated the treaty on December 15, 1978. Senator Barry Goldwater, among others, unsuccessfully challenged in court the

---

[80] *Congress and the Nation*, Vol. I, p. 64; Galdi and Shuey, p. 49-54.

[81] 69 Stat. 264 at 270; 70 Stat. B54; *Congress and the Nation*, Vol. I, p. 104.

[82] *U.S. Overseas Loans and Grants and Assistance from International Organizations*, Obligations and Loan Authorization, July 1, 1945-September 30, 1988, p. 87.

[83] *American Foreign Relations 1972, A Documentary Record*, Stebbins, Ed. by Richard P. and Elaine P. Adam, (Council on Foreign Relations) NY, New York University Press, 1976, p. 310.

President's authority to end treaties absent congressional approval (Supreme Court decision December 13, 1979).[84]

Congress passed the Taiwan Relations Act on April 10, 1979, which established unofficial relations between the two countries and provided U.S. security assurances to Taiwan.[85]

22. NORTH KOREA (1953-)

Sanctions Against North Korea

The United States has imposed a variety of sanctions on North Korea since 1953. The document noted below lists selected recent examples.[86]

Support for South Korea

The Senate on January 26, 1954 approved the Mutual Defense Treaty that the United States and South Korea signed on October 1, 1953.[87]

The United States obligated or authorized approximately $8.7 billion in military and $5.4 billion in economic assistance (loans and grants) to South Korea between 1953-1986. A major U.S. military and economic assistance program to South Korea that began in 1955 continued through the early 1970s. Emphases on military aid commenced in 1975 with strong congressional support. Economic aid terminated in 1985. Military assistance since then has slowed to a trickle.[88]

---

[84] U.S. Congress, House, *Executive-Legislative Consultations on China Policy, 1978-79*, Foreign Affairs Committee Print, Congress and Foreign Policy Series No. 1, Washington, U.S. GPO, June 1980, 42 p.; 92 Stat. 740 at 746; *Congress and the Nation*, Vol. V, p. 99 and 101.

[85] 93 Stat. 14; *Congress and the Nation*, Vol. V, p. 65-66.

[86] Galdi, Theodor W. and Robert D. Shuey, *U.S. Economic Sanctions Imposed Against Specific Countries, 1979 to Present*, p. 109-12; "Foreign Assistance Act of 1961" (75 Stat. 424).

[87] *United States Treaties and Other International Agreements*, 1953, Vol. 3, Part 5, p. 2368.

[88] *U.S. Overseas Loans and Grants and Assistance from International Organizations*, Obligations and Loan Authorizations, July 1, 1945-Sept. 30, 1988, p. 78; Dumbaugh, Kerry, *Korea and Congress, 1950-1990*, Report No. 85-171 F, Washington, Congressional Research Service, August 16, 1985, p. 2-12.

Pueblo Capture

Congress in September 1968, following North Korea's seizure of the USS *Pueblo* in January, passed a bill authorizing hostile fire pay for the ship's captured crew (HR 17780, approved September 21).[89]

President Johnson on January 25, 1968 called up approximately 14,000 men from the reserve using authority granted by a 1966 amendment to the defense appropriations bill.[90]

23. GUATEMALA (1953-54)

The United States, at the 10th Inter-American Conference held at Caracas in March 1954, won approval for a resolution declaring the "solidarity...of the American states against international communist intervention." The Senate on June 25, 1954, and the House on June 29 passed S. Con. Res. 91 affirming support for the Caracas resolution. Prior to its passage, Senate Majority Leader Knowland stated, "I do not interpret the resolution as being a blank check for a specific act of some kind, because I think that in every place in the world...the President of the United States has made it very clear...that we will operate under our constitutional procedures."[91]

Congress apparently played no direct role in U.S. efforts to oust Guatemalan President Arbenz Guzmán.

24. VIETNAM (1955-65)

Congress strongly supported the U.S. aid program to Vietnam during 1955-61, and never reduced significantly the Administration's authorization and appropriations requests. The United States during this period provided

---

[89] *U.S. Code Congressional and Administrative News*, 1968, P.L. 90-510, "Unified Services--Hostile Fire Access--Prisoners Pay".

[90] *Congress and the Nation*, Vol. I, p. 103.

[91] *Congressional Record* June 25, 1954, p. 8926-27; June 29, 1954, p. 9179; and June 25, 1954.

$1.5 to $2 billion in aid to Vietnam, excluding funds for CIA and military advisory group funds.[92]

Congress was not in session when Kennedy made his November 15, 1961 decision to increase the U.S. role in Vietnam, and little if any congressional consultation apparently occurred. The President had sufficient statutory authority to send additional personnel and equipment under the recently approved "Act for International Development of 1961" (PL-87-195), and funds were available through the 1961 foreign aid and defense appropriations bills. Moreover, in 1962 Congress voted "overwhelmingly" to approve the foreign aid sought by the administration to fulfill the new commitment.[93]

President Johnson on August 4, 1964 ordered retaliatory air strikes against North Vietnam in response to the Gulf of Tonkin incident earlier that day. On August 5 he sent a special message to Congress requesting passage of a resolution supporting "all necessary action to protect our Armed Forces and to assist nations covered by the SEATO Treaty."[94]

Congress on August 7, 1964 passed the Gulf of Tonkin Resolution (H.J. Res. 1145, approved August 10) which expressed approval for the President's action against North Vietnam and stated that the United States would be "prepared, as the President determines, to take all necessary steps, including the use of armed force, to assist any member or protocol state of the Southeast Asia Collective Defense Treaty requesting assistance in defense of its freedom."[95]

President Johnson in a May 4, 1965 special message to Congress requested an additional $700 million for "mounting military requirements in Vietnam." He emphasized that this "is not a routine appropriation. For each member of Congress who supports this request is also voting to persist in our effort to halt Communist aggression in South Viet Nam. Each is saying that the Congress and the President stand united before the world in joint determination that the independence of South Viet Nam shall be preserved and Communist attack will not succeed." Congress on May 6, 1965 passed H.J. Res. 447 ("Department of Defense Supplemental Appropriation," approved

---

[92] U.S. Congress, Senate, *The U.S. Government and the Vietnam War*, Part I, Prepared for the Committee on Foreign Relations by the Congressional Research Service, 98th Congress, 2nd Session, Washington, U.S. GPO, April 1984, p. 314-318.

[93] *Ibid.*, Part II, p. 100-01 and 126.

[94] *Congressional Quarterly Almanac*, 1964, p. 332.

[95] *U.S. Code Congressional and Administrative News*, 1964, P.L. 88-408, p. 441.

May 7) which provided the additional $700 million for Vietnam requested by the President.[96]

25. LAOS (1955-65)

The United States provided Laos with $300 million in military and economic between 1955 and 1964. Congress strongly supported those programs and never significantly reduced the Administration's requests.[97]

President Kennedy on May 15, 1962 "briefed" congressional leaders to send U.S. troops to Thailand, on Laos' west flank.[98]

President Kennedy signed the Laos neutrality agreement on July 23, 1962 as an Executive Agreement. Congress was not critical.[99]

The war nevertheless continued, as it did in Vietnam (Case 24) and Cambodia, where U.S. aid totalled about $360 million during the period 1955-63. Prince Norodom Sihanouk on November 19, 1963 ended all U.S. assistance to Cambodia claiming that U.S. military advisers were aiding anti-Government rebels.[100]

26. LEBANON (1958)

Congress in 1957 passed the "Middle East Resolution" (H.J. Res. 117, approved March 9) which authorized the President to "use armed forces to assist any such nation or group of nations (in Middle East) requesting assistance against armed aggression from any country controlled by Lebanon.

---

[96] "Additional $700 Million Requested for Viet Nam War," *Congressional Quarterly Almanac*, 1965, p. 1372-73; *U.S. Code Congressional and Administrative News*, 1965, P.L. 89-18, p. 112.

[97] Blechman, Barry M. and Stephen S. Kaplan, *Force Without War*, Washington, Brookings Institution, 1978, p.136; *The U.S. Government and the Vietnam War*, Part II, p. 318.

[98] *The U.S. Government and the Vietnam War*, Part II, p. 116.

[99] *Ibid.*, Part II, p. 117.

[100] *Congressional Quarterly Almanac*, 1963, p. 283.

Despite their ambivalence, he concluded that "authority for such an operation lay so clearly within the responsibility of the Executive that no direct objection was voiced. In any event, the issue was clear to me -- we had to go in." However, Eisenhower acknowledged later that "the government was moving in accord with the provisions of the Middle East Resolution, but if the conflict expanded into something that the Resolution did not cover, I would given time, go to the Congress for additional authorization."[101]

Eisenhower on July 15, in a speech before a joint session of Congress, justified intervention in Lebanon on the basis of Article 51 of the UN Charter.[102]

27. CUBA (1960-)

Sanctions

The United States since 1960 has imposed a variety of economic and political sanctions on Cuba. First, Congress authorized the President to cut the amount of sugar Cuba could export to the United States (H.R. 12311, PL 86-592, approved July 6, 1960). President Eisenhower on January 3, 1961 broke diplomatic relations with Cuba. President Kennedy on February 7, 1962 banned all U.S. exports to Cuba (except foodstuffs and medicines) using authority provided by Congress in the Foreign Assistance Act of 1961, which is still in effect, and prohibited Cuban imports into the United States soon thereafter.[103]

---

[101] Eisenhower, Dwight D., *The White House Years & Waging Peace*, Garden City, NY, Doubleday, 1963, p. 271-73.

[102] *Congressional Record* 85th Congress, 2nd Session, "Statement by the President," July 15, 1957, p. 13767-68; *U.S. Code Congressional and Administrative News*, 1958, "Assistance to the Republic of Lebanon," p. 5466-67; *Congressional Quarterly Almanac*, 1958, "Radio-Television Statement," p. 601-02.

[103] *U.S. Code Congressional and Administrative News*, 1960, P.L. 86-592, p. 385; *Congressional Quarterly Almanac*, 1960, p. 208; *Congress and the Nation*, Vol. I, p. 127; Galdi, Theodor W., and Robert D. Shuey, *U.S. Economic Sanctions Imposed Against Specific Foreign Countries: 1979 to the Present*, Washington, Congressional Research Service, September 9, 1989, p. 55-62; *U.S. Code Congressional and Administrative News*, "Foreign Assistance Act of 1961," 1961, p. 470.

Bay of Pigs (1961)

President Eisenhower on March 17, 1960 approved a CIA plan to unseat Castro. President Kennedy in April 1961 allowed the plan to proceed. He did not brief Congressional leaders until April 19 when the invasion had already failed.[104]

Cuban Missile Crisis (1962)

Congress during the Cuban Missile Crisis passed a joint resolution (S.J. Res. 230, approved October 3, 1962) expressing U.S. determination to stop Cuba, with force if necessary, from extending its "aggressive or subversive activities" to any part of the Western Hemisphere. The resolution also resolved to prevent the Soviets from establishing a military presence in Cuba that could threaten the United States, and to promote self determination for the Cuban people.[105]

Anti-Castro Activities (1960-65)

Congress was not involved in covert operations aimed at ousting Fidel Castro.

28. SOUTH AFRICA (1960-)

Congressional involvement in U.S. low-intensity conflict with South Africa has focused primarily on legislation mandating economic and political sanctions against that country. Congress in 1978 amended the "Export-Import Bank Act of 1945" to prohibit the bank from helping finance "any export which would contribute to enabling the government of the Republic of South Africa to maintain or enforce apartheid..."[106]

The House and Senate in 1985 both approved versions of a bill that would have imposed sanctions on South Africa. Before final Senate

---

[104] Wyden, Peter, *The Bay of Pigs: The Untold Story*, NY, Simon and Schuster, 1979, p. 25, 159-170; *Congressional Quarterly Almanac*, 1961, p. 330.

[105] 76 Stat. 697 (PL 87-733); U.S. Congress, House, *Background Information on the Use of U.S. Armed Forces in Foreign Countries*, 1975 Revision, A report prepared for the Subcommittee on International Security and Scientific Affairs of the Committee on International Relations, 94th Congress, 1st Session, U.S. GPO, Washington, 1975, p. 43.

[106] *Congressional Quarterly Almanac*, 1985, p. 85; Shuey and Galdi, p. 179-191; 92 Stat. 3724 (PL-95-630).

consideration of the bill, President Reagan on September 9 announced a package of more limited sanctions, thereby undercutting the congressional movement toward stronger action. The statement accompanying his Executive Order asserted, "If Congress sends me the present bill as reported by the Conference Committee, I would have to veto it. That need not happen. I want to work with the Congress to advance bipartisan support for America's policy toward South Africa." The President's sanctions included a ban on most loans to the South African Government, an end to the sale of computers and related equipment to South African entities enforcing apartheid, and prohibitions on the export of most nuclear production facility-related goods and technology.[107]

Congress on September 12, 1986 passed the "Comprehensive Anti-Apartheid act of 1986" (H.R. 4868) providing for numerous economic and political sanctions against South Africa. President Reagan vetoed the measure on September 26, but, Congress overrode his veto on October 2. The Act set policy goals, such as the release of political prisoners including Nelson Mandela, and an end to South African military actions against neighboring states. The Act also imposed new sanctions such as termination of air travel between the United States and South Africa, almost complete prohibition on U.S. government cooperation with South Africa's armed forces, and an end to South Africa's U.S. sugar import quota.[108]

Some Members of Congress in 1988 and 1989 attempted unsuccessfully to strengthen U.S. sanctions against South Africa.[109]

29. DOMINICAN REPUBLIC (1960-62)

Congress in 1960 declined to pass legislation, requested by the President Eisenhower, curtailing the Dominican sugar quota, partly because some

---

[107] *Congressional Quarterly Almanac*, 1985, p. 83; *U.S. Code Congressional and Administrative News*, 1985, Executive Order 12532, p. B82-85; *Congressional Quarterly Almanac*, 1985, "South Africa Sanctions," p. 28-D.

[108] 100 Stat. 1086 (PL 99-440); *Congressional Quarterly Almanac*, 1986, p. 359-73.

[109] *Congressional Quarterly Almanac*, 1988, p. 525-38; Branaman, Brenda M., *South Africa: U.S. Policy After Sanctions*, Issue Brief IB87128, Washington, Congressional Research Service, January 19, 1990, 14 p.

Members suspected that the Dominican government would get worse if Trujillo fell. A bill approved March 31, 1961, however, did comply with his request.[110]

Congress was not involved in covert operations aimed at ousting Trujillo.

30. ZAIRE (1960-64)

Congressional action in this conflict was sparse, but generally supportive. The House in 1961 rejected an amendment to a spending bill (HR 7712, P.L. 87-74) that would have reduced U.S. payments to support UN peacekeeping forces in the Congo by the amount the U.S. had spent airlifting those forces ($10.3 million).[111]

U.S. operations in Zaire were little noted by Congress, although Senator John Stennis asserted in 1964 that he strongly opposed "letting the Congo become an African Vietnam" and Senator Mike Mansfield stated that "news of increased U.S. involvement in the Congolese revolution is disturbing."[112]

Congress was not in session during "Operation Dragon Rouge."

31. BRAZIL (1961-64)

Congress was not involved in operations aimed at ousting President Goulart, but approved aid to his successor.

32. VIETNAM (1963)

Congress was not involved in the overthrow of President Diem. In the Foreign Assistance Act approved December 16, 1963, however, Congress expressed its sense that "assistance authorized by this Act should be extended to or withheld from the government of South Vietnam, in the discretion of the

---

[110] *Congressional Quarterly Almanac*, 1960, p. 208-16; and *Congressional Quarterly Almanac*, 1961, p. 129; and *U.S. Code Congressional and Administrative News*, 1961, p. 40 and 1520.

[111] *Congressional Quarterly Almanac*, 1961, p. 176.

[112] *Congressional Record*, 88th Congress, 2nd Session, August 14 and 21, 1964, p. 19531 and 20884.

President, to further the objectives of victory in the war against communism and the return to their homeland of Americans involved in that struggle." [113]

33. DOMINICAN REPUBLIC (1965-66)

Before sending troops to the Dominican Republic in 1965, President Johnson informed congressional leaders of his intentions. According to Senator Everett Dirksen, he told them that the CIA had identified at least three communists in the rebel command.[114]

The Senate Foreign Relations Committee, chaired by Senator William Fulbright, held closed hearings between April and July 1965 on the situation in the Dominican Republic. The Committee did not issue a report, but Senator Fulbright on the Senate floor made a September 15 speech that was harshly critical of the Administration's policy. He argued that the United States intervened primarily to prevent "another Cuba," rather than to save U.S. lives, and contended that fear of communist influence in the Dominican Republic was based on "fragmentary and inadequate evidence." [115]

The House of Representatives on September 20, 1965 passed H. Res. 560 expressing its sense that any country in the Western Hemisphere could through unilateral use of force stop a communist takeover anywhere else in the hemisphere. A resolution does not have the force of law.[116]

U.S. economic and military aid to the Dominican Republic continued, despite reservations expressed above. Congress also appropriated funds to support operations by Organization of American States forces.

---

[113] *U.S. Code Congressional and Administrative News*, 1963, p. 417.

[114] Wormuth and Firmage, *To Chain the Dog of War*, p. 160; *Congressional Quarterly Almanac*, 1965, p. 515.

[115] *Congressional Record*, 89th Congress, 1st Session, September 15, 1965, p. 23859.

[116] *Congressional Record*, 89th Congress, 1st Session, "Sense of the House of Representatives Relative to International Communism in the Western Hemisphere," September 20, 1965, p. 24347; *Congressional Quarterly Almanac*, 1965, p. 518.

34. GUATEMALA (1965-74)

Unclassified records suggest that the Johnson Administration did not consult with Congress about U.S. special forces combat missions in support of Guatemalan counterinsurgency operations between 1965 and 1974. Following a 1976 hearing on "Human Rights in Nicaragua, Guatemala, and El Salvador," Congressman Michael Harrington wrote the State Department, stating it "has been alleged that U.S. Government personnel -- i.e. Special Forces, Milgroups, MAAG or special contractees -- went beyond their advisory capacity and at times engaged in actual combat. More specifically, it has been alleged that 28 Americans died in Guatemala during the time period in question." He then asked for "specific instances in which U.S. personnel engaged in combat operations between 1966 to 1972." The State Department replied in part that it "has been U.S. Government policy throughout the counterinsurgency period that no U.S. military personnel be either ordered, or permitted, to participate in combat operations in Guatemala. Also, there is no evidence to indicate that any U.S. military personnel ever engaged in combat on their own initiative."[117] U.S. security assistance continued throughout the period.

35. THAILAND (1965-85)

Congressional authorization of U.S. counterinsurgency-related assistance to Thailand is difficult to separate from allocations determined by the Executive Branch.[118]

The United States reduced strong support for Thai counterinsurgency after 1969, but defeating insurgency remained an element of ongoing U.S. military and economic assistance to that country for several years thereafter. A Senate "staff report" prepared in January 1972 found that "United States support for counterinsurgency programs in Thailand is...closely related to the military assistance program and ...to the economic assistance program as well."

---

[117] U.S. Congress, Senate, *Guatemala and the Dominican Republic*, A Staff Memorandum prepared for the Foreign Relations Subcommittee on Western Hemisphere Affairs, Washington, U.S. Government Printing Office, 1971; U.S. Congress, House, *Human Rights in Nicaragua, Guatemala, and El Salvador: Implications for U.S. Policy*, Hearings before the International Relations Subcommittee on International Organizations, Washington, U.S. GPO, 1976, p. 217.

[118] Randolph, R. Sean, *The United States and Thailand: Alliance Dynamics, 1950-1985*, Berkeley, Institute of East Asian Studies, 1986, p. 85-109, 144-145; U.S. Congress, Senate, *United States Security Agreements and Commitments Abroad, Kingdom of Thailand*, Washington, U.S. GPO, 1970, p. 633-34; 632, 629, 775, 834, 629-32; *Congress and the Nation*, Vol. III, p. 935.

The report identified Special Forces and other U.S. military personnel "in some form of counterinsurgency advisory role," although in most cases the duty was "collateral." It also noted that "(p)rimary emphasis in the U.S. program will continue to be placed in bolstering Thai efforts to improve security in rural areas and to support Thai counterinsurgency oriented rural development programs." [119]

U.S. military and economic aid to Thailand continued into the mid 1980's, but was generally justified on grounds other than counterinsurgency. During 1982 testimony at a Senate Foreign Relations East Asian and Pacific Affairs Subcommittee hearing on "U.S. Policies and Programs in Southeast Asia," Deputy Assistant Secretary of Defense for East Asia and Pacific Affairs Richard Armitage stressed that U.S. military assistance to Thailand was necessary to defend that country against potential Vietnamese aggression.[120] He never mentioned the insurgency.

36. JORDAN (1970)

The Nixon Administration during the September 1970 crisis in Jordan apparently did not consult with Congress as events unfolded. Nixon later told Congress that the crisis was "the gravest threat to world peace since the administration came to office." [121]

---

[119] U.S. Congress, Senate, *Thailand, Laos, and Cambodia: January 1972*, A Staff Report prepared for the Foreign Relations Subcommittee on U.S. Security Agreements and Commitments Abroad, Washington, U.S. GPO, 1972, p. 10-17.

[120] Kerdphol, Gen. Saiyud, *The Struggle for Thailand, Counterinsurgency 1965-1985*, Bangkok, S. Research Center Co., 1986, 253 p; *Overseas Loans and Grants and Assistance from International Organizations*, Obligations and Loan Authorizations, July 1, 1945-September 30, 1987, p. 84; U.S. Congress, Senate, *U.S. Policies and Programs in Southeast Asia*, Hearings before the Foreign Relations Subcommittee on East Asian and Pacific Affairs, Washington, U.S. G.P.O., 1982, p. 7-13.

[121] Blechman and Kaplan, *Force Without War*, p. 257-79; Hersh, Seymour M., *The Price of Power, Kissinger in the Nixon White House*, New York, Summit Books, 1983, p. 234-49; Kissinger, Henry, *White House Years*, Boston, Little, Brown, p. 609-631.

Following the crisis, Congress passed the "Special Foreign Assistance Act of 1971" (H.R. 19911, approved January 8, 1971) which included $30 million in additional military assistance for Jordan.[122]

37. LIBYA (1970-)

Sanctions

Congress has authorized various sanctions against Libya, in addition to those initiated by the Executive Branch. Congress in September 1979, for example, amended the "Export Administration Act" to require the State Department to notify Congress before approving the export of goods or technology worth more than $7 million to countries repeatedly supporting acts of international terrorism, if such exports would contribute to the recipient's military potential or enhance its ability to support terrorism. The Carter Administration placed Libya on the list of offenders. Congress, in the 1982 foreign assistance appropriation measure approved December 29, 1981, added Libya to a list of nations barred from receiving direct U.S. assistance or reparations. In the International Security and Development Cooperation Act of 1985, approved on August 8, 1985, Congress specifically authorized the President to prohibit trade with Libya. Congress in 1986 amended the Arms Export Control Act to prohibit (with provision for Presidential waiver) the export of any U.S. Munitions List item to countries repeatedly supporting international terrorism. That included Libya.[123]

Military Clashes

President Reagan received strong support in Congress for his March and April 1986 military actions against Libya. Some Members, however, criticized him for failing to comply fully with the War Powers Resolution because he did not consult adequately with Congress in advance. President Reagan's first report on March 23 did not specifically mention the resolution. His April 16 statement acknowledged that in "accordance with my desire that Congress be informed on the matter, and consistent with the War Powers Resolution, I am providing this report on the employment of the U.S. Armed Forces." He added

---

[122] *U.S. Code Congressional and Administrative News*, 1970, p. 2281 (PL 91-652); *Congressional Record*, 91st Congress, Second Session, December 8, 1970, p. 40706.

[123] Galdi and Shuey, p. 123-131; "Export Administration Act of 1979," 93 Stat. 515 (P.L. 96-72); "Foreign Assistance and Related Program Appropriation Act," 95 Stat. 1655 (P.L. 97-121); "International Security and Development Cooperation Act of 1985," 99 Stat. 220 (P.L. 99-83); "Omnibus Diplomatic Security and Antiterrorism Act of 1986," 100 Stat. 874 (P.L. 99-399).

that the "self defense measures were undertaken pursuant to my authority under the constitution." [124]

38. CHILE (1970-73)

Congress did not participate in U.S. covert operations designed to oust Chilean President Allende. The Senate Select Committee that subsequently investigated the matter asserted that congressional oversight during the period April 1964 to December 1974 was "inadequate". CIA briefed Congress at various times, but the "record suggests that the briefings were often after the fact and incomplete." The Committee, in it final report for example, acknowledges 13 CIA briefings on Chile between March 1973 and December 1974 that at least in part addressed covert action; all, however, "were concerned with *past* CIA covert action..." [125]

39. IRAQ (1972-75)

Congress was not consulted regarding U.S. aid to Kurdish insurgents in Iraq. The House Select Intelligence Committee report on that subject

---

[124] *Congressional Quarterly Almanac*, 1986, "Clashes with Libya Renew War Powers Debate," p. 392; *Congressional Record*, 99th Congress, 2nd Session, April 8, 1986, "Libyan Action and War Powers," p. E 1016-17; Collier, Ellen C., *War Powers Resolution: Presidential Compliance*, Issue Brief IB81050, Washington, Congressional Research Service, November 2, 1989, p. 9-10; *Congressional Record*, 99th Congress, 2nd Session, April 16, 1986, "Report from President Reagan Regarding Use of Air and Naval Forces in Libya," p. S4334.

[125] U.S. Congress, Senate, *Covert Action in Chile, 1963-1973*, Staff Report of the Select Committee to Study Government Operations with Respect to Intelligence Activities, 94th Congress, 1st Session, Washington, U.S. GPO, December 18, 1975, p. 2, 50, 53; U.S. Congress, Senate, *Foreign and Military Intelligence (Book 1)*, Final Report of the Select Committee..., 94th Congress, 2nd Session, Washington, U.S. GPO, April 26, 1976, p. 150; U.S. Congress, Senate, *Alleged Assassination Plots Involving Foreign Leaders*, An Interim Report of the Select Committee..., 94th Congress, 1st Session, Washington, U.S. G.P.O., November 20, 1975, p. 225-227.

indicates that President Nixon and Henry Kissinger also "circumvented" the Forty Committee and kept the State Department "in the dark." [126]

40. OPEC (1974-75)

Congressional outrage over OPEC's use of oil for "international extortion" was featured in floor speeches for several months, but Congress played no direct role in the Ford Administrations's posturing *vis-à-vis* OPEC in 1975. On the contrary, congressional hearings and reports, which took a sober view of threats against OPEC, may have helped constrain military options.[127]

The Trade Act of 1974 H.R. 10710, (approved January 3, 1975) instructed the President not to designate any member of OPEC as a "beneficiary developing country." Congress subsequently established a Strategic Petroleum Reserve, and took further steps to help reduce U.S. vulnerabilities in event of another oil embargo.[128]

41. CYPRUS (1974-78)

Congress used a continuing appropriations resolution (H.J.Res. 1167, approved October 17, 1974) to impose an arms embargo on Turkey in response to that country's use of U.S.-supplied military equipment during its intervention in Cyprus. The measure forbid the Executive Branch to provide military assistance or sell "defense articles and services" to Turkey until the President certified to Congress that Turkey was "in compliance with the Foreign Assistance Act of 1961, (and) the Foreign Military Sales Act...and that substantial progress toward agreement has been made regarding military forces in Cyprus." Suspension took effect in December 1974. President Ford vetoed two similar resolutions (H.J. Res. 1131 and H.J. Res. 1163) before signing H.J.Res. 1167. Congress later approved a "suspension of military assistance to Turkey" (S. 3394, "Foreign Assistance Act of 1974," December 30, 1974), but

---

[126] "The CIA Report the President Doesn't Want You to Read, the Pike Papers: and Introduction by Aaron Latham," *Village Voice*, February 16, 1976, p. 85.

[127] U.S. Congress, House, *Oil Fields As Military Objectives*, Prepared for the International Relations Special Subcommittee on Investigation by the Congressional Research Service, Library of Congress, 94th Congress, 1st Session, Washington, U.S. GPO, 1975, 111 p.

[128] *U.S. Code Congressional and Administrative News*, 1974, (P.L. 93-618) p. 2290 and 2395-96; P.L. 94-163, December 22, 1975.

delayed implementation of the embargo until February 5, 1975. Congress included the aid suspension in yet a third measure, another continuing appropriations resolution (H.J. Res. 1178) approved on December 31, 1974. [129]

Congress in 1975 partially lifted the ban on military aid to Turkey after an intensive Administration lobbying campaign that emphasized Turkey's decision to terminate U.S. operations at bases within its borders. The act (S. 2230, approved October 6, 1975) authorized the President to provide Turkey the "defense articles and defense services" that it had contracted for under the Foreign Military Sales Act on or before February 5, 1975, when the embargo began. The measure also permitted the United States to provide military equipment Turkey needed to fulfill NATO-related defense responsibilities. Accordingly, Congress used the International Security Assistance and Arms Export Control Act of 1976 (H.R. 13680, approved June 30, 1976) to authorize the supply -- via sales credits and loan guaranties -- of not more than $125 million worth of defense articles and services needed by Turkey.[130]

The International Security Assistance Act of 1978 (S. 3075, approved September 26, 1978) fully lifted the embargo on military aid to Turkey. Before the two countries could resume "full military cooperation," however, the Act required the President to certify to Congress that the relationship would be in the national interest and that Turkey was making a good faith effort to settle the Cyprus problem. Moreover, the Act required a Presidential status report every sixty days on the situation in Cyprus as well as Presidential certification that any military aid provided to Turkey or Greece would be for defensive purposes only.[131]

42. MAYAGUEZ (1975)

President Ford on May 15, 1975 reported to Congress on U.S. use of armed force to recover the USS *Mayaguez* and crew during the previous two

---

[129] 88 Stat. 1363-65 (P.L. 93-448); *Congressional Quarterly Almanac*, 1974, "Congress Wins Restrictions on Aid to Turkey," p. 547-53; U.S. Congress, House, *Congressional-Executive Relations and the Turkish Arms Embargo*, Report Prepared for the Committee on Foreign Affairs, Congress and Foreign Policy Series No. 3, Washington, U.S. GPO, June 1981, p. 3; *U.S. Code Congressional and Administrative News*, 1974, p. 2064, 2072 (P.L. 93-559); p. 2143 (P.L. 93-570).

[130] 89 Stat. 508 (P.L. 94-104); *Congressional Quarterly Almanac*, 1975, "Turkish Aid Ban Imposed, Partially Lifted," p. 327-31; 90 Stat. 729 at 757 (P.L. 94-329)

[131] 92 Stat. 730 at 737-40 (P.L. 95-384); *Congressional Quarterly Almanac*, 1978, "Military Aid Bill: Turkey Arms Ban Lifted," p. 416-24.

days. His letter to the Speaker of the House and the President pro tempore of the Senate was "in accordance" with his "desire that the Congress be informed on this matter and taking note of Section 4(a)(1) of the War Powers Resolution..." He recounted the U.S. action and indicated that U.S. forces had "begun the process of disengagement and withdrawal." The President maintained that he ordered and conducted the operation using his "constitutional Executive power and his authority as Commander-in-Chief" of the U.S. Armed Forces.[132]

Congress generally supported the President's policy regarding the *Mayaguez*, but controversy arose over whether he had consulted adequately with Congress prior to taking action. The Administration did communicate with congressional leaders and relevant committees on May 13-14, 1975. The State Department briefed the House International Relations, Senate Foreign Relations, and House Armed Services Committees on the situation. Yet many lawmakers believed that Congress had been merely "informed" not "consulted."[133]

43. CAMBODIA (1975-)

The 1985 International Security and Development Act (S. 960, approved August 8, 1985) authorized up to $5 million in grant nonlethal military assistance and economic support funds to the "noncommunist resistance forces in Cambodia" for both FY 1986 and 1987. Section 906 of the Act banned assistance to the Khmer Rouge. All subsequent aid measures were subject to

---

[132] *American Foreign Relations 1975, A Documentary Record*, Ed by Richard P. Stebbins and Elaine P. Adams, NY, New York University Press, 1977, p. 159-60.

[133] *Congressional Quarterly Almanac*, 1975, "U.S. Merchant Ship Hijacked by Cambodians, Crew and Vessel Rescued by American Forces," p. 310-11; *Congressional Record*, 94th Congress, 1st Session, June 23, 1975, p. 20270; U.S. Congress, House, *War Powers: A Test of Compliance Relative to the Danang Sealift*, the Evacuation of Phnom Penh, the Evacuation of Saigon, and the Mayaguez Incident, Hearings Before the International Relations Subcommittee on International Security and Scientific Affairs, 94th Congress, 1st Session, Washington, U.S. GPO, p. 116-17; Collier, Ellen C., *War Powers Resolution: Presidential Compliance*, Congressional Research Issue Brief IB 81050, January 2, 1990, p. 13; U.S. Congress, House, *Seizure of the Mayaguez (Part IV)*, Reports of the Comptroller General of the United States submitted to the International Relations Subcommittee on International Political and Military Affairs, 94th Congress, 2nd Session, Washington, U.S. GPO, 1976, p. 134.

similar provisions. In addition, the Administration reportedly gave resistance groups substantially more nonlethal covert aid between FY 1986-89.[134]

Congress passed a joint resolution (H.J. Res. 602, approved October 18, 1988) "in support of the restoration of a free and independent Cambodia, the withdrawal of Vietnamese forces, and the protection of the Cambodian people from a return to power of the genocidal Khmer Rouge." The resolution also specifically declared that the United States should continue to assist the non-Communist Cambodian forces, and called for consideration of an international conference on the Cambodian situation.[135]

The Bush Administration in the spring of 1989 sought permission to provide covert lethal aid to noncommunist Cambodian resistance forces. Congress declined, and in the FY 1990 foreign assistance appropriations act (H.R. 3743, approved November 21, 1989) openly provided not more than $7 million in "Foreign Military Financing Program" funds and "Economic Support Funds" to the "Cambodian non-Communist resistance forces." A classified appendix to that act reportedly directed the Administration to obtain congressional approval before using CIA contingency funds for lethal aid to those forces.[136]

Congress and the Executive Branch both have imposed sanctions on the Cambodian Government. Congress, for example, has used annual foreign aid appropriation measures since 1976 to ban assistance or reparations to the Cambodian Government. Most recently, the provision appeared in the FY 1990 foreign assistance appropriations act (H.R. 3743, approved November 21, 1989) which prohibited such assistance to Cambodia among other countries. Additionally, Congress in the "Export-Import Bank Act Amendments of 1986" (H.R. 5548, approved October 15, 1986) placed Cambodia on a list of "specific countries deemed to be Marxist-Leninist" to which the Export-Import Bank could not provide credit. [137]

---

[134] 99 Stat. 190 at 268 (P.L. 99-83); 99 Stat. 1185 at 1311, "Further Continuing Appropriations, 1985" (approved December 19, 1985, P.L. 99-190); 100 Stat. 3341 at 3341-236, "Continuing Appropriations, Fiscal Year 1987" (approved October 30, 1986, P.L. 99-591); 101 Stat. 1329 at 1329-165, "Continuing Appropriations, Fiscal Year 1988" (approved December 22, 1987, P.L. 100-202); 102 Stat. 2268 at 2268-48, FY 1989 Foreign Assistance Appropriations Act (approved October 1, 1988, P.L. 100-461); Sutter, Robert G., *Cambodian Crisis: Problems of a Settlement and Policy Dilemmas for the United States*, Issue Brief IB89020, Washington, Congressional Research Service, January 24, 1990, p. 8-9.

[135] 102 Stat. 2504 (P.L. 100-502)

[136] Sutter, *Cambodian Crisis*, p. 10; 103 Stat. 1195 at 1245.

[137] 103 Stat. 1195 at 1219 (P.L. 101-167); 100 Stat. 1200 at 1203 (P.L. 99-472).

44. NICARAGUA (1978-79)

Congress sent mixed signals to the Executive Branch concerning actions to oust Nicaragua's President Anastasio Somoza. Some approved, some did not. Congressmen Jack Murphy and Charles Wilson, for example, opposed Congressman Ed Koch's 1977 attempt to eliminate military aid for Nicaragua. Wilson won approval for two basic human needs loans to Nicaragua in May 1977. The foreign aid bill conference committee cut out a Senate amendment which would have eliminated assistance to Nicaragua that same year, unless the President certified to Congress that aid "will serve to promote democratic processes in that country." [138]

As domestic opposition to Somoza strengthened in the fall of 1978, 78 legislators on September 21 wrote President Carter insisting that he "come publicly to the support of the Government of Nicaragua during this period of crisis." In contrast, on October 13, 86 lawmakers implored Secretary of State Cyrus Vance to "suspend all aid to the Nicaraguan government" to avoid giving "a misleading message of support" to the dictator. Finally, on June 18, 1979, 100 Representatives and 5 Senators wrote a public letter to President Carter urging support for Somoza.[139]

45. IRAN (1979-)

U.S. Hostages in Teheran

Following the seizure of the U.S. embassy in Iran, Congress voted some sanctions against that country, in addition to those imposed by the Executive Branch. Specifically, the continuing appropriations resolution for fiscal year 1980 (H.J. Res. 440, approved November 20, 1979) mandated that "none of the funds provided by this joint resolution shall be used for military or economic aid for Iran." [140]

President Carter on April 26, 1980 reported to Congress on the aborted attempt to rescue the American hostages in Iran with U.S. armed forces, because of his "desire that Congress be informed on this matter and consistent with the reporting provisions of the War Powers Resolution..." He described the operation, and stated that it had been "ordered and conducted pursuant

---

[138] Galdi and Shuey, p. 141-145; Pastor, Robert A., *Condemned to Repetition: The United States and Nicaragua*, Princeton, NJ, Princeton University Press, 1987, p. 53-54, 65-66.

[139] Pastor, 98-99,and 143.

[140] Galdi and Shuey, p. 97-103; 93 Stat. 923 at 926 (P.L. 96-123).

to the President's powers under the Constitution as Chief Executive and as Commander-in-Chief" of the U.S. Armed Forces. Moreover, he argued that the United States acted "to protect and rescue its citizens" in accordance with Article 51 of the United Nations charter.[141]

The Carter Administration apparently did not consult with, or inform, Congress about "Desert One" prior to its initiation. Acting Secretary of State Warren Christopher, in testimony before a closed session of the Senate Foreign Relations Committee on May 8, 1980 (shortly after the aborted mission), stated that the "President concluded in this case that the success of the operation and the safety of those involved depended upon total surprise and total secrecy. For that reason, he concluded that it was essential to limit knowledge of the operation to a very small group of individuals directly involved in the planning and implementing of the operation. He therefore concluded that it was not possible in this instance to engage in the consultations under section 3 of the War Powers Resolution." Foreign Relations Committee Chairman Frank Church, who objected to this line of reasoning, argued that the President cannot unilaterally determine when consultation is required, and that "consultation requires giving Congress an opportunity to participate in the decision making process." [142]

"Iran-Contra" Affair

Congress in August 1986, via the Omnibus Diplomatic Security and Antiterrorism Act of 1986 (HR 4151, approved August 27, 1986), prohibited the export of any items on the U.S. Munitions List to countries determined by the Secretary of State to have "repeatedly provided support for acts of international terrorism." The Reagan Administration had placed Iran on the list of offenders under the Export Administration Act in January 1986.[143]

The Reagan Administration did not inform Congress concerning the exchange of covert arms for hostages in Iran or the diversion of arms sales proceeds to Nicaraguan "Contras". The Senate Intelligence Committee and the House Foreign Affairs Committees held hearings on the Iran-Contra affair in December 1986, following Reagan's November 13 public revelation. Both

---

[141] U.S. Congress, House, *Use of Armed Forces in Attempted Rescue of Hostages in Iran*, Communications from the President of the United States, Washington, U.S. GPO, 1980, 2 p.

[142] U.S. Congress, Senate, *The Situation in Iran*, Hearing before the Committee on Foreign Relations, 96th Congress, 2nd Session, (Top Secret hearing held on May 8, 1980, sanitized and printed on February 18, 1981), Washington, U.S. GPO, 1980, p. iii and 4.

[143] 100 Stat. 853 at 874 (P.L. 99-399); Shuey and Galdi, p. 100. See Case 37, Libya, "Sanctions" for reference to export restrictions under the "Export Administration Act."

Houses formed special committees to conduct a more formal investigation in 1987: the House Select Committee to Investigate Covert Arms Transactions with Iran; the Senate Select Committee on Secret Military Assistance to Iran and the Nicaraguan Opposition. They issued a joint report on November 18, 1987. The bipartisan majority report harshly criticized the Administration, concluding that the "common ingredients of the Iran and Contra policies were secrecy, deception and disdain for the law." The Republican minority report defended the Administration, stating that although "President Reagan and his staff made mistakes in the Iran-Contra Affair," these were "mistakes in judgement, and nothing more. There was no constitutional crisis, no systematic disrespect for rule of law,' no grand conspiracy, and no Administration-wide dishonesty or coverup." [144]

Congress in the foreign operations appropriation act for FY 1988 (which appeared in H.J.Res. 395, the continuing appropriation resolution, approved December 22, 1987), mandated that "none of the funds appropriated or otherwise made available pursuant to this Act shall be obligated or expended to finance directly any assistance or reparations" to Iran among several other countries.[145]

46. SYRIA (1979-)

Congress has authorized various sanctions against Syria for supporting terrorism, in addition to those initiated by the Executive Branch. The Export Administration Act of 1979 (S. 737, approved September 29, 1979) required the State Department to notify Congress before approving the export of goods or technology worth more than $7 million to countries repeatedly supporting acts of international terrorism, if such exports would contribute to the recipients military potential or enhance its ability to support terrorism. The Secretary of State in December 1979 included Syria on the list of offenders. The 1982 foreign assistance appropriation act (H.R. 4559, December 29, 1981) placed Syria on a list of nations barred from receiving funds provided by the act for direct assistance or reparations. This prohibition was repeated, for example, in the FY 1988 foreign assistance appropriation act (part of H.J. Res.

---

[144] *Congressional Quarterly Almanac*, "Special Report: The Iran-Contra Affair," 1986, p. 415-50, and 1987, p. 61-111; Woldman, Joel M., "Congress and the Iran-Contra-Affair," Washington, Congressional Research Service Report 88-765 F, November 1988, 37 p.; and U.S. Congress, House, *Report of the Congressional Committees Investigating the Iran-Contra-Affair: with Supplemental, Minority, and Additional Views*, Select Committees to Investigate Covert Arms Transactions with Iran, U.S. Senate Select Committee on Secret Military Assistance to Iran and the Nicaraguan Opposition, Washington, U.S. GPO, 1987, 690 p.

[145] 101 Stat. 1329, at 1329-155 (P.L. 100-202)

395, the continuing appropriations resolution approved on December 22, 1987). The Act also bars Syria from receiving funds made available for indirect assistance or reparations, unless the President "certifies that the withholding of these funds is contrary to the national interest of the United States." The continuing appropriations resolution for FY 1984 (H.J.Res. 413, approved November 14, 1983) eliminated the economic assistance program to Syria, and with some exceptions, deobligated "all funds heretofore obligated" for such aid. Congress in August 1986, via the Omnibus Diplomatic Security and Antiterrorism Act of 1986, (H.R. 4151, approved August 27, 1986) prohibited the export of any items on the U.S. Munitions list to countries determined by the Secretary of State -- for purposes of similar export controls under the Export Administration Act, to have "repeatedly provided support for acts of international terrorism." As mentioned above, Syria had already been cited as such a country by the State Department.[146]

Congress has a limited ability to directly secure the release of the hostages. Congressional efforts focus mainly on publicizing the existence of the hostages, drawing attention to issues related to terrorism generally, and deliberating broad policy responses.[147]

47. EL SALVADOR (1979-)

Congressional oversight and prescriptions connected with this conflict have been intense. The International Security and Development Cooperation Act of 1981 (S 1196, approved December 29, 1981) authorized economic and military aid to El Salvador requested by the Reagan Administration for FY 1982 ($26 million military, $40 million Economic Support Funds (ESF), $51.1 million food and development assistance). However, the Act conditioned assistance upon a semiannual Presidential certification that the Salvadoran government was improving the human rights situation, controlling its armed forces, implementing economic and political reforms such as land reform, and moving toward democratic elections. The Reagan Administration made the requisite certifications in 1982.[148]

---

[146] Galdi and Shuey, p. 199-202; 93 Stat. 503 at 515 (P.L. 96-72); 95 Stat. 1647 at 1655 (P.L. 97-1210); 101 Stat. 1329, 1329-155, at 1329-169 (P.L. 100-202); 97 Stat. 964 at 967 (P.L. 98-151); 100 Stat. 853 at 874 (P.L. 99-399)

[147] Mark, Clyde R., *Lebanon: The Remaining U.S. Hostages*, Washington, Congressional Research Service, Issue Brief IB85183, January 22, 1990, p. 10.

[148] 95 Stat. 1519 at 1554-1557 (P.L. 97-113); Storrs, K. Larry, *El Salvador Aid: Congressional Action, 1981-1986, On President Reagan's Requests for Economic and Military Assistance for El Salvador*, Washington, Congressional Research Service Report No. 87-230 F, March 18, 1987, p. 5-6.

Since then, congressional action on requests for assistance have hinged on such issues. Some funds, for example, were withheld pending trials related to the murder of four American churchwomen in 1983.[149]

The FY 1989 foreign aid appropriation act (H.R. 4637, approved October 1, 1988) specifically $185 million in economic support funds for El Salvador, but did not earmark or reduce military aid for that country. The measure continued previously approved provisions relating to El Salvador, such as a semi-annual presidential report on that nation's progress on items such as land reform and ending death squad activity (Section 590).[150]

The FY 1990 foreign assistance appropriation (H.R. 3743, November 21, 1989) limited foreign military financing to El Salvador to "not more than" $85 million. Congress did not add restrictions on military aid sought by some members in connection with the November 16 murder of six Jesuit priests, but the Act did include conditions similar to those approved in the past (President Bush had vetoed an earlier version of this bill). Congress also passed resolutions in November 1989 (H. Con. Res. 236 and S. Res. 217) stating that the United States would reconsider aid to El Salvador if its Government did not prosecute and punish those responsible for the murder of the six priests (and two women).[151]

48. BOLIVIA (1980-86)

Congress imposed various sanctions on Bolivia for drug production during the period 1980-86 -- in addition to those initiated by the Executive Branch. The International Security and Development Cooperation Act of 1985 (S. 960, approved August 8, 1985) mandated that if the President certified that Bolivia had taken specified actions to eradicate illegal coca production, then that country could receive "up to 50 percent" of allocated military assistance and economic support funds (ESF) during FY 1986. The remaining half would be released upon Presidential certification that Bolivia achieved drug eradication targets for 1985 contained in a 1983 narcotics agreement with the United States. The measure also imposed conditions on FY 1987 aid. The FY 1986 Foreign Assistance Appropriation (part of the Further Continuing Resolution, H.J. Res 465, approved December 19, 1985) included the same conditions on FY 1986 aid, but did not address FY 1987 assistance as in the authorization.

---

[149] Storrs, p. 9-15; Stat .301 (P.L. 98-63); 97 Stat. 964 (P.L. 98-151).

[150] Storrs, *El Salvador: U.S. Aid in 1987 and 1988*, p. 10-11; 102 Stat. 2268 at 2268-10 (P.L. 100-461).

[151] Storrs, K. Larry, *El Salvador and U.S. Aid: Congressional Action in 1989*, CRS Issue Brief IB90011, January 5, 1990, 8 p.; 103 Stat. 1195 (P.L. 101-167).

The United States in June 1986 withheld $7.2 million in foreign aid to Bolivia because the country did not meet the agreed upon 1985 drug eradication targets.[152]

The Anti-Drug Abuse Act of 1986 (H.R. 5484, approved October 27, 1986) "applaud(ed)" the Bolivian government for its drug interdiction efforts. The Act amended the International Security and Development Cooperation Act passed the previous year so as to allow up to 50 percent of authorized aid upon Presidential certification that Bolivia engaged in interdiction operations to disrupt significantly the drug industry or had cooperated with the United States to do so. The remaining half could be released upon Presidential certification that Bolivia had either met the 1985 eradication targets or entered into agreement for -- and made substantial progress toward -- the plan's implementation in 1987. The FY 1987 foreign assistance appropriations measure (part of the Continuing Appropriations Resolution for FY 1987, H.J. Res. 738, October 30, 1986) incorporated the provision. Congress included similar language the following year in the foreign assistance appropriations measure for FY 1988 (part of the FY 1988 Continuing Appropriations Resolution, H.J. Res. 395, approved December 22, 1987).[153]

President Reagan did not report to Congress following the July 14, 1986 introduction of U.S. Army personnel and aircraft into Bolivia for anti-drug assistance, because he did not believe the War Powers Resolution applied. The Administration briefed 15 key members of Congress on July 14.[154]

49. AFGHANISTAN (1980-)

Congress has strongly supported the Afghan rebels and opposed Soviet intervention. Both the Senate and House approved a resolution in October 1984 (S.Con. Res. 74) resolving that it should be U.S. policy to "support effectively the people of Afghanistan in their fight for freedom." Similarly, Congress in the FY 1988-89 Foreign Relations Authorization Act (H.R. 1777, approved December 22, 1987) declared "it to be the policy of the United States...to provide such assistance to the Afghan people as will most effectively

---

[152] 99 Stat. 190 at 230 (P.L. 99-83); 99 Stat. 1185 at 1308-1309 (P.L. 99-190); and Galdi and Shuey, p. 26.

[153] 100 Stat. 3207 at 3207-65 and 3207-66 (P.L. 99-570); 100 Stat. 3341 at 3341-232 (P.L. 99-591); 101 Stat. 1329 at 1329-160 (P.L. 100-202); and Shuey and Galdi, p. 26-27.

[154] Collier, Ellen C., *War Powers Resolution: Presidential Compliance*, p. 12; and Perl, Raphael, *Narcotics and the Use of U.S. Military Personnel: Operations in Bolivia and Issues for Congress*, Congressional Research Report for Congress 86-800 F, July 29, 1986, p. 9-10.

help them resist the Soviet invaders." The Senate passed a resolution on February 29, 1988 (S.Res. 386), prior to the Soviet's decision in April to withdraw from Afghanistan, insisting that the United States should continue aid to the Afghan rebels "until it is absolutely clear that the Soviets have terminated their military occupation." This resolution apparently strengthened the Reagan Administration's stated position that the United States would continue to provide assistance to the rebels as long as the Soviet Union continued to aid the Government of Afghanistan.[155]

Congress reportedly has approved considerable funds for covert assistance through Pakistan to the Afghan resistance. In addition, Congress has openly provided non-military funds to the "Afghan people" since 1985. The International Security and Development Cooperation Act of 1985 (S. 960, August 8, 1985) authorized $15 million in humanitarian assistance (food, medicine, etc.). The foreign assistance appropriation measure for FY 1987 (part of the Continuing Appropriations Resolution, H.J. Res. 738, approved October 30, 1986) boosted the humanitarian aid to $30 million. The foreign assistance appropriation measure for FY 1988 (part of the Continuing Appropriations Resolution, H.J. Res. 395, December 22, 1987) increased humanitarian aid to $45 million. The foreign assistance appropriations act for FY 1989 (H.R. 4637, October 1, 1988) again provided $45 million in humanitarian aid to the Afghan people.[156]

Congress has imposed sanctions on the Afghan Government in addition to those initiated by the Executive Branch. For example, assistance appropriations measure for FY 1986 (part of the further Continuing Appropriations Resolution, H.J. Res 465, December 19, 1985) authorized the President to deny most-favored-nation trade (MFN) treatment to Afghan exports to the United States and to deny credits to Afghanistan. President Reagan on February 18, 1986 suspended Afghanistan's MFN status. Congress in the Export-Import Bank Act Amendments of 1986 (H.R. 5548, October 15, 1986) placed Afghanistan on a list of "specific countries deemed to be Marxist-Leninist," to which the Export-Import Bank could not provide credit.[157]

---

[155] *Congressional Record* (Daily Edition), 98th Congress, 2nd Session, October 3, 1984, p. S 12940-41, and October 4, 1984, p H 11474-75; 101 Stat. 1331 at 1420-1421 (P.L. 100-204), *Congressional Quarterly Almanac*, 1988, p. 7-S; Cronin, Richard P. and Francis T. Miko, *Afghanistan: Status, U.S. Role, and Implications of a Soviet Withdrawal*, Issue Brief IB 88049, Congressional Research Service, January 6, 1989, p. 10.

[156] *Congressional Quarterly Almanac*, 1984, p. 118 and 1987, p. 143; Prados, Alfred P., *Intelligence Budget: Contents and Releasability*, Washington, Congressional Research Service, 89-465 F, August 2, 1989, 53 p.; 99 Stat. 190 at 268 (P.L. 99-83); 100 Stat. 334 at 3341-236 (P.L. 99-591); 101 Stat. 1329 at 1329-164 (P.L. 100-202); 102 Stat. 2268 at 2268-30 (P.L. 100-461).

[157] 99 Stat. 1185 at 1314-1315 (P.L. 99-190); Galdi and Shuey p. 6; 100 Stat. 1200 (P.L. 99-472).

50. NICARAGUA (1981-)

Few low-intensity conflicts have attracted closer congressional attention and participation than Nicaragua. Congress in 1981 and again in 1982 reportedly approved $19 million in covert military aid to the anti-Government guerrillas in Nicaragua (Contras). The Defense Department appropriation (part of the Continuing Appropriations Resolution for FY 1983, H.J. Res. 631, December 21, 1982) included the first "Boland Amendment" which stated that no funds provided by the Act could be used by CIA or DOD to assist any group "for the purpose of overthrowing the Government of Nicaragua or provoking a military exchange between Nicaragua and Honduras."[158]

The Intelligence Authorization Act for Fiscal Year 1984 (H.R. 2968, approved December 9, 1983) openly authorized "not more than" $24 million in military assistance to the Contras. The Act did not contain a "Boland Amendment," but that ceiling and classified restrictions blocked CIA from using its contingency fund for Contra aid, which it had reportedly done the previous year. The Department of Defense Appropriations Act, 1984 (H.R. 4185, December 8, 1983) openly appropriated the $24 million, using the same language found in the authorization act.[159]

Congress in mid-1984 effectively ended U.S. assistance to the Contras when it removed aid from a supplemental appropriations resolution (H.J. Res. 492, approved July 2, 1984). Contra aid previously approved in 1983 had apparently been exhausted by that time. The Department of Defense Appropriations Act, 1985 (part of the Continuing Appropriations Resolution for FY 1985, H.J. Res. 648, approved October 12, 1984) included a second "Boland Amendment." The measure allowed aid only if Congress passed a joint resolution after February 28, 1985 approving "assistance for military or paramilitary operations." Congress never enacted the requisite joint resolution. The FY 1985 Intelligence Authorization Act (H.R. 5399, November 8, 1984) also prohibited Contra aid, except in accordance with H.J. Res. 648.[160]

The International Security and Development Cooperation Act of 1985 (S. 960, approved August 8, 1985) authorized $27 million in humanitarian assistance (food, clothing, medicine, etc.) to the "Nicaraguan democratic resistance." No funds from this Act, the 1961 Foreign Assistance Act, or the Arms Export Control Act ("except the funds authorized to be appropriated in

---

[158] Serafino, Nina M. and Maureen Taft-Morales, *Contra Aid: Summary and Chronology of Major Congressional Action 1981-1989*, Washington, Congressional Research Service, November 1, 1989, p. 5-6; and 96 Stat. 1830 at 1865 (P.L. 97-377).

[159] 97 Stat. 1473 at 1475 (P.L. 98-215); Serafino and Taft-Morales, *Contra Aid*, p. 6-7; 97 Stat. 1421 at 1452 (P.L. 98-212).

[160] 98 Stat. 283 (P.L. 98-332); Serafino and Taft-Morales, p. 8; 98; Stat. 1837 at 1935 (P.L. 98-473); 98 Stat. 3298 at 3304 (P.L. 98-618).

this section") could be used to "provide assistance of any kind, either directly or indirectly, to any person or group engaging in an insurgency or other act of rebellion against the Government of Nicaragua." The FY 1986 "Intelligence Authorization Act" mandated that CIA, DOD or any other "agency or entity of the United States involved in intelligence activities" could only provide contra aid during FY 1986 as specifically authorized by law-- thereby effectively prohibiting the use of CIA contingency funds.[161]

Title II of the FY 1987 Military Construction Appropriations Act (H.J. Res. 738, approved October 30, 1986) resumed military aid to the Contras, but specified that "nothing in this title shall be construed as permitting the President to furnish additional assistance to the Nicaraguan Democratic Resistance from funds other than the funds transferred under section 6(a) or otherwise specifically authorized by Congress." [162]

After the Iran-Contra affair in late 1986, Congress in early 1987 seriously considered, but did not impose, a moratorium on disbursement of already approved contra aid.[163] Following the Central American peace accord signed August 7, 1987, Congress refused military aid for FY 1988, but approved humanitarian assistance to the contras via several measures.[164]

The FY 1989 "Department of Defense Appropriation Act" (H.R. 4781, approved October 1, 1988) provided over $27 million in humanitarian assistance to the Contras, transferred from previously appropriated defense funds. It also allowed the release of undelivered military assistance to the Contras, if Congress passed a joint resolution approving a Presidential request to do so.[165]

Congress approved $49.75 million in humanitarian assistance to the contras in an act "to implement the Bipartisan Accord on Central America of March 24, 1989" (H.R. 1750, approved April 18, 1989). The Bush Administration promised that it would consult Congress prior to obligating these funds past November 30, 1989.[166]

---

[161] 99 Stat. 190 at 249-259 (P.L. 99-83); 99 Stat. 293 at 324-326 (P.L. 99-88); 99 Stat. 1002-1003 (P.L. 99-169).

[162] 100 Stat. 3341 at 3341-296 (P.L. 99-591); 100 Stat. 3190 (P.L. 99-569)

[163] Serafino and Taft-Morales, p. 13.

[164] 101 Stat. 789 (P.L. 100-120), 101 Stat. 903 (P.L. 100-162), 101 Stat. 1310 (P.L. 100-193), 101 Stat. 1314 (P.L. 100-197); 101 Stat. 1329 (P.L. 100-202); and 102 Stat. 62 (P.L. 100-276).

[165] 102 Stat. 2270 at 2270-49 (P.L. 100-463).

[166] 103 Stat. 37 (P.L. 101-14); and Serafino and Taft-Morales, p. 16.

Congress authorized sanctions against the Nicaraguan Government in addition to those initiated by the Executive Branch. The Export-Import Bank Act Amendments of 1986 (H.R. 5548, approved October 15, 1986) prohibited the Bank from providing guarantees, insurance, or credit to "Marxist-Leninist countries." The Act place Nicaragua on the list of such countries.[167]

51. FALKLANDS ISLANDS (1982)

Congress played no direct role during the Falkland Islands conflict. A number of Members made motions, but Congress acted on none.[168]

52. LEBANON (1982-84)

President Reagan in 1982 reported to Congress both times that he ordered U.S. armed forces to Lebanon. In an August 24, 1982 letter to the Speaker of the House and President Pro Tempore of the Senate he "informed" Congress about the "deployment and mission" of 800 Marines sent to Lebanon on August 25 to participate in a multinational force overseeing the withdrawal of the Palestinian Liberation Organization from Beruit. The President stated that he was reporting "consistent with the War Powers Resolution," but did not cite Section 4(a)(1), which requires Congressional authorization for the use of force past 60-90 days. The Administration on September 29 again reported to Congress "consistent with the War Powers Resolution" upon deploying 1200 Marines to participate in a Multinational Force in Lebanon. President Reagan stated that he undertook this action "pursuant" to his "constitutional authority with respect to the conduct of foreign relation and as Commander-in-Chief of the United States Armed Forces," but did not cite Section 4(a)(1) of the law, and thus did not trigger the 60-90 day time limit on use of force absent congressional authorization. Many in Congress were displeased with this approach. When Lebanon asked the United States and other countries to double the number of troops committed to the peacekeeping force, for example, 14 members of the Senate Foreign Relations Committee on December 15, 1982 wrote to the President insisting that he seek "formal Congressional

---

[167] 100 Stat. 1200 (P.L. 99-472)

[168] Preece, Charlotte Phillips, *The Falkland/Malvinas Islands Crisis*, Issue Brief IB 82052, Washington, Congressional Research Service, July 15, 1982, p. 18.

authorization...before undertaking long-term or expanded commitments or extending indefinitely the present level of operations" in Lebanon.[169]

Congress, in the Lebanon Emergency Assistance Act of 1983 (S. 639, approved June 27, 1983 after 63 people were killed in an April car bombing of the U.S. embassy) expressed concerns over authorization of the U.S. presence in Lebanon by mandating that the "President shall obtain statutory authorization from the Congress with respect to any substantial expansion in the number or role in Lebanon of United States Armed Forces..." In addition to funds already authorized for FY 1983, the act provided $150 in economic assistance and over $100 million for military sales and related aid to Lebanon. Congress had already provided considerable emergency aid to Lebanon in 1982 following Israel's June invasion. A resolution approved on June 30, 1982 (H.R. 6631), for example, authorized $50 million in humanitarian assistance to "the people of Lebanon."[170]

President Reagan on August 30, 1983, following the death of two U.S. Marines, again reported to Congress "consistent" with the War Powers Resolution and, as usual neglected to not cite section 4(a)(1) of the law. On this occasion, Congress actively sought to force him to do so. The Administration and Congress finally reached a compromise in the Multinational Force in Lebanon Resolution (S.J.Res. 159, approved October 12, 1983) which invoked section 4(a)(1) of the War Powers Resolution and placed an 18 month limit on continued U.S. troop deployment. The compromise allowed the President to maintain that he did not recognize the constitutional legality of the War Powers Resolution and that he still possessed authority under the constitution to send U.S. forces abroad.[171]

President Reagan reported to Congress on March 30, 1984 in the wake of mounting congressional and public pressure to change policy after the October 23, 1983 truck bombing of Marine Headquarters at the Beruit airport.[172]

---

[169] *Congressional Quarterly Almanac*, 1982, p. 167-171; *Weekly Compilation of Presidential Documents*, August 30, 1982, p. 1065-66; October 4, 1982, p. 1232; *Congressional Record* (Daily Edition), December 18, 1982, p. S15482 (all in *American Foreign Policy Current Documents*, 1982, p. 855-56, 871, 883-84).

[170] 97 Stat. 214 (P.L. 98-43); and 96 Stat. 138 (P.L. 97-208)

[171] *Congressional Quarterly Almanac*, 1983, p. 114; *Weekly Compilation of Presidential Documents*, September 5, 1983, p. 1186-87; 97 Stat. 805 (P.L. 98-119); and *Congress and the Nation*, vol. VI, "Lebanon Policy, War Powers," p. 156-58.

[172] *Weekly Compilation of Presidential Documents*, April 2, 1984, p. 456-457.

53. GRENADA (1983)

Congress generally supported the Reagan Administration's October 25, 1983 intervention in Grenada. The President met with key Congressional leaders at the White House on October 24, before the operation began but after the decision had been made to proceed. Speaker of the House O'Neill said the group had been briefed not asked for advice.[173]

President Reagan on October 25 reported the intervenion to the Speaker of the House and the President Pro Tempore of the Senate "in accordance with (his) desire that the Congress be informed on this matter, and consistent with the War Powers Resolution." He did not cite Section 4(a)(1) of the War Powers Resolution. [174]

The House of Representative on November 1, 1983 passed a joint resolution (H.J. Res. 402) resolving that for "purposes of section 5(b) of the War Powers Resolution, the Congress hereby determines that the requirements of Section 4(a)(1) of the War Powers Resolution became operative on October 25, 1983, when the United States Armed Forces were introduced into Grenada." The Senate included the same provision as an amendment to an unrelated resolution (H.J. Res. 308) to increase the debt limit. The amendment was later eliminated in conference.[175]

Congress following the intervention provided economic aid to Grenada. FY 1984 foreign assistance appropriation measure (part of the Continuing Appropriations Resolution, H.J. Res. 413, approved November 14, 1983), eliminated $85 million in previously allocated economic assistance to Syria and gave $15 million of the freed up funds to Grenada.[176]

---

[173] *Congressional Quarterly Almanac*, 1983, p. 135-36; and Hanover, Janice R., *Grenada: Issues Concerning the Use of U.S. Forces*, Congressional Research Service Issue Brief IB 83170, Updated February 22, 1984, p. 13.

[174] *Congressional Record* (Daily Edition), 98th Congress, 1st Session, October 31, 1983, p. H 8887; and October 28, 1983, p. S 14871, Hanover, p.13-14.

[175] *Congressional Record* (Daily Edition), 98th Congress, 1st Session, October 28, 1983, p. S14868 and S14876-77 and November 1, 1983, p. H8933-34.

[176] 97 Stat. 964 at 966 (P.L. 98-151)

54. PHILIPPINES (1984-)

The United States has supported the Philippines counterinsurgency effort since at least 1972 by providing military aid. During the period 1972-1974 it amounted to $16.7 million, $22.5 million, and $41.1 million. Additionally, in 1972 and 1973 the Philippines received $68.4 million and $124 million in economic aid.[177]

Congress specifically authorized military assistance for the Philippines at least twice during the latter half the 1970s. The International Security Assistance Act of 1977 (H.R. 6884, August 4, 1977) authorized "not more than" $19.6 million in military assistance to the Philippines. Congress in the International Security Assistance Act of 1978 (S. 3075, September 26, 1978) authorized "not more than" $17.1 million in military assistance. [178]

The International Security and Development Act of 1980 (H.R. 6942, December 16, 1980) authorized "not more than" $25 million in military assistance. During the conference on H.R. 6942, the House proposed reducing the $50 million arms loans request for the Philippines by $5 million to protest continued martial law in that country. Conferees rejected the proposal.[179]

The Foreign Assistance and Related Programs Appropriations Act, 1985 (part of H.J. Res 684, the continuing resolution approved October 12, 1984) appropriated $180 million in military and economic assistance. However, to protest Marcos' authoritarian regime, Congress shifted $45 million of the requested $60 million in military aid loans to economic aid.[180]

Congress in 1985 twice reduced the Reagan Administration's requested military aid to the Philippines to encourage economic, political, and military reforms. The International Security and Development Cooperation Act of 1985 (S. 960, August 8, 1985), authorized "not more than" $20 million in foreign military sales financing, $50 million in grant military assistance, and $110 million in economic support funds (ESF). The measure asserted that the "primary purpose of U.S. assistance," besides promoting friendly relations

---

[177] Buss, Claude A., *The United States and the Philippines: Background for Policy*, Washington, American Enterprise Institute for Public Policy Research, 1977, p. 62-66, U.S. Congress, House of Representatives, *Human Rights in South Korea and the Philippines: Implications for U.S. Policy*, International Relations Subcommittee on International Organizations, 94th Congress, 1st Session, Washington, U.S. GPO, 1975, p. 317-21.

[178] 91 Stat. 614 (PL 95-92); and 92 Stat. 730 at 732 (PL 95-384).

[179] 94 Stat. 3131 at 3138-39 (PL 96-533); *Congressional Quarterly Almanac*, 1980, p. 329-30.

[180] 98 Stat. 1884 (P.L. 98-473); and *Congressional Quarterly Almanac*, 1984, p. 398.

between the two nations, was "to encourage the restoration of internal security, both of which goals can be best served by the achievement of an open and stable democracy." Importantly, the Act shifted $30 million from military grants to economic assistance. The Foreign Assistance and Related Programs Appropriations Act, 1986 (part of H.J. Res. 465, the "Further Continuing Appropriations" December 19, 1985) further reduced Philippine military aid to $55 million. One influential member called the cut a message to President Marcos, and stated that "all of us are worried we're going to end up with a Marxist victory there, because you've got to have change to win."[181]

Congress twice boosted aid to the Philippines in 1986, following Marcos's ouster and Corazon Aquino's accession to power. The Urgent Supplemental Appropriations Act, 1986 (H.R. 4515, approved July 2, 1986), provided an additional $100 million ESF and $50 million in military assistance. The Foreign Assistance and Related Programs Appropriations Act, 1987 (H.J. Res. 738, part of the "Continuing Appropriations, Fiscal Year 1987," October 20, 1986), provided "that not less than an additional sum of $200 million shall be available only for the Philippines" in economic support funds.[182]

Congress has continued to support the Aquino government with economic and military aid. The Foreign Operations, Export Financing, and Related Programs Appropriations Act, 1988 (part of H.J. Res 395, "Continuing Appropriations, Fiscal Year 1988" December 22, 1987), appropriated $124 million in economic support funds (ESF), $125 million in military assistance, $40 million in development assistance, and $50 million for land reform, contingent on a suitable Philippine program. Similarly, in the Foreign Operations, Export Financing, and Related Programs Appropriations Act, 1989 (H.R. 4637, October 1, 1989), Congress appropriated $40 million in development assistance and $125 million in military assistance to the Philippines. The military assistance figure was $15 million higher than the original Reagan Administration request.[183]

---

[181] *Congressional Quarterly Almanac*, 1985, p. 113-14; 99 Stat. 190 at 266-67 (P.L. 99-83); *Congressional Quarterly Almanac*, 1985, p. 41 and 55; 99 Stat 1185, 1291, and 1301-02 (P.L. 99-190); *Congressional Quarterly Almanac*, 1985, p. 368.

[182] 100 Stat. 710 at 726 (P.L. 99-349); 100 Stat. 3341, 3341-214, and 3341-221 (P.L. 99-591).

[183] 101 Stat. 1329, 1329-142, and 1329-147 (P.L. 100-202); Niksch, Larry A., *Philippines: U.S. Foreign Assistance Facts*, Issue Brief IB85077, Congressional Research Service, 102 Stat. 2268, 2268-8, and 2268-16 (P.L. 100-461); *Congressional Quarterly Almanac*, 1988, p. 694.

55. PHILIPPINES (1985-86)

In addition to pressuring Marcos during 1985 by reducing military aid (see case 54), Congress contributed to his ouster by issuing several strong statements related to reforms and free elections in the Philippines.

The International Security and Development Cooperation Act of 1985 (S. 960, approved August 8, 1985) declared its sense that the United States should encourage democracy in the Philippines by making future aid contingent upon free elections in 1986 or 1987, prosecuting those responsible for Benigno Aquino's murder, and implementing changes such as economic structural reforms and enhancement of Philippine armed forces and security forces. This law also provided some military aid.[184]

Both Houses of Congress on November 14, 1985 passed H.Con.Res. 232, a concurrent resolution that stated "reinvigoration of Philippine democratic institutions offers the best means of restoring public confidence in the government and of defeating the growing Communist insurgency." The resolution noted Marcos' pledge to hold a free and fair Presidential election and set out five steps to provide "institutional guarantees for an honest election." Those measures included neutral conduct by the Philippine military, opposition access to the media, and independent monitoring of the proceedings.[185]

After the February 7, 1986 election in the Philippines, the Senate passed a resolution (S.Res. 345) expressing its sense "that the recent presidential elections in the Philippines were marked by such widespread fraud that they cannot be considered a fair reflection of the will of the people of the Philippines."[186]

56. HAITI (1985-86)

For several years prior to Haitian President Jean Claude Duvalier's February 7, 1986 ouster, Congress pressured him to implement political reform. The International Security and Development Act of 1983 (part of

---

[184] 99 Stat. 190 at 266-67 (P.L. 99-83)

[185] *Congressional Record*, 99th Congress, 1st Session, "Expressing Sense of Congress with Respect to Restoration of Democracy in the Philippines," November 14, 1985, p. 31844-31846; and *Congressional Record* (Daily Edition), 99th Congress, 1st Session, "Restoration of Democracy in the Philippines," November 14, 1985, p. S 15670-74.

[186] *Congressional Record* (Daily Edition), 99th Congress, 2nd Session, "The Presidential Election in the Philippines," February 19, 1986, p. S 1338-54.

the Continuing Appropriations Resolution for FY1984, H.J. Res. 413, approved November 14, 1983) conditioned U.S. development assistance to Haiti upon President Reagan's determination that the Duvalier government had made "a concerted and significant effort to improve the human rights." Specifically it required political reforms essential to the development of democracy in Haiti, including "the establishment of political parties, free elections, and freedom of the press." Congress incorporated essentially the same condition in the 1984 foreign aid appropriation (part of the continuing appropriation resolution for FY 1985, H.J. Res. 648, approved October 12, 1984) and the 1985 foreign aid authorization (S 960, approved August 8, 1985). The Reagan Administration did not report to Congress that Haiti had complied with the above condition and others. The United States thereupon suspended aid. The Administration made the necessary determination once Duvalier had been replaced by a new government, and Congress lifted the suspension.[187]

Following Duvalier's ouster, Congress moved to strengthen the new government of Haiti. The Special Foreign Assistance Act of 1986 (S.1917, approved October 24, 1986) expressly sought to "promote democracy in Haiti." Specifically, it earmarked $108 million for economic assistance in FY 1987, conditioned on President Reagan's determination that the interim government was making specific reforms, many of them related to democracy. The Act also provided up to $4 million in military aid, if President Reagan determined that the interim government had implemented certain human rights-related reforms.[188]

57. ANGOLA (1986-)

The Clark Amendment, included in the International Security Assistance and Arms Export Control Act of 1976 (H.R. 13680, June 30, 1976), barred "assistance of any kind" to groups conducting "military or paramilitary operations in Angola unless and until the Congress expressly authorized assistance by law..." Thus, this provision effectively banned U.S. covert assistance to anti-government forces in Angola. The International Security and Development Cooperation Act of 1980 (HR. 6942, approved December 16, 1980) repeated the Clark Amendment. The International Security and Development Cooperation Act of 1985 (S. 960, approved August 8, 1985) repealed the Clark Amendment.[189]

---

[187] 97 Stat. 964 at 971 (P.L. 98-151); 98 Stat. 1837 at 1903 (P.L. 98-473); 99 Stat. 190 at 241-42 (P.L. 99-83); and Galdi and Shuey, p. 88.

[188] 100 Stat. 3010 (P.L. 99-529)

[189] 99 Stat. 190 at 264 (P.L. 99-83); 90 Stat. 729 at 757-758 (P.L. 94-329); and 94 Stat. 3131 at 3141 (P.L. 96-533).

Following repeal of the Clark Amendment, the Reagan Administration reportedly provided $15 million in covert assistance to UNITA during FY1986. Chairman of the House Intelligence Committee Lee Hamilton opposed this action and sought unsuccessfully to revive the Clark Amendment. The covert assistance program apparently continued, reportedly growing to $45-50 million by FY 1989.[190]

The Foreign Relations Authorization Act, Fiscal Years 1988 and 1989 (H.R. 1777, December, 22, 1987) sensed that "the United States should continue to work toward a peaceful resolution to the Angolan conflict," including "the complete withdrawal of all foreign forces and Soviet military advisers."[191]

Congress has authorized sanctions against the Angolan government, in addition to those imposed by the Executive Branch. The Continuing Appropriations Resolution for FY 1988 (H.J. Res. 395, approved December 22, 1987) banned direct and indirect assistance or reparations to Angola among other countries. This ban had first been instituted in the FY 1978 foreign assistance appropriations act (H.R. 7797, October 31, 1977).[192]

58. NARCO CONFLICT (1986-)

Congress passed the Anti-Drug Abuse Act of 1986 (H.R. 5484, approved October 27, 1986) which contained the Internationl Narcotics Control Act of 1986 (Title II) and the National Drug Interdiction Improvement Act of 1986 (Title III). The Narcotics Control Act authorized approximately $75 million for international narcotics control assistance in FY 1987. The Act also established "restrictions on the provision of United States assistance" to "every major illicit drug producing country or major drug transit country." It required withholding of half of U.S. assistance unless the President certified that the country in question had cooperated with the United States, or acted unilaterally to stop the production or flow of drugs. The President could ignore this sanction if "vital" national interests would be jeopardized by withholding assistance. The Narcotics Control Act also required a report every six months listing drug producing/transporting countries. The Interdiction Act contained the Defense Drug Interdiction Assistance Act which set out numerous provisions related to the Defense Department's role, and it

---

[190] *Congressional Quarterly Almanac*, 1986, p. 387-88; and *Washington Post*, November 30, 1989, "CIA Plane Carrying Arms to Angolan Rebels Crashes," p. 1.

[191] 101 stat. 1331 at 1414-1415 (P.L. 100-204)

[192] 101 Stat. 1329 at 1329-155, 1329-169 (P.L. 100-202); and 91 Stat. 1230 at 1235 (P.L. 95-148).

authorized $138 million in FY 1987 to refurbish specific aircraft for drug interdiction purposes.[193]

Congress in 1987, as part of the Defense Authorization Act for FY 1988 and 89 (H.R. 1748, December 4, 1987) required a "GAO study of the capabilities of the United States to control drug smuggling into the United States." Specifically, the provision indicated that the report should cover the role of U.S. armed forces in drug interdiction activities, as well as what effect a greater role in these operations would have on them.[194]

Congress in 1988 passed another major "Anti-Drug Abuse Act" (H.R. 5210, approved November 18, 1988). It included a massive International Narcotics Control Act, which authorized $101 million for international narcotics-control programs in FY 1989. Among numerous other provisions, it cut off all U.S. aid to drug producing/transporting countries absent certification. It allowed Congress to overturn a Persidential certification via resolution within 45 days.[195]

Congress in 1988 addressed the Pentagon's role in the drug war within the Defense Authorization Act (H.R. 4481, approved September 29, 1988) and Appropriations Acts (H.R. 4781, approved October 1, 1988). Title XI of the authorization act provided for "drug interdiction and law enforcement support." The measure's main thrust required "military support for civilian law enforcement agencies" in carrying out drug interdiction, and authorized $300 million for this objective ,plus $66 million for balloon transported radars to detect low flying aircraft entering the United States. The defense appropriations act provided the $300 million.[196]

Congress in 1989 passed several measures related to the narco conflict. The Foreign Assistance Appropriations Act for FY 1990 (H.R. 3743, November 21, 1990), provided $270 million for anti-narcotics related activities. The National Defense Authorization Act of FY 1990 and 1991 (H.R. 2461, November 29, 1989) authorized $450 million for FY90 drug interdiction and law enforcement support activities by the Defense Department. The International Narcotics Control Act of 1989 (H.R. 3611, December 13, 1989)

---

[193] 100 Stat. 3207 at 3207-60, 3207-73 (P.L. 99-570); *Congressional Quarterly Almanac*, 1986, "Congress Clears Massive Anti-Drug Measure," p. 92-106.

[194] 101 Stat. 1019 at 1162 (P.L. 100-180).

[195] 102 Stat. 4181 at 4261 (P.L. 100-690); *Congressional Quarterly Almanac*, 1988, "Election-Year Anto-Drug Bill Enacted," p. 85-88.

[196] 102 Stat. 1918 at 2042 (P.L. 100-456); 102 Stat. 2270 at 2270-16 (P.L. 100-463); and *Congressional Quarterly Almanac*, 1988, "Pentagon Anti-Drug Efforts," p. 432.

among many other provisions, authorized $125 million in military and law enforcement assistance to Bolivia, Columbia, and Peru for FY 1990.[197]

59. PERSIAN GULF (1987-88)

Congress in the FY 1988 continuing resolution appropriated $100 million to cover most of the above normal costs for FY 1988 associated with the Persian Gulf operation (H.J. Res. 395, approved December 22, 1987). The Navy had absorbed FY 1987 costs by deferring maintenance projects. The FY 1989 Defense Appropriations bill (H.R. 4781, approved October 1, 1988) included $60 million to pay for Persian Gulf operations by the Navy.[198]

Congress and the Reagan Administration disputed Persian Gulf policy throughout 1987-88. Many in Congress wanted to invoke the War Powers Resolution. Over 100 House members brought suit in federal court to force the Administration to do so (dismissed December 18, 1987). The House approved an amendment to the Coast Guard authorization bill in July 1987 that would have delayed reflagging Kuwaiti ships for 90 days (H.R. 2342). The Senate in October adopted the Byrd-Warner Resolution (S.J. Res. 194) which would have established special rules to expedite Senate condsideration of measures against U.S. Persian Gulf policy. The only provision that became law was a section of the FY 1987 Supplemental Appropriations Act (H.R. 1827, approved July 11, 1987) that required the Secretary of Defense to report to Congress on plans to protect Kuwaiti ships. In 1988 Congress again debated Persian Gulf policy, but did not pass any laws that constrained the Administration.[199]

The Reagan Administration reported to Congress six times after various hostilities in the Persian Gulf. Congress never invoked the War Powers

---

[197] 103 Stat. 1195 (P.L. 101-167); 103 Stat. 1352 at 1562 (P.L. 101-189); 103 Stat. 1954 (P.L. 101-231); Perl, Raphael F., *Drug Control: International Policy and Options*, Issue Brief IB88093, Washington, Congressional Research Service, March 19, 1990, 15 p.

[198] O'Rouke, Ronald, *Persian Gulf: U.S. Military Operations*, Issue Brief IB87145, Washington, Congressional Research Service, January 19, 1989; 101 Stat. 1329 (P.L. 100-102); *Congressional Quarterly Almanac*, 1988, p. 655-66; 102 Stat. 2270 (P.L. 100-463).

[199] *Congressional Quarterly Almanac*, 1987, "Hill Challenges Reagan on Persian Gulf Policy," p. 254 and 261; 101 Stat. 391 at 399 (P.L. 100-71); *Congressional Quarterly Almanac*, 1988, "Persian Gulf Escorts Continue, Despite Debate," pp 434-439.

Resolution to impose a time limit on use of U.S. forces, which involved large naval deployments.[200]

60. PANAMA (1987-90)

Congress initiated sanctions against Panama beginning in 1987, in addition to those imposed by the Executive Branch. The foreign assistance appropriations act for FY 1988 (included as part of the FY 1988 Continuing Appropriations Resolution H.J. Res. 395, December 22, 1987) prohibited U.S. assistance to Panama, and barred using funds from the Act for joint military exercises in that country, unless the U.S. President certified that the Panamanian Government was controlling the military, moving toward free elections, and providing constitutional guarantees such as freedom of the press. A separate section provided for the "elimination of the sugar quota allocation of Panama." Congress essentially repeated these conditions and sanctions over the next two years in the foreign assistance appropriations acts for FY 1989 (H.R. 4637, October 1, 1988) and FY 1990 (H.R. 3743, November 21, 1989).[201]

Congress expressed its sentiments regarding Panama during this period via non-binding resolutions. The House passed H. Res. 399 on March 10, 1988 which demanded Noriega's removal from power and requested that the President "consider seriously the range of additional economic and political sanctions available to the United States that could be used to enourage the re-establishment of civilian authority in Panama." The Senate on March 25 1988 passed S.Con.Res. 108 which asked the President to implement "additional diplomatic, political and economic pressure" against Noriega.[202]

Following the unsuccessful coup in October 1989, many in Congress criticized the Bush administration for not helping the conspirators oust Noriega. The Administration insisted that the Executive Branch must be

---

[200] Collier, Ellen C., *War Powers Resolution: Presidential Compliance*, Issue Brief 81050, Washington, Congressional Research Service, February 16, 1990, 17 p.

[201] 101 Stat. 1329 at 1329-174 (P.L. 100-202); 102 Stat. 2268 at 2268-40 (P.L. 100-461); and 103 Stat. 1195 at 1239 (P.L. 101-167).

[202] *Congressional Quarterly Almanac*, 1988, "U.S. Fails to Oust Panama's Noriega," p. 549-557.

circumspect in supporting coup attempts and cited the Executive Order that bans political assassination.[203]

Congress generally supported the December 20, 1989 U.S. intervention of Panama that removed Noriega from power. The Administration briefed congressional leaders prior to the military action. On December 21, President Bush reported to Congress concerning the intervention "consistent with the War Powers Resolution." Compliance with the War Powers Resolution for the most part did not become a serious issue in Congress.[204]

Following Operation Just Cause, President Bush began lifting sanctions against Panama and announced his intention to seek an economic assistance program worth approximately $1 billion. Congress swiftly passed the Urgent Assistance for Democracy in Panama Act of 1990 (H.R. 3952, approved February 14, 1990) which authorized $42 million. The Act also allowed Panama to again receive U.S. aid and trade benefits.[205]

---

[203] *Congressional Quarterly*, October 7, 1989, "Failed Coup Against Noriega Stirs Hill Frustrations," p. 2660; October 14, 1989, "Abortive Coup Spurs Debate Over How Much to Help," p. 2723-26; October, 21, 1989, "Administration Seeks Leeway in Helping Future Coups," p. 2812.

[204] Sullivan, Mark P., *Panamanian-U.S. Relations: Issues for Congress*, Issue Brief IB9044, Washington, Congressional Research Service, February 13, 1990, p. 5; *Congressional Quarterly*, "Invasion, Noriega Ouster Win Support on Capitol Hill," December 23, 1989, p. 353235; Collier, Ellen C., *War Powers Resolution: Presidential Compliance*, Issue Brief IB81050, Washington, Congressional Research Service, 2-5.

[205] P.L. 101-243; *Congressional Quarterly*, "Congress Rushes to Approve Emergency Aid Package," February 10, 1990, p. 404-05; Sullivan, Mark P., *Panama-U.S. Relations: Issues for Congress*, p. 6 and 10.

Annex C

GLOSSARY

ANTITERRORISM   Defensive measures that reduce the vulnerability of people and property to terrorism. *See also* Counterterrorism; Terrorism.

AREA ORIENTATION   Organizing, training, equipping, and otherwise preparing individuals and groups to operate in a particular geographic region.

ASSASSINATION   Premeditated murder for political or social purposes.

CIVIC ACTION   Political, economic, and social programs undertaken by indigenous governments, occupying powers, other groups, and/or outsiders to strengthen the internal security of a state or territory. Public works, agriculture, education, and training are representative projects.

CIVIC AFFAIRS   Nonmilitary functions that foreign armed forces perform for, and by agreement with, indigenous governments in peacetime or war; executive, legislative, and judicial authority that foreign armed forces exercise in occupied countries or territories.

CIVIL MILITARY OPERATIONS   Activities designed to establish favorable relations between foreign armed forces and indigenous governments/populations and thereby facilitate mission accomplishment.

CLANDESTINE OPERATIONS   Activities conducted so secretly that no one but sponsors, planners, and implementors know they are taking place. *See also* Covert operations; Overt operations.

COLD WAR   A term used to describe U.S.-Soviet non-violent conflict from 1946 at least until 1989. *See also* Nonviolent conflict.

COLLECTIVE SECURITY   Multilateral measures by two or more partners to ensure successful accomplishment of respective deterrent, offensive, or defensive objectives. *See also* Foreign internal defense.

COMBATTING TERRORISM   Deterrent, offensive, and defensive measures, both active and passive, taken to diminish threats from domestic and transnational terrorists. *See also* Antiterrorism; Counterterrorism; Terrorism; Transnational terrorism.

CONFLICT   Hostile intent and activities in relations between nations or between nations and subnational groups. *See also* High-intensity conflict; Low-intensity conflict; Mid-intensity conflict; Nonviolent conflict; Peace; War.

CONFLICT SPECTRUM   A continuum of hostilities that ranges from sub-crisis maneuvering to the most violent form of general war.

CONVENTIONAL FORCES, OPERATIONS, WEAPONS   Regular military organizations, hostilities, and hardware that exclude nuclear, chemical, and biological capabilities. *See also* General purpose forces; Special operations; Special operations forces.

COUNTERINSURGENCY   1. Political, economic, social, military, and paramilitary measures that indigenous governments and associates use to forestall or defeat insurgencies. 2. Similar measures occupying powers use to forestall or defeat resistance movements. *See also* Insurgency; Resistance.

COUNTERREVOLUTION   Operations by losers and associates against the regime installed by winners of a successful insurgency.

COUNTERTERRORISM   Measures designed to deter, and if necessary defeat, terrorism. *See also* Antiterrorism; Terrorism.

COUNTRY TEAM   Senior members of all U.S. official organizations in a foreign country, headed by the ambassador or principal U.S. diplomatic representative. Members commonly include military and CIA.

COUP D'ETAT   Brief violence or bloodless action by a small, conspiratorial group to overthrow a government and seize political power. *See also* Insurgency.

COVERT OPERATIONS   Activities that conceal the identity of sponsors and facilitate plausible denial of involvement if they are detected and accused. *See also* Clandestine operations; Overt operations.

DETERRENCE   Steps to prevent opponents from initiating aggressive action and to inhibit escalation if such actions occur. Promises of punishment and reward both may contribute.

DEVELOPING NATION   A country, not necessarily poor, in transition from traditional culture and relatively simple economy to different structures, values, and lifestyles associated with industrialization and modernity. Feelings of political and social dislocation, coupled with rising expectations the government finds difficult to satisfy, sometimes cause serious internal security problems. *See also* Nation building.

DIPLOMACY   Skill in accomplishing foreign policy objectives during peacetime and war, especially the settlement of disputes and the development of mutually satisfactory agreements through ongoing representation, negotiations, and other dialogue.

DOCTRINE   Principles that guide and provide uniformity to applications of national power under specified conditions in peacetime and war. Doctrine differs from policy, which does not necessarily demand uniform practices and is subject to more frequent change.   *See also* National policies.

ECONOMIC ASSISTANCE   Money, supplies, equipment, advice, education, training, and other nonmilitary aid, provided free of charge or paid for by cash, credit, or barter, calculated especially to abet nation building by an ally or other associate, alleviate balance of payment problems, and/or fund specified infrastructure.   *See also* Foreign assistance; Military assistance; Security assistance.

ECONOMIC SUPPORT FUNDS   Foreign aid that addresses economic, structural, and development requirements in countries of particular security and political interest to the United States.   ESF often facilitate military base rights agreements, access rights agreements or alleviate balance of payments problems.   *See also* Economic aid; Foreign aid.

ECONOMIC WARFARE   The purposeful manipulation of trade, foreign aid programs, financial transactions, and other matters that influence the production, distribution, and consumption of goods/services with the intent to coerce, damage, or destroy opponents.   *See also* Sanctions.

E & E   *See* Evasion and escape.

ESCAPE AND EVASION   *See* Evasion and escape.

ESF   *See* Economic support funds.

EXFILTRATION   The covert or clandestine movement of individuals or groups through enemy defenses from hostile to friendly territory by land, sea, or air in peacetime and war.   *See also* Evasion and escape; Infiltration.

EVASION AND ESCAPE   1. Avoidance/elusion of enemy control, followed by exfiltration;   2. A clandestine, compartmented network of people and facilities to improve prospects of success.   *See also* Exfiltration.

EXPEDITIONARY FORCES   Any military formation designed to operate in foreign countries during peacetime or war.   *See also* Punitive expedition; Protective expedition.

FID   *See* Foreign internal defense.

FOREIGN ASSISTANCE   Aid to an ally or other associate for political, humanitarian, economic, and/or security reasons that may be altruistic or self-serving. *See also* Economic assistance; Military assistance; Security assistance.

FOREIGN INTERNAL DEFENSE   Participation by civilian and military agencies of a government in programs another government undertakes to forestall or defeat insurgency, transnational terrorism, or lawlessness. *See also* Collective security; Internal defense.

GENERAL PURPOSE FORCES   Deployable military forces, less those designed primarily to accomplish strategic nuclear, mobility, or special operations missions. *See also* Conventional forces; Special operations forces.

GUERRILLA   Armed member of any paramilitary insurgent or resistance group engaged in guerrilla warfare. *See also* Guerrilla warfare; Paramilitary; Underground.

GUERRILLA WARFARE   1. Hit and run operations by paramilitary insurgent or resistant groups against regular armed forces, other irregulars, or noncombatants; 2. Similar operations by regular armed force. *See also* Guerrilla.

HANDS OFF OPPOSITION   Nonviolent operations designed to reduce the capabilities of opponents or influence their actions in desired ways. *See also* Nonviolent conflict.

HANDS OFF SUPPORT   Nonviolent operations designed to increase the capabilities of friends, influence their actions in desired ways, and/or sway neutrals favorably. *See also* Nonviolent conflict.

HIC   *See* High-intensity conflict.

HIGH-INTENSITY CONFLICT (from U.S. perspective)   1. Any war in which any belligerent employs nuclear, lethal chemical, or biological weapons so liberally that survival of the United States and/or its allies is at stake; 2. Any other war which causes casualties and damage so severe that the United States must mobilize most of its military and industrial resources to avoid defeat. *See also* Conflict; Low-intensity conflict; Mid-intensity conflict.

HOSTAGE   Any person or property illegally held captive or in peril until redeemed, rescued, or voluntarily released. *See also* Hostage rescue.

HOSTAGE RESCUE   Diplomacy , negotiations, sanctions, and armed action, singly or in some combination, to secure the safe release of persons or property held for redemption, preferably without meeting the holder's demands. *See also* Hostage; Rescue.

HOST COUNTRY   A nation within which foreign organizations and officials operate in response to official invitation and/or international agreement.

HUMAN INTELLIGENCE   Intelligence derived from information collected by agents, scouts, informants, and other individuals, rather than technological instruments. Overt, covert, and clandestine (espionage) operations all are involved. *See also* Intelligence.

HUMANITARIAN ASSISTANCE   Aid designed to improve public welfare in a foreign country, especially food, shelter, medical and dental care, sanitation, utilities, and rudimentary surface transportation.

HUMINT   *See* Human intelligence.

ID   *See* Internal defense

INCIDENTS   Brief, small-scale armed clashes that generally occur during crises in "peacetime" or cold war.

INFILTRATION   1. The covert or clandestine movement of individuals and groups through enemy defenses from friendly to hostile territory by land, sea, or air in "peacetime" and war; 2. Similar movement within or between hostile sectors. *See also* Exfiltration.

INFORMATION   Unprocessed data, regardless of type or derivation, that can be converted into intelligence. *See also* Intelligence.

INFRASTRUCTURE   Organizations, fabrications, facilities, and installations that control and support military, paramilitary, law enforcement, and/or subversive activities.

INSTRUMENTS OF NATIONAL POWER   Armed forces, diplomacy, reform, threats, assistance, sanctions, covert operations, psychological operations, and other means used to implement a nation's plans and programs. *See also* National power.

INSURGENCY   Extended, organized efforts by domestic groups to overthrow the established order (not necessarily a government), seize political power by subversive and coercive means, and sometimes (not always) alter social systems. *See also* Counterinsurgency; Coup d'etat; Guerrilla warfare; Insurgency phases; Resistance; Subversion; Underground.

INSURGENCY PHASES   I, insurgent infrastructure development and preservation, underground activities; II, progressive expansion, which combines Phase I with guerrilla warfare; III, open employment of large paramilitary formations, which supplement Phase I and II operations.

INSURRECTION   *See* Insurgency.

INTELLIGENCE   Products resulting from the collection, evaluation, analysis, integration, and interpretation of information. *See also* Human Intelligence; Information.

INTERESTS   *See* National interests.

INTERNAL DEFENSE   All measures a government takes to forestall or defeat subversion, insurgency, transnational terrorism, or lawlessness within its own territory. *See also* Foreign internal defense; Internal development.

INTERNAL DEVELOPMENT   All measures a government takes to promote political, economic, social, judicial, and other institutions that serve society. *See also* Internal defense.

IRREGULAR FORCES, OPERATIONS   Individuals and groups, not part of any official military or law enforcement apparatus, that engage primarily in insurgency, resistance, and/or transnational terrorism. *See also* Paramilitary; Regular forces, operations.

LAW ENFORCEMENT (FORCES, OPERATIONS)   Police, gendarmes, border guards, coast guards, and other lightly-armed forces whose primary purpose is to maintain order within the boundaries of a nation, in accord with local, regional, and (sometimes) international legal mandates.

LIC   *See* Low-intensity conflict.

LOW-INTENSITY CONFLICT (from U.S. perspective)   Hostilities that range from political, economic, psychological, technological, and other nonviolent warfare that does not qualify as normal peacetime competition through armed combat that inflicts few casualties on U.S. personnel and/or causes little damage to U.S. property. *See also* Conflict; High-intensity conflict; Mid-intensity conflict.

MIC   *See* Mid-intensity conflict.

MID-INTENSITY CONFLICT (from U.S. perspective)   Armed combat that inflicts moderate casualties on U.S. personnel and/or causes moderate damage to U.S. property. The Korean and Vietnam Wars are illustrative. *See also* Conflict; High-intensity conflict; Low-intensity conflict.

MILITARY ASSISTANCE   Money, weapons, equipment, supplies, advice, education, training, construction, services, and other aid, provided free of charge or paid for by cash, credit, or barter, calculated to improve the armed forces of an ally or other associate. *See also* Economic assistance; Foreign assistance; Security assistance.

MILITARY FORCES, OPERATIONS   Regular land, sea, and aerospace armed forces of a nation, active and reserve, whose primary purposes are to deter, defeat, or otherwise deal with the full range of external armed aggression against national security interests, wherever required; secondarily, they assist law enforcement/internal security forces, as directed. *See also* Law enforcement, Paramilitary; Regular.

MILITARY STRATEGY   The art and science of employing military power under all circumstances to attain national security objectives by applying force or threats of force. *See also* Strategy; Tactics.

NARCO CONFLICT   Hostilities associated with operations designed to reduce, and if possible, eradicate the production of illegal drugs, interdict shipments, and prevent distribution.

NATIONAL INTERESTS   Highly generalized expressions of a state's compelling wants and needs. Survival, security, peace, prosperity, and power are representative. National security interests are primarily concerned with preserving the state from harm.

NATIONAL OBJECTIVES   Fundamental goals, aims, and purposes of a state toward which policies are directed and energies are applied. They may be short-, mid-, or long-range in nature. Those associated with national security are concerned primarily with shielding national interests from foreign and domestic threats.

NATIONAL POLICIES   Broad courses of action or statements of guidance that a government adopts in pursuit of national objectives. *See also* Doctrine.

NATIONAL POWER   The sum total of any state's capabilities or potential derived from political, economic, military, geographic, social, scientific, technological, and informational resources. *See also* Instruments of national power.

NATION BUILDING   Activities by a developing country, unilaterally or with outside assistance, to create or strengthen popular acceptance of political, economic, legal, social, and other institutions, thereby enhancing internal security. *See also* Developing nation.

NET ASSESSMENT   The dispassionate comparison of capabilities possessed by competing countries or coalitions to ascertain relative abilities to achieve objectives, despite opposition by the other.

NONVIOLENT CONFLICT   International dispute wherein political, economic, technological, sociological, and psychological measures are orchestrated to attain security objectives. Armed forces deploy primarily to impress; employment is confined to incidents and skirmishes. *See also* Conflict; Peace.

OBJECTIVES   *See* National objectives.

OPERATIONAL CONTINUUM   A term intended to replace "conflict spectrum" in JCS doctrine. It comprises three political-military aspects of international relations: war, conflict, and peacetime competition. A fourth aspect, routine peaceful competiton, involves situations in which military power plays no part. *See also* Conflict spectrum.

OVERT OPERATIONS   Activities conducted openly, without concealing the identity of the sponsor or participants.   *See also* Clandestine operations; Covert operations.

PARAMILITARY FORCES, OPERATIONS   1. Land, sea, and air forces of a nation which have a distinctive chain of command, primarily perform internal security functions beyond the ability of law enforcement units, and supplement the regular military establishment as required; 2, Guerrillas and other armed irregulars that use quasimilitary tactics and techniques. *See also* Law enforcement; Military forces; Regular forces; Security troops.

PEACE   A condition characterized by the absence of hostile activities and/or intent in the relations between two or more competitors. *See also* Conflict.

PEACEFUL COMPETITION   *See* Peace

PEACEKEEPING   Nonviolent efforts of a military force, interposed between belligerents by mutual consent, to maintain a truce or otherwise discourage hostilities. *See also* Peacemaking.

PEACEMAKING   Efforts by a military force to prevent armed conflict in a specified locale or terminate hostilities by force, if necessary. *See also* Peacekeeping.

POLICIES   *See* National policies.

POLITICAL WARFARE   The malicious manipulation of international relations with the intent to coerce, damage, or destroy opponents.

POSTURING   Bombast, bluff, military shows of force, and other nonviolent actions taken to influence opponents in desired ways. *See also* Show of force.

PROPAGANDA   Any form of communication designed to influence the opinions, emotions, attitudes, or behavior of any group in ways intended to suit the sponsor, directly or indirectly.

PROTECTIVE EXPEDITION   Any military formation deployed primarily to deter attacks against its nation's interests in a foreign country and defend those interests if deterrence fails. *See also* Punitive expedition.

PROTECTORATE   Any state or territory that, by invitation or acquiescence, is governed or controlled by a more powerful nation.

PROXY OPERATIONS   A form of limited warfare in which a competitor seeks to avoid direct confrontation with opponents, yet accomplish security objectives at reduced cost and risk, by relying on *de facto* or *de jura* surrogates.

PSYCHOLOGICAL OPERATIONS   The planned use of propaganda and actions to influence the opinions, emotions, attitudes, and behavior of friends, neutrals, and enemies in ways that assist accomplishment of security objectives. *See also* Propaganda; Psychological warfare.

PSYCHOLOGICAL WARFARE   The planned use of propaganda and actions to influence the opinions, emotions, attitudes, and behavior of enemies in ways that assist accomplishment of security objectives. *See also* Propaganda; Psychological operations.

PSYOP   *See* Psychological operations.

PSWAR   *See* Psychological warfare.

RAID   Short, surprise attack to achieve a specific purpose that excludes intent to hold territory.

REBELLION   An armed uprising, usually unsuccessful, against established authority. Motives need not be the same as those that inspire insurgency or resistance. *See also* Insurgency; Resistance.

REFORM   Political, economic, social, and/or military measures by a regime to prevent, reduce, or eradicate widespread dissatisfaction, and thereby strengthen popular support.

REGULAR FORCES, OPERATIONS   1. Active and reserve military establishments that are organized, trained, and equipped for conventional or nuclear/biological/chemical conflict. Regular forces may engage in irregular activities. 2. Law enforcement elements. *See also* Irregular.

RESCUE   Armed operations to free prisoners of war or other captives. *See also* Hostage rescue; Retrieval.

RESISTANCE   Organized efforts by all or part of a population to importune and, if possible, oust a regime installed by an occupying power. Forces and tactics are similar to those of insurgency. *See also* Rescue.

RETRIEVAL   Armed operations to recover captured materiel or documents. *See also* Rescue.

REVOLUTIONARY WAR   *See* insurgency.

ROUTINE PEACEFUL COMPETITION   *See* Peace.

SANCTIONS   Political and/or economic punishment, undertaken unilaterally or multilaterally, to convince opponents they should cease undesirable practices or otherwise bow to the wielder's will.

SECURITY ASSISTANCE   Foreign aid provided primarily to improve the ability of an ally or associate to resist internal/external aggression and/or contribute more effectively to an alliance. *See also* Economic assistance; Foreign assistance; Military assistance.

SHOW OF FORCE   Military deployments taken to influence opponents, allies, and/or neutrals in desired ways without resort to combat. *See also* Posturing.

SOF   *See* Special operations forces.

SO/LIC   *See* Special operations; Low-intensity conflict.

SPECIAL ACTIVITIES   U.S. operations, planned and executed so that the role of the United States Government is not apparent or acknowledged publicly, are solely a CIA responsibility in peacetime. Covert activities must be approved by the President.

SPECIAL OPERATIONS   1. Insurgency, counterinsurgency, resistance, transnational terrorism, counterterrorism; 2. Unorthodox, comparatively low-cost, potentially high-payoff, often covert or clandestine methods that national, subnational, and theater leaders employ independently in "peacetime" or to support nuclear/biological/chemical and/or conventional warfare. *See also* Conventional forces, operations; Special operations forces.

SPECIAL OPERATIONS FORCES   Individuals and small, carefully selected military, paramilitary, and civilian units with unusual (occasionally unique) skills, which are superlatively trained for specific rather than general purposes, and designed to undertake unorthodox tasks that conventional forces could accomplish only with far greater difficulty and far less effectiveness, if at all. SOF, however, are not needed for all special operations. *See also* Conventional forces, operations; Special operations.

SPECIAL WARFARE   *See* Special operations.

SPECTRUM OF CONFLICT   *See* Conflict spectrum.

STRATEGY   The art and science of applying power of all types, directly and indirectly, under all circumstances to exert desired degrees of control over opponents, and thereby achieve security objectives. *See also* Military strategy; Tactics.

SUBNATIONAL GROUP A nongovernmental organization whose members profess common aspirations that may be political, economic, and/or social, usually possess military or paramilitary capabilities, and oppose official authority in particular places for particular reasons. The Palestinian Liberation Organization, Viet Cong, Contras, Kurds, and Basque separatists are representative.

SUBVERSION   Measures intended to undermine the morale, discipline, will, and/or loyalty of a populace to a regime, using insidious, mainly psychological means.

"SURGICAL" STRIKE   Any attack designed to eliminate or stringently limit casualties among people or damage to property not specifically targeted.

TACTICS Detailed methods used to implement strategic designs. Military tactics involve the employment of units in combat, including the arrangement and maneuvering of units in relation to each other and/or to the enemy. *See also* Strategy.

TECHNOLOGICAL WARFARE   The malicious manipulation of research, development, test, and engineering programs, as well as resultant products, with the intent to coerce, deprive, and/or deceive opponents.

TERRORISM   Public, repetitive violence or threats of violence to achieve sociopolitical objectives by inspiring widespread fear among people not personally involved and disrupting community routines so severely that compliance with terrorist demands seems preferable to further disorder. *See also* Terrorist; Transnational terrorism.

TERRORIST   Anyone who, with whatever motive and for whatever purpose, practices terrorism. *See also* Terrorism; Transnational terrorism.

THIRD WORLD   *See* Developing nation.

THREAT   The combined capabilities, intentions, and (sometimes) actions of actual or potential enemies to prevent or interfere with the fulfillment of national interests and/or objectives at particular times and places.

TRANSNATIONAL TERRORISM   Terrorism that is staged in, and perhaps supported by, one country, but takes place in another country or countries.

UNCONVENTIONAL WARFARE   Activities by a foreign government or group that assists insurgents or resistance movements in another country.

UNDERGROUND   An illegal, partly clandestine, partly covert organization that plans and controls an insurgency or resistance movement; conducts covert or clandestine operations, such as subversion, sabotage, and terror; and conducts logistic/administrative support activities that include recruitment, indoctrination, training, intelligence, supply, communication, and fund raising. *See also* Guerrilla.

UW   *See* Unconventional warfare.

WAR   Conflict that usually is construed to include substantial armed combat. *See also* Conflict.

ANNEX D

ABBREVIATIONS AND ACRONYMS

CENTO	Central Treaty Organization
CLIC	Center for Low-intentsity Conflict
DMZ	Demilitarized Zone
DOD	Department of Defense
DRV	Democratic Republic of Vietnam
E&E	Evasion and escape
ESF	Economic support funds
FID	Foreign internal defense
HIC	High-intensity conflict
HUK	Hukbalahap
HUMINT	Human intelligence
ID	Internal defense
LIC	Low-intensity conflict
MFO	Multinational Force and Observers
MIC	Mid-intensity conflict
NATO	North Atlantic Treaty Organization
NSC	National Security Council
OAS	Organization of American States
OECS	Organization of Eastern Caribbean States
OPEC	Organization of Petroleum Exporting Countries
OSS	Office of Strategic Services
PL	Public Law
PLF	Palestinian Liberation Front
PLO	Palestinian Liberation Organization
POW	Prisioner of War
PRC	People's Republic of China
PSYOP	Psychological operations
PSYWAR	Psychological warfare
ROK	Republic of Korea
RVN	Republic of Vietnam
SCUBA	Self-contained underwater breathing apparatus
SDS	Students for a Democratic Society

SEATO	Southeast Asia Treaty Organization
SO	Special operations
SOCOM	Special Operations Command
SOF	Special operations forces
SO/LIC	Special operations/low-intensity conflict

UAR	United Arab Republic
UN	United Nations
USSOCOM	U.S. Special Operations Command

INDEX

ABOUT THE AUTHOR

John M. Collins, Senior Specialist in National Defense at the Library of Congress, Washington, D.C., is well qualified to write this unique study of U.S. small wars in the Twentieth Century. He has 49 years of experience, much of it as a military strategist, contingency planner, and policy analyst. Senior national security officials and members of the media, industry, research institutes, and academic communities around the world respect his assessments.

An AUSA Institute of Land Warfare Book

The Association of the United States Army, or AUSA, was founded in 1950 as a not-for-profit organization dedicated to education concerning the role of the U.S. Army, to providing material for military professional development, and to the promotion of proper recognition and appreciation of the profession of arms. Its constituencies include those who serve in the Army today, including Army National Guard, Army Reserve, and Army civilians, and the retirees and veterans who have served in the past, and all their families. A large number of public-minded citizens and business leaders are also an important constituency. The Association seeks to educate the public, elected and appointed officials, and leaders of defense industry on crucial issues involving the adequacy of our national defense, particularly those issues affecting land warfare.

In 1988 AUSA established within its existing organization a new entity known as the Institute of Land Warfare. Its purpose is to extend the educational work of AUSA by sponsoring scholarly publications, to include books, monographs, and essays on key defense issues, as well as workshops and symposia. Among the volumes chosen for designation as "An AUSA Institute of Land Warfare Book" are both new texts and reprints of titles of enduring value that are no longer in print. Topics include history, policy issues, strategy, and tactics. Publication as an AUSA Book does not indicate that the Association of the United States Army and the publisher agree with everything in the book, but does suggest that the AUSA and the publisher believe this book will stimulate the thinking of AUSA members and others concerned about important issues.